D0203727

Why Some Children Succeed Despite the Odds

Why Some Children Succeed Despite the Odds

Edited by
Warren A. Rhodes
and
Waln K. Brown

FOREWORD BY ROBERT D. FELNER

New York
Westport, Connecticut
London

Library of Congress Cataloging-in-Publication Data

Why some children succeed despite the odds / edited by Warren A. Rhodes and Waln K. Brown; foreword by Robert D. Felner.
p. cm.
Includes bibliographical references and index.
ISBN 0-275-93705-4 (alk. paper)
1. Child mental health. 2. Resilience (Personality trait) in children. 3. Stress in children. 4. Mental illness—Prevention.
I. Rhodes, Warren Allen, 1948- . II. Brown, Waln K., 1944-
RJ489.W445 1991
362.7—dc20 90-49203

British Library Cataloguing in Publication Data is available.

Library of Congress Catalog Card Number: 90-49203
ISBN: 0-275-93705-4

First published in 1991

Praeger Publishers, One Madison Avenue, New York, NY 10010
An imprint of Greenwood Publishing Group, Inc.

Printed in the United States of America

The paper used in this book complies with the Permanent Paper Standard issued by the National Information Standards Organization (Z39.48-1984).

10 9 8 7 6 5 4 3 2 1

To
Barbara and Mandisa

Contents

Foreword
Robert D. Felner ix

Acknowledgments xiii

1. Introduction and Review of the Literature 1
Warren A. Rhodes and Waln K. Brown

2. Children of Divorce: Some Do Cope 7
Bonnie E. Robson

3. Resiliency in Black Children from Single-Parent Families 23
Mark A. Fine and Andrew I. Schwebel

4. Stepchildren: Burying the Cinderella Myth 41
Marilyn Coleman and Lawrence H. Ganong

5. Foster Family Care: Solution or Problem? 55
Edith Fein and Anthony N. Maluccio

6. Children Who Lose a Sibling 67
Helen Rosen

7. Risk and Resilience in Teenagers Who Avoid Pregnancy 79
Howard Stevenson and Warren A. Rhodes

8. Factors Affecting Positive Long-Term Outcome in Attention Deficit Hyperactive Disorder 93
Lily Hechtman

9. Forging Competence in Developmentally Delayed Children: Grounds for Optimism, Directions for Intervention 107
Kofi Marfo

10. Help for the Runaway Child 131
Richard L. Jenkins

11. Socializing the Unsocialized Delinquent 141
Richard L. Jenkins

12. Guidelines from Follow-Up Surveys of Adult Subjects Who Were Adjudicated Delinquent as Juveniles 149
Waln K. Brown, Timothy P. Miller, Richard L. Jenkins, and Warren A. Rhodes

13. Resisting the Powers of Religious Cults 159
Lita Linzer-Schwartz

14. Factors That Promote Invulnerability and Resiliency in At-Risk Children 171
Waln K. Brown and Warren A. Rhodes

Author Index 179

Subject Index 187

About the Contributors 193

Foreword

Robert D. Felner

> In applying clinical ways of thinking formulated out of experience with broken adults, we were slow to see how the language of adequacy to meet life's challenges could become the subject matter of pyschological science. Thus there are thousands of studies of maladjustment for each one that deals directly with the ways of managing life's problems with personal strength and adequacy. The language of problems, difficulties, inadequacies, of antisocial or delinquent conduct, or of ambivalence and anxiety is familiar. We know that there are devices for correcting, bypassing, or overcoming threats, but for the most part these have not been studied.
>
> Murphy, 1962

Since the time that Lois Murphy wrote these words, the study of "positive mental health" has come into vogue in psychology and related disciplines. Coping, life skills, social skills, mastery, hardiness, empowerment, self-esteem, and social competence are all constructs that have moved into the forefront of attention and study. Indeed, that ubiquitous and "traditional" bastion of psychopathology and the illness model of disorder, the "Diagnostic and Statistical Manual of the Mental Disorders" (DSM-III-R) now devotes an entire diagnostic axis to the consideration of the highest level of functioning of the person on positive mental health. Explicit in this addition is the recognition that "ratings of highest level of functioning during the past year will frequently have prognostic significance" and that "ratings of current functioning will generally reflect the current need for treatment or care," even given the presence of other dysfunction (DSM-III-R, 1987 p. 20).

Over the past two decades, spurred by the ground-breaking efforts of Norman Garmezy and others (e.g. Garmezy and Neuchterlein, 1972), the spotlight of attention has gradually begun to shine more brightly on the path for the search for positive mental health characteristics. Adding fuel to this movement was the increasing emphasis on prevention over remediation and treatment, and the need that accompanied it to understand the nature of those human characteristics that might successfully "inoculate" individuals against the potentially devastating effects of social and economic disadvantage, major stresses or traumas, and other developmentally hazardous conditions that so often are encountered on life's journey. But, viable strategies for pursuing this path have often proven more elusive. With the history of the study of disorder so firmly entrenched in clarifying disorder, our conceptual frameworks and empirical sophistication about how best to articulate the nature of positive mental health and adaptation, especially in relation to disorder, was seriously underdeveloped. Indeed, careful reading of the chapters in this volume and elsewhere reveals an almost bewildering array of definitions and inclusive elements for positive mental health.

A consideration of our differential facility in considering conditions of disorder versus health illustrates this point. We have a number of well-developed approaches for making relatively clear distinctions among different "pathological" conditions. Classic works on topologies of behavioral problems, and more recent studies of DSM-III-R that indicate the relative reliability with which clinicians can distinguish at least among the superordinate categories of dysfunction (American Psychiatric Association, DSM-III-R, 1987), nicely demonstrate our sophistication in this area. Lengthy debates over the past century about intrapsychic versus behavioral or cognitive substrates for the disorders with which we are concerned have helped to make the figure and ground of what questions to ask, if not their answers, very well defined. This definition enables researchers to examine the relative contributions of each process to etiological pathways, critical issues that must be addressed to allow for adequate intervention. For positive mental health, these distinctions and processes are far less clear.

Emerging from this confusion has been a strategy that, once articulated, has the compelling parsimony of both good science and good common sense. Others have observed that "blinding glimpses of the obvious" are often those that make for the most exciting and important scientific advances. For us, this is the study of resilience. The study of resilience in mental health comes from the simple, yet elegant, observation that many of those children and youth who are exposed to the slings, arrows, hardships, and risk conditions of life, which have been shown to strongly predict disorder, do not themselves develop disorder. Rather than ask "Why do children and youth develop X?" we can now ask the far more positive and intriguing question of "Why, under conditions of heightened stress and hazard, do many children successfully navigate these treacherous waters and often emerge stronger?" Using this as a basic paradigm for research, those interested in positive mental health outcomes and prevention have begun the pursuit of the "active ingredients" of resilience with great vigor, as shown in the chapters that follow.

In this quest not only is both an elegant and appropriate question and research paradigm necessary but, as any graduate student knows, it is a basic principle in psychology that before a construct can be adequately investigated it must be carefully defined and delineated. Further, if this is done well, a testable hypothesis about its function and form can and should be formulated. The precision with which resilience has often been defined leaves much to be desired when viewed against these criteria. Blurred distinctions between such concepts as risk, vulnerability, "protective factors," and resilience are just an illustration of the sources of some of this confusion. The authors of the chapters that follow offer us a number of important and exciting facets for resilience that provide firm building blocks for constructing a far more solid foundation to our understanding of this critical construct.

The research and theory reported in this volume warm the heart of this "preventionist" because of the promise it holds for developing a knowledge base for prevention that will yield viable, humane, positive, non-victim-blaming, and far more effective approaches for reducing the damage often done to children and youth before they have a chance to fully develop their capacities. Others have argued that breaking the cycle of social and economic disadvantage and the negative health and adaptive outcomes associated with these and other harsh life conditions is "Within Our Reach." The authors of the works in this volume have taken us a step closer to this goal and made the "reach" just a little easier. Through such accomplishments our "stretch" will be reduced and our reach more certain.

REFERENCES

American Psychiatric Association (1987). *Diagnostic and statistical manual of mental disorders,* Third Edition, revised (DSM-III-R). Washington, DC: American Psychiatric Association.

Garmezy, N. and Neuchterlein, K. (1972). Invulnerable children: The fact and fiction of competence and disadvantage. *American Journal of Orthopsychiatry, 42,* 328-329.

Murphy, Lois. (1962). *Paths Toward Mastery.* New York: Basic Books.

Acknowledgments

This book would not have been possible without the dedicated assistance of several individuals. We are pleased to express our deep gratitude to them.

To the contributors who graciously consented to share their research, perceptions, and ideas with our audience: We thank you for your professionalism as demonstrated in the excellent quality of the manuscripts you submitted in a timely fashion—qualities that all editors can truly appreciate. We encourage you to persist in your efforts to unravel the mysteries surrounding "resiliency."

To Ms. Barbara Rhodes, Dr. Richard Jenkins, Ms. Shirley Gravely-Currie, Dr. Larcy McCarley, Ms. Hazel Johnson-Jones, and Dr. Marcella Copes: We greatly appreciate your editorial assistance.

To Ms. Stephanie Jackson and Ms. Terri Nicholls: Thanks for your patience and expert clerical support.

To Dr. Thom Moore: Thanks for your wisdom, encouragement, and just being there.

To Dr. Robert Felner: Special thanks for sharing your insights.

Chapter 1

Introduction and Review of the Literature

Warren A. Rhodes and
Waln K. Brown

The study of "resilient" and "invulnerable" children has proved a new and different focus in the primary prevention of mental illness (Garmezy, 1971). Traditionally, the major focus of primary prevention in mental illness is on the child who has developed emotional or behavioral problems, or is "at risk" to develop some form of psychopathology. Accordingly, the identification of early childhood dysfunctions related to later psychological adversities has taken on tremendous importance.

It is generally accepted that childhood experiences are precursors (indeed, causative factors) for later psychological dysfunctions. Many personality theories and views on the development of psychopathologies are based upon the concept that early traumatic life experiences have profound effects on adult functioning. It is further assumed that primary prevention efforts would be greatly improved if professionals could accurately identify factors that place children "at risk" of developing social, emotional, or psychological difficulties. Effective intervention efforts can be designed only after these risk factors are identified. The research literature is replete with studies that have attempted, with varying degrees of success, to identify early childhood indicators of later adult dysfunctions.

This volume, with its focus on "resilient" children, suggests an alternative approach to primary prevention of mental illness. Resilient children are those who, because of stressful life events, are at risk of developing later psychological dysfunctions, but do not. As examples: every teenage parent does not quit school and live on welfare; most behaviorally disordered children do not become dysfunctional adults; not all high school dropouts fail to make a good living; and many adjudicated delinquents do not become adult offenders.

This volume addresses this key question: What factors promote a healthy adjustment for those children who thrive when others, with similar characteristics or circumstances, succumb to adversity? Understanding factors that contribute to promoting a healthy adjustment in these resilient children is a major change in focus for mental health professionals concerned with primary prevention. A complete understanding of these resilient children could help primary prevention specialists create precursor conditions that enhance the chances of producing resilient children. Furthermore, it would help intervention specialists to identify and promote coping mechanisms for nonresilient children (Anthony, 1987) and provide the foundation for building a psychology of wellness (Cowen and Work, 1988).

An extensive review of the literature on resiliency, invulnerability, and related concepts revealed a dearth of research in this area. Despite the fact that the concept of studying "positive outcomes" would seem painfully obvious and that some researchers have been investigating this theme for at least two decades, there is still very little known about what factors contribute to some children overcoming odds to which others succumb.

Most investigators credit Garmezy (1971, 1974) and his colleagues (Garmezy and Neuchterlien, 1972; Garmezy et al., 1979), and Anthony (1974) with providing the historical bases for the concept of "invulnerability in childhood." Garmezy and Anthony have contributed a wealth of knowledge on the general nature of invulnerable or resilient children. Although slow in coming, primary prevention efforts in mental illness have finally begun to focus on factors that promote a healthy adjustment despite adverse circumstances (for example, Brown, 1978; O'Grady and Metz, 1987; Lewis et al., 1988; Werner and Smith, 1988).

While there are investigations of specific populations of resilient children (for example, Garmezy, 1974; Anthony, 1987; Werner and Smith, 1988), a review of the literature revealed a limited number of volumes that compiled the investigations on different populations of resilient children. These few volumes can only begin to provide clues to the mystery of resiliency.

Given the wide range of stress-producing factors that may occur throughout childhood and even prior to birth (e.g., in utero cocaine addiction), it is understandable that past volumes would provide limited coverage. For example, Garmezy and Rutter's volume (1989) offered readers an understanding of the neurochemical and physiological aspects of stress, a description of stress-producing factors that occur during infancy and early childhood, and an understanding of coping mechanisms associated with resiliency—all considered within the context of childhood development. The volume understandably offered limited coverage of stress-producing factors that occur during middle childhood and beyond. Anthony and Cohler (1987) extended the topics discussed in Garmezy and Rutter's volume (initially published in 1983).

The authors of this volume have been studying the concept of "positive outcomes" of the juvenile justice system, hoping to discover why some adjudicated delinquents manage to overcome their delinquent/criminal activities and become nonrecidivists (Gable and Brown, 1978; Brown, 1979, 1980, 1981a, 1988a; Brown, Miller and Jenkins, 1987, 1989; Jenkins and Brown, 1988; Brown et al., 1989a, 1989b). The authors have also attempted to discern how they, as "positive outcomes" of the juvenile justice system, managed their own turnarounds (Brown, 1978, 1981b, 1983, 1988b; Rhodes, 1987, 1988). Nonetheless, the number and types of resilient childhood populations that have undergone investigation is limited.

The current volume seeks to extend the work on resilience and positive outcomes by focusing on a different set of childhood and adolescent adversities (stress factors), which tend to produce psychological dysfunctions, and on the resilient children who overcome them. It also includes a description of several youth populations that have received little or no attention from the resiliency literature. Included in the following chapters are such topics as teens who avoid pregnancy, adolescents who resist the powers of religious cults, children who lose a sibling, runaway children, youths with attention deficit hyperactive disorder, black children from single-parent families, developmentally delayed children, children of divorce, children in foster family care, and stepchildren. By including such topics, the current volume hopes to: (1) expand the knowledge base about resilient and invulnerable children; (2) promote the study of resiliency in diverse populations of at-risk children; and (3) identify factors that promote resiliency.

REFERENCES

Anthony, E. J. (1974). The syndrome of the psychologically invulnerable child. In E. J. Anthony and C. Koupernik (Eds.), *The child in his family: Children at psychiatric risk* (International Yearbook, Vol. 3). New York: Wiley.

______. (1987). Risk, vulnerability, and resilience: An overview. In E. J. Anthony and B. J. Cohler (Eds.), *The invulnerable child.* New York: The Guilford Press.

Anthony, E. J. and Cohler, B. J. (1987). *The invulnerable child.* New York: The Guilford Press.

Brown, W. K. (1978). The vulnerable child and positive outcomes: A case history of delinquent behavior in perspective. In E. J. Anthony, C. Koupernik, and C. Chiland (Eds.), *The child in his family: Vulnerable children* (International Yearbook, Vol. 4). New York: Wiley.

______. (1979). Social adaption of former delinquents. *International Journal of Offender Therapy and Comparative Criminology, 23,* 117-128.

______. (1980). Social adaption of delinquents. *International Journal of Offender Therapy and Comparative Criminology, 24,* 58-66.

______. (1981a). Maturation as a factor in delinquency devolution. *Behavior Disorders, 6,* 206-209.

______. (1981b). A case history of delinquency devolution. *Criminal Justice and Behavior, 8,* 425-438.

______. (1983). *The other side of delinquency.* New Brunswick, NJ: Rutgers.

______. (1988a). Delinquents who reform. *Pennsylvania Juvenile Court Judges' Newsletter, 12,* 8-10.

______. (1988b). The post-intervention experience: A self-report examination of deviancy devolution. In R. L. Jenkins and W. K. Brown (Eds.), *The abandonment of delinquent behavior: Promoting the turnaround.* New York: Praeger.

Brown, W. K., Miller, T. P., and Jenkins, R. L. (1987). The favorable effect of juvenile court adjudication of delinquent youth on the first contact with the juvenile justice system. *Juvenile and Family Court Journal, 38,* 21-26.

______. (1989). The fallacy of radical nonintervention. *Annals of Clinical Psychiatry, 1,* 55-57.

Brown, W. K., Miller, T. P., Jenkins, R. L., and Rhodes, W. A. (1989a). The effect of early juvenile court adjudication on adult outcome. *International Journal of Offender Therapy and Comparative Criminology, 33,* 177-183.

______. (1989b). How delinquents view their problems in retrospect. *Juvenile and Family Court Journal, 40,* 29-36.

Cowen, E. L., and Work, W. C. (1988). Resilient children, psychological wellness, and primary prevention. *American Journal of Community Psychology, 16,* 591-607.

Gable, R. L., and Brown, W. K. (1978). Positive outcomes: A new approach to delinquency research. *Juvenile and Family Court Journal, 29,* 57-64.

Garmezy, N. (1971). Vulnerability research and the issue of primary prevention. *American Journal of Orthopsychiatry, 41,* 101-116.

______. (1974). The study of competence in children at risk for severe psychopathology. In E. J. Anthony and C. Koupernik (Eds.), *The child in his family: Children at psychiatric risk* (International Yearbook, Vol. 3). New York: Wiley.

Garmezy, N., Masten, A., Nordstrom, L., and Terrorese, M. (1979). The nature of competence in normal and deviant children. In M. W. Kent and J. E. Rolf (Eds.), *The primary prevention of psychopathology* (Vol. 3). Hanover, NH: University Press of New England.

Garmezy, N. and Neuchterlein, K. (1972). Invulnerable children: The facts and fiction of competence and disadvantage. *American Journal of Orthopsychiatry, 42,* 328-329.

Garmezy, N. and Rutter, M. (1989). *Stress, coping, and development in children.* New York: McGraw-Hill.

Jenkins, R. L. and Brown, W. K. (1988). *The abandonment of delinquent behavior: Promoting the turnaround.* New York: Praeger.

Lewis, R. J., Dlugokinski, E. L., Caputo, L. M., and Griffin, R. B. (1988). Children at risk for emotional disorders: Risk and resource dimensions. *Clinical Psychology Review, 8,* 417-440.

O'Grady, D. O. and Metz, R. J. (1987). Resilience in children at high risk for psychological disorder. *Journal of Pediatric Psychology, 12,* 3-23.

Rhodes, W. (1987). *From the jail house to the white house.* York, PA: Gladden Press.

______. (1988). Imagery as a motivating factor in delinquency involvement and cessation. In R. L. Jenkins and W. K. Brown (Eds.), *The abandonment of delinquent behavior: Promoting the turnaround.* New York: Praeger.

Werner, E. E. and Smith, R. S. (1988). *Vulnerable but invincible.* New York: Adam, Bannister and Cox.

Chapter 2

Children of Divorce: Some Do Cope

Bonnie E. Robson

Today children are likely to grow up experiencing more than one family pattern. In addition to the traditional family unit of a set of biological parents, their children, and possibly other blood relatives, there are single, widowed, separated, divorced, adoptive, and selective parent families, as well as blended or remarried families. Most children who have lived in more than one family structure have experienced parental separation or divorce (Rutter, 1979). Approximately one-third of the children in North America have parents who separate before the children are 18 years of age (Glick, 1979). Of children born in the 1980s, 40-50 percent will spend some time in a single-parent home (McDermott, 1970). Although the divorce rate peaked in 1982 and the plateau effect is expected to hold, it is predicted that during the 1990s almost half of Canadian families and 45 percent of American families will be of the remarried form (Statistics Canada, 1983). This is not surprising given that 80 percent of divorced men and 75 percent of divorced women remarry (Rae-Grant and Awad, 1983). These statistics suggest that 25 percent of all children will be part of a remarried family; others will live with parents who are in a blended common-law union. The process continues for some children as 47 percent of second marriages dissolve.

Under the best of circumstances, divorce is stressful and has marked effects on all concerned. The literature on divorce indicates clearly that the women, men, and children who experience a separation and divorce are at comparative risk for mental health problems. The divorced adult is at disproportionate risk of a major psychiatric disorder; the mental illness rates of the separated and divorced are as high as twenty times those of the married (Grad and Stainsbury, 1966; Srole et al., 1962).

Divorce is associated with depression and suicide, alcoholism, and even some physical illness, such as diabetes and some neoplasms among adults (National Center for Health Statistics, 1970a, 1970b; Dorian et al., 1982).

Parental separation and divorce is the factor most strongly associated with attempted suicide by adolescents (Garfinkel, 1979). For almost two decades, we have been aware that children with divorced parents are overrepresented in psychiatric populations (Kalter, 1977). One can readily see why such experts as Hetherington, Cox, and Cox (1979) state that every family breakdown has its victim or victims. But the view that divorce will inevitably have a disastrous outcome is incorrect.

Bob was 15 when his parents separated. He has a younger brother and sister. He feels that the divorce process gave him a greater understanding of his parents. He says, "You get a certain amount of strength having gone through something and survived it all. I felt stronger than a lot of kids whose parents are still married." Now 18, Bob will finish high school this year. He works part-time as a dishwasher and in his spare time is a volunteer broadcaster (Robson, 1979, p. 11).[1]

For some children and adolescents the divorce process might encourage healthy development. This is not to suggest that these "invulnerable" children have escaped unscathed, but rather that they may experience the divorce as a growth-enhancing process, albeit a painful and initially distressing event.

Five years after their parents' separation, two-thirds of the children in Kelly and Wallerstein's longitudinal study were coping well and described as emotionally healthy, while one-third were still very distressed and described as intensely unhappy (Wallerstein, 1980). Thus some children cope; some do not. Longitudinal studies are vital because divorce is not a single event. The legal act of divorce is an indicator of an ongoing process that had a history and points to future stresses. Divorce signals the failure of a marriage, usually after attempts to rescue it and a trial separation. Divorce signals the beginning of new family relationships and interactions.

Rutter (1971, p. 54) states: "There is a most regrettable tendency to focus gloomily on the ills of mankind and on all that can and does go wrong. It is quite exceptional for anyone to study the development of those important individuals who overcome adversity, who survive stress and rise above disadvantage." Because of the lack of rigorous scientific evaluative studies of interventions to promote healthy outcomes of the divorce process, we must make inferences based on (1) the research on those who are showing adverse reactions, (2) descriptions of programs that are subjectively reported to be of assistance, and (3) on the subjective histories of those children and adolescents who are coping well.

Based on this material we can look at what factors within the child promote a healthy adaptation or what coping strategies the child can employ to handle the ongoing stresses. These are the child-related variables that differentiate the vulnerable from the invulnerable child. Second, we can look at what factors in the parents and in the parent-child relationship support a positive response. So important among the parental variables that it has evolved into a separate area is the level of conflict between the parents or the nature of the relationship both before and after the separation and divorce and sometimes after the remarriage. This area includes the legal process and questions surrounding custody and access. Finally we can look at what additional supports and stressors in the immediate environment impinge on the child and how preventive programs may assist the child. For example, encouraging continuation of visiting with both sets of grandparents, helping the child to maintain contact with a teacher who values the child, and specific intervention programs like school-based groups may be indicated.

CHILD VARIABLES

Age

Most research in this field is cross-sectional, but the longitudinal study by Wallerstein and Kelly (1980) established that the adaptation and the responses of children to their parents' separation and divorce are dependent on their age and developmental stage at the time of the separation. If the response of the parents to the child is appropriate to the developmental phase, then the child is likely to respond better.

Infants have little cognitive understanding but react to parent loss even at an early age. They regress and show feeding and toileting problems and disturbed sleep patterns. Parents need to provide predictable routines and as few as possible environmental changes. Where it is feasible the nonresident parent should visit the infant once or twice a week in the infant's home.[2]

Children aged about two to five fear abandonment. They believe that the parent that they live with can leave as easily as the parent who has already left. This fear is entirely appropriate for this stage of development and many children whose parents' marriage is intact will express similar concerns. Children whose parents separate can be whiny, frightened, regress as infants do, and become highly resistant to change. A preschooler who previously enjoyed overnight visits with the grandparents may scream with fright if this is proposed after the separation. Some information about the separation is helpful to these children. In one study they found that 80 percent of preschoolers were given no information as to why one parent was no longer living in the home (Wallerstein and Kelly, 1980). The child asks, "Where's Daddy?" Her mother replies, "He's gone away." This is insufficient. When confronted by their pediatrician, many parents justify this action by asserting that the child would not understand. With any difficult issue, children need to be given information appropriate to their developmental stage; but they do deserve an explanation. Preschool children need routines and firm discipline.

Early school-age children (aged six to eight) are known for the predominant sense of guilt they feel for their parents' separation. These children normally show a great deal of sadness and openly grieve. They look distraught and yearn for the departing parent. Often, they use denial as a defense. One young girl told me that she pretends that her father is at work in another city so that he can't come home. She is only sad when she sees him because then she knows that her pretending is not true. Parents of school-age children need to acknowledge the sadness. Frequent regular visiting with the nonresident parent is essential, as are consistent rules in each home and regular school attendance. Some of these children begin to complain of minor physical symptoms to avoid school. Because of the sadness many parents are tempted to let the child stay home from school even when the child is not very sick. The school routine seems to help the child adjust to the other changes in his or her life and should not be interrupted unless absolutely necessary.

Older school-age children (aged nine to twelve) seem less distressed but more alienated. These children experience loyalty conflicts and seem to need to find out which parent is to blame for the separation. These children can understand incompatibility but seem loath to accept this reason. They express concern about their parents' remarriage and tend as a group to dislike stepparents. They worry about custody and can be easily drawn into the litigation. Initially they may react with shock, surprise, or disbelief to the separation. A child in this age group can become very dependent on one parent to the exclusion of the other parent. Parents with children in this developmental group should avoid blaming the other parent or putting the other parent down. These children must be kept out of the custody issues if more serious behavior disorders are to be avoided. Every effort should be made to encourage these children to visit the nonresident parent, even though they may be resistant. Gardiner (1985) calls this display of resistance the "parental alienation syndrome."

Adolescents experience more acutely the loss of the family unit than the loss or partial loss of one parent. They express concerns about their own future marriage, their parents' adjustment, and their younger siblings' reactions. They may take on too much responsibility too soon. They experience loyalty conflicts not over who is to blame, if anyone, but how they can share themselves equally with both parents. Most adolescents with separated parents at some point have feelings of low self-confidence and abnormality. They long to be "normal" and view teenagers whose parents are not separated as lucky. Later, these same teenagers feel they are the lucky ones, who are more mature than their peers. They talk of having survived. It is crucial for parents of teens to maintain a parent-child relationship. This means not becoming dependent on the teenager for emotional support, for too much financial assistance, or for too much housework and chores. Parents must remember that the tasks of physical, psychological, and social growth during the adolescent years are formidable. Teenagers, because they enjoy a sense of grandiosity, may welcome an opportunity to take on too much responsibility too soon and may be loath to part with it. Firm guidelines must be discussed and enforced if delinquent or promiscuous behavior and depression are to be avoided. Adolescents do well with peer support and teens should be encouraged by their parents to set aside time for normal peer interaction.

Sex

Hetherington (1979) found that girls in mother custody homes were better adjusted. Thus it appears that there is an interaction between the sex of the child and that of the custodial parent. Children of the same sex as the custodial parent adjust better. Hetherington, Cox, and Cox (1979) felt that girls recovered faster and, within two years of parental separation, were less likely than boys to feel that peers and teachers responded to them negatively. However, several authors (Kurdek, Blish, and Siesky, 1981; Santrok and Warshak, 1979; Saucier and Ambert, 1986) have challenged the validity of a difference in response and adjustment between boys and girls.

Academic Achievement

Even early studies showed that children who were doing well in school and who were able to focus on their educational achievements seemed invulnerable to parental separation (Rutter, 1979). The establishment of a positive relationship with one particular teacher or mentor who likes the student seems important. The Toronto Family Study (Robson et al., 1986) confirmed that children who had a stable academic background and who had never required tutoring or special education were more likely to cope well. As well, the less school changes the children experienced before the separation, the better they did after the separation.

Self-Image

Research from adolescent girls' groups has confirmed the impression that there is a tendency to a lower self-concept among girls whose parents are separated (Parish and Taylor, 1979). Those who were coping well were those who had their self-confidence bolstered by success in sports, academics, employment, or the creative arts (Robson, 1979). Unfortunately, some teenage girls rely on their appearance and attractiveness to compensate for feelings of low self-worth. This is common in girls who have little or no contact with their fathers (Hetherington, 1972). They seek attention from men and demonstrate early heterosexual behavior as compared with daughters of widows, who were found to be more shy around men.

Sarah, who is 18 and lives with her mother and younger sister, recalls that she became somewhat promiscuous after the separation, when her father and older brother moved out. She felt that her promiscuity was a substitute for an affectionate relationship with her father. "Before the separation I didn't know anything about sex. After I went out a lot, I got to know guys a lot. I didn't know the dangers when I was 12-13. I needed a lot of male companionship; I missed my father. At 13, I used to turn to male companions, taxi drivers, my brother's friends just to talk to. When I was 14, I looked 17 and that was a problem. Some girls might say, 'Hey, wow!' but since I wasn't [17], I had trouble with guys thinking I was older than I was. I had to have the police around the house a couple of times because they were annoying me. I got in with the wrong gang, smoking and drinking. I was hauled down an alleyway. Now I am 18 and a normal human being. I've gotten to know different types of males." In retrospect, Sarah feels she would have been wiser to spend more time visiting with her father (Robson, 1979, p. 189).

Sexuality and Marriage

The normal developmental fear of homosexuality during adolescence appears to be increased among students with divorced parents. They express fears about disturbed gender identity formation as a result of living with only one parent, particularly if that parent has preferred an opposite-sex child. Not being of the preferred gender is an issue for both males and females. Adolescents who are coping well express these fears openly to one or both parents. A parent who is aware of the child's fear that the parent would have preferred a child of the opposite sex—and especially when this fear has some validity—can assist the child to understand that a parent loves a child regardless of such preference. In the situation where one parent is neglectful, the other parent must help the child to value him- or herself. It is unfortunate when a boy lives with his mother, who seems angry at all men, especially the boy whom she openly accuses of being "just like your father." Another relative or friend can help the mother to appreciate that she is asking the boy to reject all parts of the father. In devaluing the father, she is devaluing the son; risking the development of a poor self-image in her son. Similarly, fathers need to take great care not to put down their daughters, especially not to denigrate them for being female.

A study of 400 18- and 19-year-old college students revealed that those with divorced or separated parents were anxious about their future marriages (Robson, 1985). They were less likely to want children. If they planned to marry, they thought they should delay it until they were older, perhaps in their late twenties. More of the students reported that they planned to live with their partners prior to marriage because of their anxiety that their own marriage might end in divorce. Wallerstein and Kelly (1980) reported similar concerns in their interviews with younger adolescents. Family life courses in schools often address these concerns and receive mixed reviews from teens with separated parents. Some feel that they are of no use in reducing the anxieties and others felt that the information helped.

PARENT VARIABLES

Unavailability or Dependency

For the last 60 years, the literature on psychological development has related the concepts of protection, safety and a secure base to the nurturant caregiver—most commonly the biological mother. It is from this secure base that healthy children separate and reach out to explore the world, and to which they attempt to return in times of stress. Proximity-seeking with the significant figure is seen in adults in states of regression (Bowlby, 1969). After marital separation men and women seek proximity with their "attachment figures." Here women seem advantaged. Unlike men, women often have a network of female friends to whom they can turn at times of stress for advice and support. With a separation, women can retreat to this network. Men, on the other hand, have lost their primary maternal support with the loss of their wives.

In marriage, men in this century have been encouraged to rely on their spouses as once they did on their mothers. They adhere to the refrain, "I want a girl just like the girl that married dear old Dad." To return to a secure base, many divorced men seek a replacement for their wives/mothers and remarry precipitately or rely on their teenage daughters to fill the gap emotionally. The latter arrangement works well until the father remarries and the daughter is displaced from her position of prominence in running the home.

One year past separation, both men and women are anxious, depressed, and angry, and they feel rejected and incompetent. Hetherington et al. (1978) found that, despite the better social network, the feelings were more sustained for women. Alternatively, Huntington (1986), in a study of 184 fathers attending a divorce counseling center, reported that men were lower than women on their overall adjustment level. "They were less happy to be out of their former marriages and had fewer negative feelings toward their ex-wives" (p. 54). It appears that both parents are at risk for emotional withdrawal from the children. Children and adolescents who can find support from other sources—relatives, friends, religious or health care counselors—will fare better. They are less likely to turn to unavailable parents for comfort (Robson et al., 1986).

Loss of Discipline and Parental Rules

Discipline seems very important in determining how children cope. Younger children find reassurance in structure and feel safe if there is consistency in the environment, especially in family rules or traditions. Single parents may have more difficulty in maintaining consistent limits, even if they are not emotionally preoccupied. Most teenagers say that their parents are less strict after the separation (Robson, 1979). This can lead to a sense of maturity and responsibility if the adolescent is able to handle the freedom.

Jim feels: "Since the divorce, I'm more independent than I used to be. I don't have to be dependent on my parents. My father's working and he lets us have more freedom—but we don't take advantage of it." Duncan adds that although he feels he is more mature, he missed a great deal through this loss of discipline. He even goes so far as to say that it feels like a loss of family life and parental caring. "I think the loss of discipline is a loss too. You know, sometimes when I go call on my friend to go to a party or something, his father or mother is always sitting there: 'Where are you going? Who's the person you're going with? What time are you coming home?' He says 12:30, his father says 11:30. It's always an hour earlier. We go out and it's kind of strange because I can stay out as late as I want, but I always feel like they're telling me, too. I kind of miss it" (Robson, 1979, p. 169).

The type of discipline experienced by the adolescent before the separation and his or her response to the discipline affects the adjustment. As noted above, if the parent is too lax it can lead to a greater sense of maturity or it can allow the adolescent to become out of control. Equally, if children and adolescents have been hit or report hitting out at their parents before the separation, they are much more likely to be disturbed than children who have firm limits but no physical exchange (Robson et al. 1986).

Abandoning Parent

Worse than the emotional withdrawal of a depressed or angry parent or the loss of parental rules may be the total abandonment by one parent. Huntington (1986) reports on one group of divorcing men who "seem to feel very little" (p. 63). These men seem capable of only shallow relationships and low-level intimacy. "They are the 'easy come easy go' men with narcissistic character disorders. . . . They quickly move on to new relationships and leave their children behind with remarkable lack of bereavement. These are the true 'disappearing' fathers'' (pg. 63 and 64).

Support for these children can come only by building on the relationship with the other parent. In one unique program, Crossman and Adams (1980) used crisis theory and social facilitation programs with preschool children. This intervention is based on the theory that children of divorce need adult-child interaction in addition to the mother-child interaction in a single-parent family in order to mediate the negative consequences of one parent's availability. In a carefully designed double control study, the preschool children with separated parents made gains in locus of control and intelligence testing.

Fortunately, many men develop stronger ties to their children than they had before the separation, being more likely to spend time alone with their children in more intense and meaningful ways (Rosenthal and Keshet 1981). The amount of contact between the father and the child can produce a significant change in a father's perception of his functioning as a parent after divorce. Thus, contact with the child may improve the father's emotional availability to the child.

LEVELS OF CONFLICT BETWEEN PARENTS

One undisputed, repeatedly replicated finding of the research in separation and divorce is that ongoing parental discord is a high-risk factor for maladaptive behavior (Chess et al., 1983; Rutter, 1971; Ellison, 1983). Further, Ellison (1983) has demonstrated that harmony between divorced parents positively correlated with children's assessment of their own psychological adjustment. Hetherington et al. (1978) found that after the separation, women retained some feelings of attachment to their spouses but, at the same time, felt angry, resentful, and hostile toward them. The ambivalent feelings between ex-spouses usually declined after the first year of separation, but the anger and resentment were sustained longer in women than in men. Interparent hostility and conflict was not greatly reduced in the opinion of the children. Five years after the separation, two-thirds of the children said that there were ongoing hostile interactions between their parents.

How do the children and adolescents make a healthy adaptation to this hostility? Given differences in developmental stages, most children advise others caught between parental hostility to protect oneself from getting involved. The general feeling is that the bitter parent is beyond the help of his or her own children. Margaret agrees: ''The more you offer to help, the more they ask. Everything that goes wrong is his [the father's] fault. If the car doesn't start, 'That bum left me with a bum car.' He didn't leave her with anything. You just have to listen and let it blow away'' (Robson, 1979, p. 122).

Healthy adolescents coping with parental hostilities employ a distancing through cognitive understanding. For example, one boy explained why his mother was constantly berating his father; he saw that she felt abandoned and was hurt when he [the father] left. For this boy, his attempts at understanding gave him a sense of maturity, as well as the normal adolescent striving for independence.

Custody and Visitation

We may deplore the fact that custody and access disputes are a two-party litigation and often ignore the wishes of the children. However, those children who are protected by their parents from the involvement in custody and visitation disputes and the ensuing loyalty conflicts seem to be better adjusted. Certainly, it seems preferable not to involve children in testifying against one parent, nor do children respond well to being allowed to read lawyers' letters or court transcripts.

Should children be involved in determining custody and visitation decisions? Some authors suggest that those who are involved adapt better, while others suggest that no-fault divorce is protective (Gardiner, 1985). Conciliation counseling, to assist families through the legal procedures surrounding a divorce, and family mediation, to simplify the procedures by proper preparation of the couple for the legalities, can help to reduce the adverse effects on the children (Puig-Antich, 1980). Many children report that their parents seemed to be acting pleasantly to each other—certainly with respect—until the legal proceedings began. Jill, 16 and an only child, reports, "Court brings out the bitterness. My parents haven't seen each other since the divorce in court" (Robson, 1979 p. 34).

Type of Custody and Visitation

Wallerstein and Kelly (1980) found that some fathers who do not have custody have more contact with their children after the divorce than before; also, both boys and girls benefit in their self-esteem and sexual identity when continuing access to both parents is harmoniously arranged. Rutter's cohort study (1979) shows that children of divorce are protected by having a good relationship with at least one parent, and suggests there is value in having access to both parents unless there are strong contradictions to this. In recent years, concern for both the children's welfare and the continuation of parents' rights has led several states to follow California's example of awarding "joint custody" as the preferred arrangement. While this term is used in a number of contexts, the California Civil Code, Section 4600 defines it as "physical custody shall be shared by the parents to assure the child frequent and continuing con-

tact with both parents." The Ilfeld, Ilfeld, and Alexander (1982) study of 414 consecutive cases in Los Angeles showed there was a significant decrease in relitigation rates when joint custody was arranged. In 18 cases where joint custody was ordered over the opposition of both parents, the relitigation rate was no higher than parents given sole custody. In a case control study with 40 joint custody families, Greif (1979) reported that joint custody promotes the involvement of the father and, through his involvement, gives a better concept and model of the parental role.

There are a number of potential negative factors to be considered. In a study of 32 children from 24 families with joint custody, Steinman (1981) found that joint custody did not solve the loyalty conflicts felt by most children, that one-third felt burdened by the conflicting demands of living in two homes, and that one-quarter were anxious about transportation arrangements back and forth. Wallerstein (1983) indicates that joint custody is more likely to be disrupting in the development of preschool children and adolescents. Thus, whether joint custody is better than other arrangments is still unclear. Certainly, contact with both parents appears to be of value to children.

Visiting

The court decision on access is the beginning of a new chapter, not the end of hostility. The bitterness does not subside (Westman et al., 1970). The adolescent can often view the struggle as an observer rather than as an active participant.

> Bitterness doesn't go away. It's like death—it's a pain you have to live with. In some ways it's worse than death 'cause it's living still. You see the person. Then all the hurt comes back. You lose the person and you're left with all the hurt. At first it's the child's responsibility not to talk too much about the absent parent. Let the parent get used to the idea of who you are living with—it helps a parent to be less rivalous—maybe not visit for a while—makes Mom more secure. My Mom fears every time my sister visits my father she's going to stay forever (Robson, 1979, p. 123).

Adolescents who have adapted in this way report that younger siblings are less able to take this observer position. This seems a healthy position at least during the early years, and one of which family therapists, mediators, and divorce counselors should be cognizant. It is important to assist the adolescent to maintain this stance. With younger children, resources outside the family may be needed to assist with visiting and with counseling for the parents. The goal of this assistance would be to protect the children from enmeshment.

SUPPORT SYSTEMS

Poverty

Most single mothers suffer a decline in economic resources with concurrent loss of social status and reduced standard of living (Hetherington et al., 1978; Wallerstein and Kelly, 1980). Ten years after divorce, 79 percent of fathers of minor children have defaulted on child support payments (Hetherington et al., 1985). Of single-parent households headed by females with children under 18, 52 percent fall below the poverty line (U.S. Census, 1977). Even in wealthy families, the burden of supporting two households rather than one makes for a dramatic drop in income after separation. Despite this, there may be a positive aspect for some teens who make a financial contribution to the family and feel that this is a positive coping strategy. Laurie was negative about getting a job and helping pay for her father's debts. "I kind of resented it at first. I'm making this money so why am I giving it to my mom when I could be spending it? But then, once I thought about it, I figured I had a lot of time. After a while I felt more mature and said, 'At least I can help out now.' It was a good feeling inside."

Peers

The Toronto Family Study (Robson et al. 1986) explored to whom the child and adolescent would turn if they had an academic problem, an emotional difficulty, or a situational crisis. The invulnerable children had a supportive peer group and were able to rely on their custodial parent and siblings for advice. This was one of the most crucial factors in differentiating the vulnerable from the invulnerable. The children and adolescents who were depressed or behaviorally disturbed reported that they had few friends before the separation and few or no friends after the separation, but that they were more likely to rely on these few friends to talk over problems.

Few of either the vulnerable or the invulnerable children in our sample sought counseling within the school; they did not regard guidance counselors, teachers, principals, or school social workers as helping resources. They did not use psychologists or psychiatrists of their own volition. Those involved in counseling appeared to become involved on the advice or insistence of their parent(s).

Because vulnerable children make less use of their families for support and rely more heavily on fewer friends who are more likely to have separated parents, peer support groups in the schools seem an appropriate support measure for them. Children's divorce groups led by elementary school counselors have been found to be extremely successful (Wil-

kinson and Bleck, 1976). Common themes of these groups are loneliness, fears of separation or abandonment, and feelings of guilt. While acknowledging that preventive programs based on a crisis intervention model can be effective initially, Kalter, Pickar, and Lesowitz (1984) believe that children go through a reworking at "nodal developmental points." They recommend that groups within the school setting should assist children "to negotiate more effectively the developmental tasks associated with both divorce and postdivorce experiences" (p. 617). They recommend groups for students at the point of entry or leaving junior or senior high school and as preparation for college or university entrance.

In addition to school groups, community support may be provided through educational groups for divorcing parents and their children. Freeman's study (1984) showed that children who participated in an eight-week educational group were better adjusted than those who were wait-listed. They showed improvement in classroom behavior, and their parents reported that they were more achievement-oriented. They had developed more specific coping repertoires and responses to stress.

SUMMARY

Although almost half the nation's children will experience a parental separation of divorce, the majority eventually cope well. For some, the process improves their self-images and develops characterlogical strengths. It is established that the reaction of the children is dependent on their stage of development at the time of the separation. Factors in the child that promote healthy adaptation include the ability to tolerate ambivalence and advanced cognitive development; good academic performance; and an interest in school, ability, talent, or sport carried on outside the home. Adolescent girls who rely more on academic achievement, employment, or success in sports or the arts for self-image seem able to cope easier than those who focus on social popularity or physical attraction.

There appears to be an interaction between the sex of the child and that of the custodial parent. Children living with the same-sexed parent are better adjusted. Before this finding is applied to custody decisions, more longitudinal research needs to be completed. Certainly, post-separation, the maintenance of frequent and positive contact with both parents is important. But if this is not possible, a positive relationship with one parent seems to promote a healthier adaptation than ongoing interparent hostility. The only protection the child has from interparent hostility is to isolate the blaming parent or isolate him- or herself. Children with a good relationship with a teacher, coach, or mentor do well.

Adolescents who are given some sense of responsibility through financial contribution to the family, but who are not burdened, have an excellent sense of their self-worth. Parents who provide consistency in rules and discipline are providing a sense of security for children of all ages, including adolescents. The establishment of new family traditions is often almost of equal importance. Social supports for children and adolescents after divorce include the establishment of government agencies to ensure the child's right to support payments and the establishment of community education and peer self-help groups.

It must be noted that the suggestions made here to promote healthy adaptation are based in the main on clinical reports and subjective studies—not on carefully controlled and well-designed demonstrations. The current studies raise many questions that will be answered by future researchers. Some of these undoubtedly will be children of parents who are currently in the divorce process and whose interest will be stimulated by their own success in coping with the stresses.

NOTES

1. Some of the stories and histories presented here are taken from the transcripts of conversations with adolescent volunteers who described themselves as coping well. Their participations in the exchange of ideas with other adolescents with divorced parents in groups, their individual interviews, and their structured questionnaire formed the basis for a book for other teens (Robson, 1979).

2. The descriptions of the developmental responses related to the parents' separation and divorce, their needs, and the helpful or appropriate responses of parents is based on a chart prepared by the author (Robson, 1982).

REFERENCES

Bowlby, J. (1969). *Attachment and loss: Vol. I: Attachment.* London: Hogarth Press.

Chess, S., Thomas, A., Kern, S., Mittleman, M., and Cohen, J. (1983). Early parental attitudes toward divorce and separation and young adult outcome: Findings of a longitudinal study. *Journal of American Academy of Child Psychiatry, 22*(1), 47-51.

Crossman, S. M. and Adams, G. R. (1980). Divorce, single parenting and child development. *Journal of Psychology, 106,* 205-217.

Dorian, B. J., Keystone, E., Garfinkel, P. E., and Brown, G. M. (1982). Alternatives in lymphocyte subpopulations and functions during psychological stress. *Clinical and Experimental Immunology, 50,* 132-138.

Ellison, E. S. (1983). Issues concerning parental harmony and children's psychosocial adjustment. *American Journal of Orthopsychiatry, 53*(1), 73-80.

Freeman, R. (1984). *Children in families experiencing separation and divorce: An investigation of the effects of brief intervention.* Toronto: Family Service Association of Metropolitan Toronto Press.

Gardiner, R. (1985). Recent trends in divorce and custody litigation. *Academic Forum,* 29, 3.

Garfinkel, B. D. (1979). *Suicidal behavior in a pediatric population.* Proceedings

Communications, Tenth International Congress for Suicide Prevention and Crisis Intervention, Ottawa, June 17-20.

Glick, P. C. (1979). Children of divorced parents in demographic perspective. *Journal of Social Issues, 35,* 170-182.

Grad, J. and Stainsbury, P. (1966). Evaluating the community psychiatric service in Chinchester: Results. *Milbank Memorial Fund Quarterly, 44,* 146-178.

Greif, J. B. (1979). Fathers, children and joint custody. *American Journal of Orthopsychiatry, 49*(2), 311-319.

Hetherington, E. M. (1972). Effects of father absence on the personality development in adolescent daughters. *Developmental Psychology, 7,* 313-326.

______. (1979). Play and social interaction in children following divorce. *Journal of Social Issues, 35*(4), 26-49.

Hetherington, E. M., Cox, M. and Cox, R. (1978). The aftermath of divorce. In J. Stevens and M. Matthews (Eds.), *Mother-child relations.* Washington, DC: National Association of Young Children.

______. (1979). Family interactions and the social emotional and cognitive development of children following divorce. In J. C. Vaughan and J. B. Brazelton (Eds.), *The family: Setting priorities.* New York: Science and Medicine Publishers.

______. (1985). Long-term effects of divorce and remarriage on the adjustment of children. *Journal of American Academy of Child Psychiatry, 24,* 518-530.

Huntington, D. S. (1986). Fathers: The forgotten figures in divorce. In J. W. Jacobs (Ed.), *Divorce and fatherhood.* Washington, DC: American Psychiatric Association, 53-83.

Ilfeld, Jr., F. W., Ilfeld, H. Z., and Alexander, J. R. (1982). Does joint custody work? A first look at outcome data of relitigation. *American Journal of Orthopsychiatry, 139*(1), 62-66.

Kalter, N. (1977). Children of divorce in an out-patient psychiatric population. *American Journal of Orthopsychiatry, 47,* 40-51.

Kalter, N., Pickar, J., and Lesowitz, M. (1984). School-based developmental facilitation groups for children of divorce: A preventive intervention. *American Journal of Orthopsychiatry, 51,* 85-100.

Kurdek, L. A., Blish, D., and Siesky, A. (1981). *Correlates of children's long-term adjustment to their parents' divorce.* New York: Basic Books.

McDermott, J. F. (1970). Divorce and its psychiatric sequelas in children. *Archives of General Psychiatry, 23*(5), 421-427.

National Center for Health Statistics (1970a). *Morality from selected census by marital status: Series 20, 8a, and 8b.* Washington, DC: U.S. Government Printing Office.

______. (1970b). *Selected symptoms of psychological distress: Series 11:37.* Washington, DC: U.S. Government Printing Office.

Parish, T. S. and Taylor, J. C. (1979). The impact of divorce and subsequent father absence on children's and adolescents' self concepts. *Journal of Youth and Adolescence, 8*(4), 427-432.

Puig-Antich, J. (1980). Affective disorders in childhood: A review and perspective. *Psychiatry Clinics of North America, 3,* 403-424.

Rae-Grant, Q. and Awad, G. (1983). The effects of marital breakdown. In P. D. Steinhauer and Q. Rae-Grant (Eds.), *Psychological problems of the child in the family.* New York: Basic Books.

Robson, B. (1979). *My parents are divorced, too.* Toronto: Dorset.

______. (1982). A developmental approach to the treatment of children of divorcing parents. In J. C. Hansen and L. Messinger, *Therapy with remarriage families.* Rockville, MD: Aspen System Corporation.

______. (1985). Marriage concepts of older adolescents. *Canadian Journal of Psychiatry, 30,* 169-172.

Robson, B., Homatides, G., Johnson, L., and Orlando, F. (1986). *Toronto family study.* Toronto: Board of Education Press.

Rosenthal, K. M. and Keshet, H. F. (1981). *Fathers without partners: A study of fathers and the family after marital separation.* Totowa, NJ: Rowman and Littlefield.

Rutter, M. (1971). Parent-child separation: Psychological effects on the children. *Journal of Child Psychology and Psychiatry, 12,* 233-260.

______. (1979). Invulnerability or why some children are not damaged by stress. In S. J. Shamsie (Ed.), *New directions in children's mental health,* New York: Spectrum, 53-75.

Santrock, W. J. and Warshak, R. A. (1979). Father custody and social development in boys and girls. *Journal of Social Issues, 35,* 112-125.

Saucier, J. and Ambert, A. (1986). Adolescents' perception of self and of immediate environment by parental marital status: A controlled study. *Canadian Journal of Psychiatry, 31*(6), 505-512.

Srole, L., Langer, T. S., Michael, S. T., Oplu, M. K., and Rennie, T.A.C. (1962). *Mental health in the metropolis.* New York: McGraw-Hill.

Statistics Canada (1983). *Divorce: Law and the family in Canada.* Ottawa: Ministry of Supply and Services.

Steinman, S. (1981). The experience of children in a joint custody arrangement: A report of a study. *American Journal of Orthopsychiatry, 51*(3), 403-414.

U.S. Bureau of the Census (1977). *Current population reports series, Advance Report.* Washington, DC: U.S. Government Printing Office.

Wallerstein, J. S. (1980). The impact of divorce on children. *Psychiatric Clinics of North America, 3*(3), 455-468.

______. (1983). Separation, divorce and remarriage. In M. D. Levine, W. B. Carey and A. C. Crocker (Eds.), *Developmental-behavioral pediatrics.* Philadelphia: W. B. Saunders.

Wallerstein, J. S. and Kelly, J. B. (1980). *Surviving the breakup: How children and parents cope with divorce.* New York: Basic Books.

Westman, J. C., Cline, D. W., Swift, W. J., and Kramer, P. A. (1970). Role of child psychiatry in divorce. *Archives of General Psychiatry, 23*(5), 416-420.

Wilkinson, G. S. and Bleck, R. T. (1976). Children's divorce groups. *Elementary School Guidance and Counseling, 11,* 205-213.

Chapter 3

Resiliency in Black Children from Single-Parent Families

Mark A. Fine and
Andrew I. Schwebel

Resiliency, a concept that has received considerable attention in the mental health literature in recent years (Garmezy, 1985, 1987; Rutter, 1985; Werner, 1989), has been defined as the "positive pole of individual differences in people's response to stress and adversity" (Rutter, 1987, p. 316). Several recent studies have focused on those children who are resilient—that is, those who were able to maintain positive mental health despite facing stressful situations typically associated with increased risk for disorder (Garmezy, 1987; Rutter, 1985; Werner, 1989; Werner and Smith, 1982). The findings from these investigators are remarkably consistent, although they used different research methods, studied different populations, and focused on different stressors. Specifically, they found (Garmezy, 1985) that resilient children possess: (1) favorable personality characteristics (e.g., high self-esteem and self-control, an internal locus of control, positive mood, social responsiveness, and flexibility); (2) a supportive family milieu that encourages and facilitates coping efforts; and (3) a warm, supportive social environment that encourages and reinforces coping attempts.

In contrast to children who are resilient, some become alienated. Typically, they feel powerless to affect their circumstances and feel threatened rather than challenged as situations unfold in their lives (Maddi, Hoover, and Kobasa, 1982). Besides being less able to take advantage of opportunities for growth, alienated youngsters, in contrast to resilient ones, cope less successfully with negative events that confront them. Moreover, for those individuals who are alienated, encountering these negative events is associated with other unfavorable consequences, such as stress-related health problems (Cohen and Hoberman, 1983).

The fact that some children can successfully emerge from high-risk environments is encouraging and has led researchers to attempt to identify those factors that serve to assist these children in coping with their difficult circumstances. The term "protective processes" is used to describe these factors. Rutter (1987) proposed that several protective factors can contribute to fostering a resiliency in children that protects them from psychiatric disorders: (1) reduction of risk impact, including altering exposure to and interpretation of risks; (2) reduction of negative chain reactions that exacerbate the effects of the risk; (3) the establishment and maintenance of self-esteem and self-efficacy; and (4) the opening up of opportunities, particularly in educational and occupational settings. Garmezy's (1985) description of protective factors is quite similar to Rutter's, emphasizing both the child's inner resources and the need for support and opportunities from the family and community.

This chapter focuses on one group of individuals who have traditionally been perceived as particularly vulnerable within society—children in black single-parent families. They face stressors both because of their experience as an oppressed minority and because they lack the stability and resources provided by living in a two-parent family. Nevertheless, many black children adjust and excel in these circumstances. While research evidence is sparse, certain characteristics (discussed later) found in many black single-parent families appear to foster resilience and "protect" children from adverse consequences (e.g., mental disorders, delinquency, and so on).

The purpose of this chapter is to review the existing literature related to the adjustment of black children in single-parent families with a focus on identifying those factors that may facilitate positive adaptation. Garmezy's categorization of protective mechanisms will be used to organize this review. Following this presentation, a theoretical model will be proposed that may have heuristic value to researchers and applied value to clinicians in that it explains why some black children seem to be resilient to the negative effects of living in single-parent households and, in some instances, to those stemming from family disruption.

CONSIDERATIONS IN ASSESSING THE ADJUSTMENT OF CHILDREN IN SINGLE-PARENT FAMILIES

Before reviewing the existing literature on the adjustment of children in single-parent families, it is important to consider several issues that influence the interpretation of the results from these studies. First, there are important racial differences in the origins of single-parent status. Among black children, 22.8 percent live with divorced parents, 27.0 percent with married parents whose spouses are absent, 5.4 percent with widowed parents, and 44.8 percent with never-married parents. The comparable percentages for white children are 52.7 percent with divorced parents, 25.3 percent with married parents whose spouses are absent, 9.7 percent with widowed parents, and 12.4 percent with never-married parents (U.S. Bureau of the Census, 1984a). Thus, while divorce is the primary cause of single parenthood among white families, out-of-wedlock parenthood is the modal cause among black families. In addition, it is important to note that because blacks are significantly less likely to remarry following divorce (Glick, 1984), some black children will remain in single-parent families longer than their white counterparts. These structural differences may affect the adjustment of black and white children in single-parent families, as will be discussed further.

Second, during the past two decades, there has been a substantial, well-documented increase in the percentage of American families headed by only one parent (Glick, 1984; Norton and Glick, 1986). Census data demonstrate that black families were and are more likely to be headed by one parent than their white counterparts. More specifically, in 1970, 33 percent of black families were one-parent households, increasing to 50.1 percent in 1980 and 51.9 percent in 1983. During the same time period, the comparable percentages for white families were 8.9 percent, 16.1 percent, and 17.4 percent, respectively (U.S. Bureau of the Census, 1984b). These differences persist when socioeconomic status is controlled (U.S. Bureau of the Census, 1984a). Since single-parenthood is more commonly experienced by black children than white ones, it may be inappropriate to draw conclusions regarding the adjustment of black children in single-parent families using data collected from white children.

Third, the models used to interpret data collected in studies assessing the adjustment of black children affect the conclusions one draws. More specifically, each of the three models that have been used to understand the functioning of black families (Fine, Schwebel, and Myers, 1987) takes a unique perspective on black families. The *pathology* model emphasizes the pathological and negative aspects of black life and assumes that their lower socioeconomic status is attributable to a variety of unhealthy psychological and social characteristics, including the prevalence of single-parent families (see Moynihan, 1965). The *structural-functional* model maintains that black families have developed positively and uniquely in response to oppressive social forces and that what some perceive to be problems (e.g., single-parenthood) may actually be attempted solutions to problems. Finally, the *emergent* model (to be discussed later) recognizes positive and adaptive features of black families and sees them as products of an interaction between African cultural heritage and the environmental circumstances in the United States.

There are value differences across the three models on the following dimensions: (1) the extent to which black families should be assessed by standards developed in mainstream "white" culture; (2) the relative importance of assessing stability in terms of socioeconomic status, as opposed to socioemotional constructs; and (3) the role of African heritage in the lives of modern Africa-American families. Fine et al. (1987) indicated that the particular model used by researchers influences the conclusions drawn from their data. They further argued that conflicting findings in the literature on black families can at least partly be understood by recognizing the impact of differing, underlying, and only implicitly stated assumptions and values held by researchers.

At present, and in Fine et al., it is argued that the values adopted, whether explicitly stated or not, influence all aspects of the investigatory process. As a result, researchers often find results that are consistent with the particular model of black family functioning that they have adopted. For example, many investigators implicitly adopting the pathology model focus their studies on poor, black, single-parent families. This focus typically reflects the acceptance of several underlying assumptions, including that socioeconomic status is the primary measure of adjustment and that differences between poor black and other types of families reflect pathology among the former. However, studies of this segment of the black population may have limited generalizability to middle and upper socioeconomic status black single-parent families. In sum, it is especially important in this area of research to attempt to identify the assumptions and values underlying the investigations.

EFFECTS OF LIVING IN SINGLE-PARENT FAMILIES ON CHILDREN

Much of the recent research conducted on the effects of living in single-parent families on children is focused on children whose parents have divorced. However, as Kurdek (1987) and Demo and Acock (1988) noted, most investigations assessing adjustment to divorce have used small, nonrepresentative, white, middle-class, voluntary samples. White subjects were used almost exclusively in the major longitudinal investigations (Guidubaldi et al., 1986; Hetherington, Cox, and Cox, 1985; Wallerstein, 1984). Because black family members were not adequately sampled, only with great caution and only because no alternative data exist should one attempt to generalize from these findings to understand the single-parent experience for children in the black community.

Recognizing these limitations in the research literature, the effects of living in single-parent families have generally been described in terms of negative outcomes. A substantial body of both clinical reports and empirical findings has demonstrated that most children experience the transition into a single-parent home (especially after divorce or the death of a parent [Schwebel, Fine, and Moreland, 1988]) as a stressful life event and exhibit short-term developmental disruptions, behavioral disorders, and emotional distress (Guidubaldi and Perry, 1985; Hetherington, 1981; Kurdek, 1987; Wallerstein, 1984). In the first few years following their parents' divorce, children show more antisocial and impulsive behavior; more aggression and noncompliance; more dependency, anxiety, and depression; more difficulties in social relationships; and more problem behavior in school than do their counterparts from intact families. Demo and Acock's (1988) review suggests that, after their parents' divorce, young children experience temporary negative affects in personal adjustment, but that adolescents are more affected by parental discord than family structure (two versus one-parent families). This theme—that parental discord is a more potent factor than is family structure in influencing child adjustment—is commonly cited in the research literature (Emery, 1982). One implication of this finding is that well-functioning single-parent families may foster child adjustment more effectively than two-parent families with parental discord.

Clinical and research reports suggest that the undesirable effects of becoming and being a member of a single-parent home are reduced in severity over time. However, long-term follow-ups of children in the Hetherington, Cox, and Cox (1978) and Wallerstein and Kelly (1980) studies revealed that some difficulties persist. Specifically, those from divorced families encountered more negative life changes than children from intact families, and these negative changes were associated with behavior problems six years following divorce (Hetherington et al., 1985). While most of the children in the Wallerstein (1984) ten-year longitudinal study were performing adequately in school, many spoke sorrowfully of their emotional and financial deprivation and wished for the more enriching life that they envisioned within intact families.

Despite these largely negative findings, some investigators have emphasized the potential beneficial effects of living in single-parent families. Kurdek and Siesky (1980) characterized children in father-absent families as androgynous, partly because children in these families often assume a variety of domestic responsibilities to compensate for the absence of the nonresidential parent (Weiss, 1979). In addition, adolescents living in single-parent families have been described as having high levels of maturity, feelings of efficacy, and an internal locus of control (Guidubaldi and Perry, 1985; Wallerstein and Kelly, 1984; Weiss, 1979).

In sum, the research reviewed in this section and most reports in the literature that have examined the impact of being raised in single-parent families have studied children whose parents divorced. Given the losses associated with divorce, children may fare relatively better in single-parent homes originating from other beginnings (e.g., mothers who never married). Because mothers who never married are the major factor in establishing single-parenthood for black children and because divorce is the modal origin of single-parent status for white children, there is reason to believe that some of the findings discussed in this section (based on primarily white samples) may not generalize to black children.

PROTECTIVE FACTORS AMONG BLACK CHILDREN FROM SINGLE-PARENT FAMILIES

To better understand why some black children emerge from single-parent families with favorable outcomes and others do not, the existing research on the adjustment of black children from single-parent families will be reviewed, following the resilience-promoting categories proposed by Garmezy (1985, 1987): personality factors in the child, the availability of a supportive family milieu, and access to an external support system that encourages and reinforces a child's coping attempts. The focus will be on socioemotional adjustment and not socioeconomic status, an important element of well-being that is beyond the scope of this review.

Personality Factors in the Child

Garmezy (1987) suggests that certain personality characteristics in children, particularly high self-esteem, are adaptive in adjusting to stressful circumstances. The studies described later report findings related to black children's self-esteem and other personality dispositions that may foster resilience.

Studies of children in two different age ranges suggest that black single-parent families are at least as able as two-parent families in fostering self-esteem in children. Rubin (1974) administered a self-concept questionnaire to 280 black fifth and sixth graders and found no significant differences between those from two-parent and single-parent households. According to Rubin, the availability of male role models outside the home was important for these children.

Hartnagel (1970) studied 113 black and 162 white adolescents from both single- and two-parent families. His results indicated that adolescents from single-parent black families had significantly lower mean differences between their actual and ideal self-concepts than did white adolescents from single-parent families. No racial differences emerged among adolescents from two-parent families. Although mothers were not assessed, Hartnagel suggested that black single mothers were more effective than their white counterparts in fostering a sense of competency in their children. Similarly, Hunt and Hunt (1975, 1977) analyzed survey data from 1,917 white and black adolescents and found that single-parenthood had damaging effects on white but not black adolescents' self-images. In fact, black male adolescents from single-parent families had higher self-images than did black males from two-parent families. This effect cut across social class.

Other studies examined variables likely associated with self-esteem and drew similar conclusions. Hurley (1972) assessed the vocational aspirations of 182 black and white working-class adolescents and observed no detrimental effects from living in single-parent families. He suggests that society, and peer groups in particular, may compensate for father absence.

Most research shows academic achievement among black children is unrelated to family structure (Hunt and Hunt, 1975; 1977; Shinn, 1978). Svanum, Bringle, and McLaughlin (1982) found, after controlling for socioeconomic status, that there were no significant differences in cognitive functioning for black (or white) children from father-present and father-absent homes. Further, Milne et al. (1986), using two nationally representative data bases, found that the effects of maternal employment on the academic achievement of black elementary school students from single-parent families were positive, while the effects on white children from single-parent families were mixed or nonsignificant. In addition to suggesting that black children from single-parent families benefit from their mothers working, this study also demonstrates that the same phenomenon (i.e., maternal employment) can have different effects on black and white children.

Assertiveness is another personality characteristic that may foster resilience in adjustment to a single-parent household. In an ethological study of factors associated with naturally occuring assertive behavior among preschool children, Weigel (1985) found that the most assertive children tended to be black, older, male, and from single-parent homes. These racial differences existed independently of social class. Weigel suggests that black parents may be preparing their children for life in a racially stratified society by reinforcing assertive/aggressive behavior. Whatever its origin, this assertive disposition may serve black children well in adapting to life in single-parent families.

Another indicator of the presence of favorable personality characteristics that foster resiliency is the quality of children's adjustment in single-parent homes. Fine and McKenry (1990) compared the adjustment of white and black children in divorced families using parental reports from the National Survey of Families and Households. They found that black parents assessed the quality of their children's lives more positively than white parents. In addition, white mothers indicated that they were more likely to take their children to see a therapist than were black mothers. While focusing only on divorce and not single-parenthood in general, this study suggests that black children, at least from their parents' perceptions, are less likely to encounter adjustment difficulties serious enough to require professional assistance. It should be noted that not all investigators have concluded that there are racial differences in child adjustment in single-parent families. McLanahan and Booth (1989), in their review of mother-only families, concluded that child adjustment does not differ according to race.

Supportive Family Milieu

Garmezy (1987) argues that a supportive, stable, and cohesive family climate—particularly nonconflictual relations between the parents and good parent-child relationships—serve a protective function for children. This section considers studies assessing whether these conditions are or are not met in black single-parent families.

First, a number of reports suggest that black single-parent families are cohesive, flexibly led, as school-achievement oriented as two-parent families, and may tap into external support to help them achieve their goals. Savage, Adair, and Friedman (1978) studied 200 black parent-absent families, including separated, divorced, widowed, parent-incarcerated, and male-headed. Their findings indicated that the majority of mothers in all groups reported that cohesiveness within their families was either "good" or "very good." Nobers (1968) investigated the effectiveness of black and white single mothers and their adolescents. Using a sample of 48 lower class mothers equally divided by race and family status, he found that black mothers were more "flexible" than their white counterparts.

Scheinfeld (1983), in his survey of 33 lower income, urban black families, found no differences between intact and single-parent families with respect to either boys' achievement and school performance or maternal attitudes. In addition, mothers of high achievers expressed ideals for their sons that emphasized self-motivation and active and engaged learning styles. Similar findings have been reported by Radin (1971), Slaughter (1969), and Prom-Jackson, Johnson, and Wallace (1987). The latter authors found that parents of academically talented black youth had high aspirations for and high expectations of their children.

In a study of family role strain (defined as stress resulting from fulfilling family role obligations) among 51 employed black women, Katz and Piotrkowski (1983) found that nonmarried mothers experienced no greater levels than did their married counterparts. Family size appeared to be a more important contributor to family role strain than the simple presence or absence of a husband. St. Pierre (1982) conducted in-depth interviews with 25 black, single mothers in the areas of family finances, attitudes toward males, parenting, and sense of family. Respondents developed innovative ways of meeting financial obligations. Although maintaining a somewhat negative attitude toward the fathers of their children and toward males in general, he found that these women nevertheless coped fairly well and reported a strong sense of organization and cohesiveness within the family.

Numerous authors have noted that black family members may benefit from an extensive kinship network. The extended family system's members can assist single parents, performing functions and serving roles that might otherwise go unprovided. Tienda and Angel (1982) documented that 28.2 percent of black single-mother homes contained adults and/or children from outside the nuclear family, in contrast to only 16.5 percent of white female-headed units. The racial differences remained even after adjustments were made for socioeconomic and demographic characteristics.

Extracting data from national longitudinal surveys, Takai (1981) found that many black single women use kinship support to replace the lost income of their ex-husbands more successfully than do white women. In a longitudinal study of black families in Mississippi and Chicago, Shimkin, Shimkin, and Frate (1978) found that extended families, sometimes consisting of over 100 individuals, were quite adaptive in terms of family members' survival and social mobility. Similarly, Stack (1974), Billingsley (1968), Aschenbrenner (1978), Malson (1983), Taylor (1986), McAdoo (1978), and Wilson (1986) have reported that the extensive extended family system served as an adaptive resource, often supporting members' upward mobility. These studies have not compared extended family networks in single-parent with those in two-parent families.

Not all investigators have concluded that single mothers have access to a sufficient amount of social support. Kin network members may assist with material needs, but they may also interfere with mothers' parenting styles (McLanahan & Booth, 1989). All in all, Milardo (1987) claims interference from kin tends to outweigh support from friends, so that single mothers experience a net negative amount of support. In contrast, those in friendship networks provide more emotional than material support, and are especially useful when the mother is attempting to change her predivorce identity and establish a new career (McLanahan, Wedemeyer, and Adelberg, 1981).

In evaluating any given family, rather than the modal family, Lindblad-Goldberg, Dukes, and Lasley's (1988) study of 70 "functional" and 56 "dysfunctional" poor, single-parent, black families is useful. They found similarities between the two types of families in the sizes and structural composition of their social networks, but mothers from the functional families were more likely to be voluntarily interdependent on others and to report that the relationships with others were reciprocal. In contrast, mothers from dysfunctional families indicated that they provided more emotional and instrumental support than they received from network members, especially family members.

Garmezy (1987), in describing the family milieu that promotes resiliency, referred to the importance of nonconflictual relations among family members. While the investigation of Dancy and Handal (1984), who studied 40 black adolescents from single-parent homes and a matched group of 40 from intact families, did not find differences in conflict level between one- and two-parent homes, it did provide support for Garmezy's position. More specifically, subjects' perceptions of family climate, psychological adjustment, and peer relationships were not related to their parents' marital status, but rather to the level of perceived conflict in the family. Dancy and Handal concluded that family structure was less important in determining the adolescents' adjustment than the amount of conflict perceived within the family.

Other research has identified factors in single-parent black families that operate to discourage the development of a resiliency-promoting atmosphere in the home. For example, McLanahan and Booth (1989) note that mother-only families face numerous stressors, including economic instability (and often poverty), loss of social support, a potential loss of social status, and possible changes in residence. These stressors (particularly related to divorce) may make it more difficult for single-parent families to provide a supportive milieu.

Other studies indicated that living in single-parent homes is related to lower levels of satisfaction among black single parents, which, in turn, may negatively affect children. Broman (1988), using data from the National Survey of Black Americans, found that divorced and separated blacks had lower levels of satisfaction than married peers. Similarly, Zollar and Williams (1987) reported that married black adults (of both genders) tended to be happier with their marriages and their lives than were unmarried black persons.

External Support System

The third protective factor that promotes resiliency is an external support system that encourages and reinforces a child's coping efforts, and strengthens these by inculcating positive values. The kind of support necessary is illustrated by the findings of Rutter et al. (1979)—lower delinquency rates in children were associated with a number of classroom management techniques, including the use of a high level of structure in the classroom, an emphasis on homework and exams, allowing students to assume responsibility for their actions and activities, and the teacher maintaining a prosocial atmosphere. In the context of single-parent families, the presence of strong social networks may ease the parents' and, consequently, the child's adjustment (Milardo, 1987; Savage, Adair, and Friedman, 1978).

The involvement of fathers can be influential in the lives of their children living in single-parent homes. They can function at the core of their children's nonhousehold support system and can provide some of the discipline necessary for effective coping, problem-solving, and living. Morris (1977) studied professionally employed blacks, now living in middle-class neighborhoods who grew up in single-parent families. These individuals felt that their fathers, although they did not live with them, were nevertheless important and they did not remember experiencing as youngsters a feeling that their homes were "broken."

Many black children living in single-parent households lack the opportunity to develop supportive relationships with their fathers. Furstenberg et al. (1983), in their analysis of a nationally representative sample of American children aged 11 to 16, found that black fathers were less likely to have seen their children in the past five years than either whites or other minorities, possibly because they were never married to the mothers or because their marriages dissolved when the children were very young. The Furstenberg et al. data do not directly address the issue of whether there are other males involved in the children's lives, as males in the community may provide support and serve as role models. Dancy and Handal's (1984) study noted that 75 percent of the adolescents in single-parent black families reported having males available to them at the time of their parents' divorce: of these men, 44 percent were uncles, 22 percent were grandfathers, 22 percent were mothers' boyfriends, and 11 percent were others, including friends and older brothers. Willie's (1976) study of over 200 families also demonstrated that single-parent family units do not lack male role models. In the case of a male figure providing support, the child benefits directly and indirectly, as the adult male help-giver eases the mother's adjustment and, consequently, the child's (Milardo, 1987; Savage et al., 1978).

Many black children from single-parent homes also benefit from the supportive social environment typically afforded to children in black communities. Some authors (King, 1976; Nobles, 1978; Staples, 1976) maintain that the black community values children in unique ways: they are prized regardless of their parentage and of their personal achievement, they are given love and nurturance in either one- or two-parent homes, and they are indirectly benefitted because their mothers and fathers gain community recognition for being parents, regardless of their marital status. With reference to children born out of wedlock, King (1976) maintains that there is no such entity as a black "illegitimate" child because, in his view, all youngsters, regardless of their parents' marital status, belong to, are valued by, and are cared for by the entire black community.

Others also argue that the black community is more accepting of single-parent status than are white individuals and this acceptance, in turn, may facilitate the adjustment of black children. Peters and Deford (1978) suggest that blacks consider the single-parent home as a viable family structure. Two factors undoubtedly contribute to this. First, a relative shortage of black men relative to black women (Darity and Myers, 1984) fosters the greater prevalence of single-parent families in the black community. Second, those black single-parent families that are successfully functioning encourage and support individuals considering and assuming that parental role.

The nature of the black community also benefits children in single-parent families directly, and indirectly, in at least one other way. Ball

(1983) interviewed low-income black families in Florida and found that his subjects had highly developed networks of kin and friends with whom they interacted frequently. While respondents seldom requested support from network members to assist with major problems, the interviewees were reassured simply by knowing that a supportive network was available if a pressing need emerged. Ball suggested that low-income parents recognize their friends' and relatives' limited ability to help financially.

INTEGRATING RESILIENCE AND ADJUSTMENT OF CHILDREN IN BLACK SINGLE-PARENT FAMILIES: A THEORETICAL MODEL

Numerous scholars have used the "emergent" model of black family functioning to explain why some black children adjust well to living in single-parent families. The discussion that follows explores the relation between the concept of resilience and the emergent model and how this model might explain the experiences and reactions of members of black single-parent families. Nobles (1974, p. 11) notes: "The black family, we contend, can only be understood or is best understood as a unit deriving its primary characteristics, form, and definition from its African nature."

Nobles identifies two African traditions with significant implications for black single-parent, American families: the importance of the tribe's survival and oneness of being. These traditions manifest themselves as a prime form of cohesion in the black community, promoting a sense of social solidarity and extending the family beyond traditional blood lines to the community as a whole. As a result, Nobles (1978) identified special characteristics of black families. They (1) are comprised of several households; (2) have multiple parenting and interfamilial consensual adoptions; (3) are child-centered; (4) have a close network of relationships between families not necessarily related by blood; and (5) have flexible and interchangeable role definitions and performance. These features have obvious value to the health of single-parent families and, moreover, provide the kinds of conditions that nurture the development of "protective factors" that also promote resilience.

Sudarkasa (1980), who studied cultural patterns of continental African societies, explains that when Africans marry, they do not begin new families, but rather join existing ones. The consanguineal core of the family, consisting of all blood relatives, is considerably more focal to African extended families than is the conjugal relationship, consisting of the marital pair. Although divorce is rare in African societies, when it does occur, the family remains stable, readjusting in a variety of ways to restore equilibrium.

This principle that consanguinity is primary in African family patterns has important implications for modern black families. As Sudarkasa (1975, p. 238) stated:

> Among blacks, households centered around consanguineal relatives have as much legitimacy . . . as family units as do households centered around conjugal unions. When this fact is understood, it becomes clear that the instability of conjugal relations cannot be taken as the sole measure of instability of the family. That black families exhibit considerable stability over time and space is evidenced by the enduring linkages and bonds of mutual obligation found among networks of consanguineal kin.

Empirical support for Sudarkasa's thesis pertaining to African roots in African-American families was generated in studies by Hauenstein (1977) and Brown, Perry, and Harburg (1977) comparing black and white wives. Hauenstein found that black women were more satisfied with their maternal role, felt it important to be good mothers and earn the respect of their children, while, at the same time, were more critical and independent with respect to evaluating the quality of their marriages than were white wives. In the Brown et al. study, results also suggested that black women at various stages of divorce were more critical of and dissatisfied with their husbands than were white women. Consistent with the Sudarkasa thesis, it appears that the maternal role is more highly valued for black women than is the marital relationship, and that they were willing to end the latter if it was not satisfying. Again, Sudarkasa's thesis suggests why and how the protective factors and resiliency would develop in many black single-parent households.

CONCLUSIONS

This review suggests that certain characteristics of black families may promote resiliency and help some black children effectively adjust to living in single-parent families. However, the literature does not support the conclusion that black children cope more effectively in single-parent homes than they would in two-parent families, or that black children in single-parent families adjust more positively than white children in such families. Rather, the conclusion that follows from this review is that some black children benefit from protective factors identified as being common in the black community.

More research is needed on how black children adjust to single-parenthood. Major longitudinal studies (paralleling those conducted with primarily white populations) would provide data with both theoretical and clinical value. Investigators planning to conduct such research should be aware that some black scholars suggest that differing investigatory methods are necessary to gain an understanding of the unique aspects of black culture. Dixon (1976), for example, proposes that, for a researcher to understand, appreciate, and be consistent with the traditional African notion of "universal unity," all studies conducted in the black community should utilize participant-observation methods.

While clinicians should and typically do avoid drawing implications about family functioning merely from knowledge of a given family's structure, it is particularly critical to do so with clients from black single-parent families. In order to assess the support and resources they may generate to help the unit and its members adjust, clinical interviews must routinely ask about factors that stimulate the resiliency-promoting protective factors; that is, the extent of aid from extended family members and friends, the amount of participation by fathers or other male figures, the parents' views of children, the adjustment to single-parenthood, and so forth. With the additional information provided by responses to these inquiries, more sensitive and effective interventions can be designed.

REFERENCES

Aschenbrenner, J. (1978). Continuities and variation in black family structure. In D. B. Shimkin, E. M. Shimkin, and D. A. Frate (Eds.), *The extended family in black societies.* The Hague: Mouton Publishers.

Ball, R. E. (1983). Family and friends: A supportive network for low-income American black families. *Journal of Comparative Family Studies,* 14(1), 51-65.

Billingsley, A. (1968). *Black families in white America.* Englewood Cliffs, NJ: Prentice-Hall.

Broman, C. L. (1988). Satisfaction among blacks: The significance of marriage and parenthood. *Journal of Marriage and the Family, 50,* 45-51.

Brown, P., Perry, L., and Harburg, E. (1977). Sex role attitudes and psychological outcomes for black and white women experiencing marital dissolution. *Journal of Marriage and the Family, 39,* 549-562.

Cohen, S. and Hoberman, H. (1983). Positive events and social supports as buffers of life change stress. *Journal of Applied Social Psychology, 13,* 99-121.

Dancy, B. L. and Handal, P. J. (1984). Perceived family climate, psychological adjustment, and peer relationship of black adolescents: A function of parental marital status or perceived family conflict? *Journal of Community Psychology, 12,* 222-229.

Darity, W. A. and Myers, S. J. (1984). Does welfare dependency cause female headship? The case of the black family. *Journal of Marriage and the Family, 46,* 765-779.

Demo, D. H. and Acock, A. C. (1988). The impact of divorce on children. *Journal of Marriage and the Family, 50,* 619-648.

Dixon, V. (1976). World views and research methodology. In L. King and V. Dixon, and W. Nobles (Eds.), *African philosophy: Assumptions and paradigms for research on black persons.* Los Angeles: Fanon Center.

Emery, R. E. (1982). Interparental conflict and the children of discord and divorce. *Psychological Bulletin, 92,* 310-330.

Fine, M. A. and McKenry, P. (1990). Patterns of black and white adjustment to divorce. Manuscript in preparation.

Fine, M. A., Schwebel, A. I., and Myers, L. J. (1987). Family stability in black families: Values underlying three different perspectives. *Journal of Comparative Family Studies, 18,* 1-23.

Furstenberg, F. F., Nord, C. W., Peterson, J. L., and Zill, N. (1983). The life course of children of divorce: marital disruption and parental contact. *American Sociological Review, 48,* 656-668.

Garmezy, N. (1985). Stress-resistant children: The search for protective factors. In J. E. Stevenson (Ed.), *Recent research in developmental psychopathology* (pp. 213-233). Oxford: Pergamon Press.

______. (1987). Stress, competence, and development: Continuities in the study of schizophrenic adults, children vulnerable to psychopathology, and the search for stress-resistant children. *American Journal of Orthopsychiatry, 57,* 159-174.

Glick, P. C. (1984). Marriage, divorce, and living arrangements: Prospective changes. *Journal of Family Issues, 5,* 7-26.

Guidubaldi, J., Cleminshaw, H. K., Perry, J. D., Nastasi, B. K., and Lightel, J. (1986). The role of selected family environment factors in children's post-divorce adjustment. *Family Relations, 35,* 141-151.

Guidubaldi, J. and Perry, J. D. (1985). Divorce and mental health sequelae for children. *Journal of the American Academy of Child Psychiatry, 24,* 531-537.

Hartnagel, T. F. (1970). Father absence and self-conception among lower class white and Negro boys. *Social Problems, 18,* 152-163.

Hauenstein, L. (1977). Attitudes of married women toward work and family: Comparisons of housewives and working wives in four socioecologically different neighborhoods. *Final Report, U.S. Public Health Service.* Rockville, MD: NIMH.

Hetherington, E. M. (1981). Children and divorce. In R. Henderson (Ed.), *Parent-child interaction: Theory, research and prospect* (pp. 33-58). New York: Academic Press.

Hetherington, E. M., Cox, M., and Cox, R. (1978). The aftermath of divorce. In J. H. Stevens, Jr. and M. Mathews (Eds.), *Mother-child, father-child relationships* (pp. 149-176). Washington, DC: National Association for Education of Young Children.

______. (1985). Effects of divorce and remarriage on the adjustment of children. *Journal of the American Academy of Child Psychiatry, 24,* 518-530.

Hunt, L. L. and Hunt, J. G. (1975). Race and the father-son connection: The conditional relevance of father absence for the orientations and identities of adolescent boys. *Social Problems, 23,* 35-52.

Hunt, J. G. and Hunt, L. L. (1977). Race, daughters, and father-loss: does absence make the girl grow stronger? *Social Problems, 25,* 90-102.

Hurley, R. B. (1972). Race, fatherlessness, and vocational development: An exploration of relationships between membership in nuclear or fatherless families and level of occupational aspiration and expectation, self-esteem, extrinsic work values and person-orientation among a sample of black and white adolescent boys. Unpublished doctoral dissertation, New York University.

Katz, M. H. and Piotrkowski, C. S. (1983). Correlates of family role strain among employed black women. *Family Relations, 32,* 331-339.

King, J. R. (1976). African survivals in the black American family: Key factors in stability. *Journal of Afro-American Issues, 4,* 153-167.

Kurdek, L. A. (1987). Children's adjustment to parental divorce: An ecological perspective. In J. P. Vincent (Ed.), *Advances in family intervention, assessment and theory* (Vol. 4). (pp. 1-32). Greenwich, CT: JAI Press.

Kurdek, L. A. and Siesky, A. E. (1980). Sex role self-concepts of single divorced parents and their children. *Journal of Divorce, 3,* 249-261.

Lindblad-Goldberg, M., Dukes, J. L., and Lasley, J. H. (1988). Stress in black, low-income, single-parent families: Normative and dysfunctional patterns. *American Journal of Orthopsychiatry 58,* 104-120.

Maddi, S., Hoover, M., and Kobasa, S. (1982). Alienation and exploratory behavior. *Journal of Personality and Social Psychology, 42,* 884-890.

Malson, M. (1983). The social-support systems of black families. *Marriage and Family Review, 5,* 37-57.

McAdoo, H. (1978). Factors related to stability in upwardly mobile black families. *Journal of Marriage and the Family, 40,* 761-776.

McLanahan, S. and Booth, K. (1989). Mother-only families: Problems, prospects, and politics. *Journal of Marriage and the Family, 51,* 557-580.

McLanahan, S. S., Wedemeyer, N., and Adelberg, T. (1981). Network structure, social support and psychological well-being in the single-parent family. *Journal of Marriage and the Family, 43,* 601-612.

Milardo, R. M. (1987). Changes in social networks of women and men following divorce: A review. *Journal of Family Issues, 8,* 78-96.

Milne, A. M., Myers, D. E., Rosenthal, A. S., and Ginsburg, A. (1986). Single parents, working mothers, and the educational achievement of school children. *Sociology of Education, 59,* 125-139.

Morris, R. B. (1977). Strengths of the black community: An investigation of the black community and broken homes. Unpublished doctoral dissertation, Columbia University Teachers College, New York.

Moynihan, D. P. (1965). *The Negro family: The case for national action.* Washington, DC: Office of Policy Planning and Research, U.S. Department of Labor.

Nobers, D. R. (1968). The effects of father absence and mothers' characteristics on the identification of adolescent white and Negro males. Unpublished doctoral dissertation, St. Louis University.

Nobles, W. (1974). Africanity: Its role in black families. *The Black Scholar, 5,* 10-17.

______. (1978). Toward an empirical and theoretical framework for defining black families. *Journal of Marriage and the Family, 40,* 679-688.

Norton, A. J. and Glick, P. C. (1986). One parent families: A social and economic profile. *Family Relations, 35,* 9-17.

Peters, M. and Deford, C. (1978). The solo mother. In R. Staples (Ed.), *The black family: Essays and studies.* Belmont, CA: Wadsworth.

Prom-Jackson, S., Johnson, S. T., and Wallace, M. B. (1987). Home environment, talented minority youth, and school achievement. *Journal of Negro Education, 56,* 111-121.

Radin, N. (1971). Maternal warmth, achievement motivation, and cognitive functioning in lower-class pre-school children. *Child Development, 42,* 1560-1565.

Rubin, R. H. (1974). Adult male absence and the self-attitudes of black children. *Child Study Journal, 4,* 33-46.

Rutter, M. (1985). Resilience in the face of adversity: Protective factors and resistance to psychiatric disorder. *British Journal of Psychiatry, 147,* 598-611.

______. (1987). Psychosocial resilience and protective mechanisms. *American Journal of Orthospsychiatry, 57,* 316-331.

Rutter, M., Maughan, B., Mortimore, P., Ouston, J., and Smith, A. (1979). *Fifteen thousand hours: Secondary schools and their effects on children.* Cambridge, MA: Harvard University Press.

Savage, J. E., Adair, A. V., and Friedman, P. (1978). Community and social variables related to black parent-absent families. *Journal of Marriage and the Family, 40,* 779-785.

Scheinfeld, D. R. (1983). Family relationships and school achievement among boys of lower-income urban black families. *American Journal of Orthopsychiatry, 53,* 127-143.

Schwebel, A. I., Fine, M. A., and Moreland, J. R. (1988). Clinical work with divorced and widowed fathers: The adjusting family model. In P. Bronstein and C. P. Cowan (Eds.), *Fatherhood today: Men's changing role in the family.* New York: Wiley.

Shimkin, D. B., Shimkin, E. M., and Frate, D. A. (Eds.) (1978). *The extended family in black societies.* The Hague: Mouton Publishers.

Shinn, M. (1978). Father absence and children's cognitive development. *Psychological Bulletin, 85,* 295-324.

Slaughter, D. (1969). Maternal antecedents of the academic achievement behaviors of Afro-American Head Start children. *Educational Horizons, 48,* 24-28.

Stack, C. B. (1974). *All our kin: Strategies for survival in a black community.* New York: Harper and Row.

Staples, R. (1976). *Introduction to black sociology.* New York: McGraw-Hill.

St. Pierre, M. (1982). Black female single-parent family life: A preliminary sociological perspective. *The Black Sociologist, 9,* 28-47.

Sudarkasa, N. (1975). An exposition of the value premises underlying black family studies. *Journal of the National Medical Association, 67,* 235-239.

______. (1980). African and Afro-American structure: A comparison. *The Black Scholar, 11,* 37-60.

Svanum, S., Bringle, R. G., and McLaughlin, J. E. (1982). Father absence and cognitive performance in a large sample of six- to eleven-year-old children. *Child Development, 53,* 136-143.

Takai, R. T. (1981). Marital separation in first marriages and remarriages of women: An examination of divergent patterns. *Dissertation Abstracts International, 42,* 2, 875A.

Taylor, R. J. (1986). Receipt of support from family among black Americans: Demographic and familial differences. *Journal of Marriage and the Family, 48,* 67-77.

Tienda, M. and Angel, R. (1982). Headship and household composition among blacks, hispanics, and other whites. *Social Forces, 61,* 508-531.

U.S. Bureau of the Census (1984a). Current Population Reports. Series P-20, No. 389, *Marital status and living arrangements: March, 1983.* Washington, DC: U.S. Government Printing Office.

______. (1984b). Current Population Reports. Series P-20, No. 388, *Household and family characteristics: June, 1983.* Washington, DC: U.S. Government Printing Office.

Wallerstein, J. (1984). Children of divorce: Preliminary report of a ten-year follow-up of young children. *American Journal of Orthopsychiatry, 54,* 444-458.

Wallerstein, J. and Kelly, J. (1980). *Surviving the breakup: How children and parents cope with divorce.* New York: Basic Books.

Weigel, R. M. (1985). Demographic factors affecting assertive and defensive behavior in preschool children: An ethological study. *Aggressive Behavior, 11,* 27-40.

Weiss, R. (1979). *Going it alone.* New York: Basic Books.

Werner, E. E. (1989). High-risk children in young adulthood: A longitudinal study from birth to 32 years. *American Journal of Orthopsychiatry, 59,* 72-81.

Werner, E. E. and Smith, B. A. (1982). *Vulnerable but invincible: A longitudinal study of resilient children and youth.* New York: McGraw-Hill.

Willie, C. V. (1976). *A new look at black families.* Bayside, NY: General Hall.

Wilson, M. (1986). The black extended family: An analytical consideration. *Developmental Psychology, 22,* 246-258.

Zollar, A. C. and Williams, J. S. (1987). The contribution of marriage to the life satisfaction of black adults. *Journal of Marriage and the Family, 49,* 87-92.

Chapter 4

Stepchildren: Burying the Cinderella Myth

Marilyn Coleman and
Lawrence H. Ganong

Stepchildren have an image problem. If stepchildren were consumer products, their advertising firm would be fired and a new one called in to devise a fresh marketing scheme. When people think of the term "stepchild," they often think of a child who is neglected, abused, and perhaps unwanted. In fact, the very idea of stepchildren doing well is so atypical that the term stepchild is sometimes used as a metaphor to refer to a person, group, or organization who is ignored, mistreated, or "in the way" (Coleman and Ganong, 1987). This negative image of stepchildren is widely held. For example, counselors, social workers, nurses, student teachers, and college students have been found to hold negative perceptions of stepchildren (Ganong, Coleman, and Mapes, in press).

In spite of prevailing negative attitudes about stepchildren, there are countless examples of well-known, successful stepchildren. One of the most famous American presidents, Abraham Lincoln, was a stepchild; Gerald Ford is a more recent president who is also a stepchild. First Lady Barbara Bush is a stepchild, as was her predecessor, Nancy Reagan. Author John Irving and even Superman (Christopher Reeve) are stepchildren, as was the famous artist, James M. Whistler (Whistler's mother was really his *step*mother). The list could go on and on, but the point has been made; many stepchildren do well in life, even though prevailing cultural myths and attitudes seem to suggest that this is not likely.

RESEARCH ON STEPCHILDREN

There are a large number of stepfamilies and stepchildren in American society. Demographer Paul Glick (1989) has predicted that over 35 percent of the children born in the early 1980s can expect to live with a stepparent before age 18. The actual number of stepchildren is not known, however, since most samples have excluded stepfamilies following parental death, do not include families formed by cohabiting couples, or are limited to assessing residential steprelationships only (Coleman and Ganong, in press). The 1990 Census was the first one to measure steprelationships; previously, estimates of the number of stepchildren were derived from subsamples. However, even the 1990 Census greatly underestimated the number of stepchildren, because only those living in stepfamily *households* were counted. An unknown number of children reside primarily with one parent but visit their other parent and stepparent. Another group, the growing number of children living in de facto (cohabitating) stepfamily households, is basically ignored.

Unfortunately, despite the relatively large number of stepchildren, the body of research on them has been slow to develop. The early literature on stepchildren was written primarily by clinicians, and even now publications by clinicians are more numerous than those by researchers. In fact, most of the empirical studies of stepchildren have been conducted in the past ten years (Coleman and Ganong, in press). Of these studies, few focused on positive outcomes for stepchildren (Coleman and Ganong, in press). Researchers appear to be little different from the general population in attitudes and assumptions regarding stepchildren; most have not shown interest in examining why some stepchildren and their families are "successful."

Two major perspectives have dominated the research on stepchildren. The most common framework is a problem-oriented perspective that examines what are generally predicted to be negative effects of parental remarriage on children. Not surprisingly, this framework has provided little insight into the successful functioning and development of stepchildren. A more recent approach looks at stepchildren and steprelationships from a normative-adaptive perspective. This approach, which emphasizes describing and understanding stepfamily relationships, is more likely to yield information about positive stepchild outcomes.

Problem-Oriented Perspective

Deficit Comparison. One of the most prevalent problem-oriented perspectives is the deficit-comparison approach, a model that assumes stepchildren will be at a deficit when compared with children from nuclear families. Deficit-comparison studies tended to focus on psychological outcome variables. Self-esteem, depression, and psychosomatic symptoms are examples of commonly measured variables. These studies have been characterized by simple designs that ignore potentially important mediating variables. For example, stepfather, stepmother, and complex stepfamilies (i.e., those households containing children from both spouses' previous relationships) frequently were grouped together. Other structural variations, such as the child's age at remarriage, the number of siblings and stepsiblings, the amount of contact with the nonresidential parent, the number of years the child had lived in the stepfamily, and the number of years the child lived in a single-parent household were also often ignored. Despite the conceptual and methodological limitations of the deficit-comparison approach, it can be concluded from these studies that stepchildren as a group do not differ much from other children (Coleman and Ganong, in press; Ganong and Coleman, 1984; 1986).

Stressful Family Transitions. Another problem-oriented perspective examines the effects of stressful family transitions on children. The most common study design has been a comparison of stepchildren to children in other types of families, especially nuclear families. A major problem with this body of literature is that conclusions were drawn about family *transitions* based entirely on cross-sectional data.

Another problem with these studies has been that behavioral ratings of children from only one person were often used. Typically, the rater knew the family status of the child prior to rating the child's behavior. If the rater held expectations for stepchildren that were negative, as has been indicated in other studies (Coleman and Ganong, in press), these expectations may have unduly affected the ratings. In some studies it was not clear whether a biological parent or stepparent was rating the children's behavior. This is important to know because stepparents typically evaluate stepchildren's behavior less positively than biological parents rate their own children's behavior (Coleman and Ganong, 1986). Studies that include teacher ratings of stepchildren are also problematic in that teachers judge children believed to be from nuclear families more positively than children believed to reside in other family forms (Guttman and Broudo, 1989). Even parent raters may be susceptible to stereotypes related to the effects of divorce and remarriage on children and may "see" problems in their children's behavior that are not there (Ferri, 1984).

Social class was not accounted for in many of the problem-oriented studies. Although Zill (1988) found that stepchildren's academic performance was slightly lower than nuclear family children, Ferri (1984) found that differences in academic performance disappeared between stepchildren and nuclear family children when she statistically controlled for social class. Social class is obviously an important mediating variable that should not be ignored.

Socialization Hypothesis. Another perspective, one we have called the socialization hypothesis (Coleman and Ganong, in press), also focused on problems. The theoretical underpinnings of this perspective come from psychoanalytic and social learning theories. Essentially, marital disruptions and remarriage are viewed as limiting children's exposure to important role models, and diminishing or terminating children's contact with important sources of reinforcement, resulting in inadequate socialization. Somewhat related to this view is an approach that could be called the "additional adult"hypothesis. This, in essence, is a belief that the stepparent takes the place of the "missing" parent.

Although the socialization perspective has been frequently used in studying children of divorce, it has less often been employed in the study of stepchildren. It has mainly served as the conceptual framework for investigations of stepchildren's attitudes and behaviors related to marriage, divorce, and parenthood. The only consistent difference found when comparing the attitudes of children in nuclear families, in single-parent families, and in stepfamilies was that stepchildren have more positive attitudes toward divorce than children from the other two types of families (Coleman and Ganong, 1984; Kinnaird and Gerrard, 1986). The findings from studies of behavior were too mixed to draw meaningful conclusions about whether the socialization experiences of stepchildren help or hinder their adult marital and parental careers (Coleman and Ganong, in press). The additional adult hypothesis also has not received uniform support (Coleman and Ganong, in press).

Biological Discrimination. From studies using a framework we have labeled the biological discrimination hypothesis (Coleman and Ganong, in press), it has been concluded that stepfathers interact more negatively with stepchildren than with biological children, because they lack the motivational and emotional genetic ties necessary to parent adequately (Flinn, 1988). Studies of physical and sexual abuse are often formulated from this perspective, and they generally report that stepchildren are more at risk for abuse and neglect than children in nuclear families (Lightcap, Kurland, and Burgess, 1982).

With some notable exceptions, particularly in the areas of abuse and neglect, problem-oriented research conducted from a variety of conceptual frameworks has not consistently documented negative effects for children in stepfamilies. It is difficult, if not impossible, however, to discern from these studies why some stepchildren do well and others do not. The normative-adaptive perspective does provide some clues.

Why Do Some Stepchildren Do Well?

What are the correlates of successful outcomes for stepchildren? Why do some stepchildren flourish and others wilt? Although these questions have not been specifically addressed in empirical research to date, we can make some inferences from recent studies on stepchildren and their families.

Structural Predictors: Age and Sex. Since few studies specifically addressed positive outcome variables for stepchildren, not many firm conclusions can be drawn about predictors of positive outcomes. However, some researchers have indicated that the age and gender of stepchildren and the gender of stepparents are important variables to consider.

Children who are younger when parents remarry appear to adapt better to stepparents and stepfamily living than preadolescents and adolescents (Duberman, 1973). A response from a teenager we interviewed illustrated this point, "I didn't like it when they dated, but once they got married it was okay. I started calling him dad right away. It's good they got married when I was 9. I wanted a dad like the other kids. It would be a lot harder now—for me and for them." Another adolescent we interviewed said: "I was real little when they got married. Joe's my father; he does everything for me." However, there is little evidence, other than anecdotal, concerning the effects of age at parental remarriage on children's well-being.

Sex differences in stepchildren's adaptation to stepparents have yielded contradictory findings (Amato, 1987; Bray, 1988). Most studies have not found sex differences for stepchild adaptation (Clingempeel and Segal, 1986; Ferri, 1984; Isaacs and Leon, 1988). Self-esteem does not appear to differ between the sexes, nor are there large differences in attitudes toward marriage and family life (Coleman and Ganong, in press). Although some studies have reported that girls with stepfathers have more behavior problems than boys with stepfathers (Hetherington, Cox, and Cox, 1985; Peterson and Zill, 1986), others found that the effect depended upon the behavior being assessed (Baydar, 1988; Needle, Su, and Doherty, 1990). Clearly, more research is needed to examine the predictive value of stepchild gender on subsequent development of the child.

The sex of the stepparent also has been considered crucial by some investigators. Stepfathers interact with stepchildren more easily than stepmothers (Hobart and Brown, 1988) and report that they feel more comfortable in the stepparent role (Ahrons and Wallisch, 1987). There may be many reasons for this. Stepmothers often end up doing the major parenting tasks, including discipline, while stepfathers sometimes take a more passive part in the rearing of their stepchildren. Children are likely to have more complaints against the "person who makes them eat their vegetables" than about a shadowy background figure who interacts mostly with their mother. It also may be that, because of societal attitudes that carry over into the home, children have trouble relating to and accepting a second mother figure or a substitute mother figure. The mother is often considered to be the person most important to the child. If that person is missing from the child's life, the child may view him- or herself as deficient or lacking in some way.

Other structural predictors of child outcomes that have been studied include: having a half-sibling, the presence of stepsiblings, sharing a residence with a stepparent versus visiting the stepparent, and the amount of contact with nonresidential biological parent (Coleman and Ganong, in press). In general, none of these has been implicated as being clearly related to the well-being of stepchildren. In fact, the research on structural predictors has not yet been fruitful.

Clinical Propositions. Much of what is "known" about successful outcomes for stepchildren comes from clinical writers. Clinical opinion and expertise and clinical case studies have been rich sources for ideas about the hows and whys of positive stepfamily development. Generally, two sources of influences on positive outcomes for stepchildren have been postulated by clinicians: (1) resources "brought" by the stepparent and (2) contributions "created" or developed by the children. We will discuss both of these sources separately, and will include any relevant empirical or theoretical support.

Resources Brought by the Stepparent

Most clinical writings, and the bulk of research to date, have examined the stressful aspects of parental remarriage. The advent of a stepparent is typically seen as a situation presenting problems for the child to overcome. This is no doubt true for many stepchildren, but it does not tell us why some children adapt better than others, nor does it clarify why some children flourish in stepfamilies. However, a few clinical writers have identified what they believe are potential assets that stepparents and stepfamilies bring to children.

1. Having two adults in the home is better for children, for the most part, than having only one parental supervisor. As one adolescent stepchild commented about his stepfather, "he makes it his business to know my business." Although most stepchildren have two living biological parents, research has consistently found that nearly half of noncustodial fathers have very little, if any, contact with their children (Furstenberg and Nord, 1985; Seltzer and Bianchi, 1988). Even when they maintain contact, they often live too far away from the child to provide daily supervision and care. Children may get more attention and more loving care if there are two adults in the home to provide it. "You have two sets of parents; you get two sets of Christmas presents and twice the love" (quotes from a child who was asked, "What do you like best about living in a stepfamily?").

It should be noted that clinicians have long identified stepparent discipline as a volatile issue in stepfamilies (Visher and Visher, 1988). Stepchildren, particularly adolescents, may not welcome the supervision and control of any unrelated adult, stepparents included. When we asked stepchildren in a recent study, "What would you like your stepparent to be more involved in and why?" the most common response was "nothing." Many of these adolescents clearly were not seeking more parenting behavior from their stepparents. Several indicated they would like their stepparent to be *less* involved in certain aspects of their lives, especially school work, social life, punishment, and telling them what to do. For many adolescents, this held true for their biological parents as well. We do not deny that stepparent attempts to discipline may result in conflict; however, some degree of behavior monitoring may reduce behavior problems outside the home and may contribute to the optimal development of stepchildren.

We noted earlier that some research has been done on the "additional adult" hypothesis. Although this work has not uniformly found that the stepparent adds greater supervision and control (Steinberg, 1987), there is evidence to suggest that the addition of a stepparent into the household may facilitate stepchild development in some areas, such as the enhancement of academic achievement (Ganong and Coleman, 1984). This is yet another area in which more research is needed. When do stepparents effectively serve as substitute parents? Are there areas of child development in which stepparents do not function as the "added adult"? These and other questions remain unanswered.

2. Children in stepfamilies may be observing a model of a satisfying, functional marital relationship for the first time. Not only might this reduce stress (if the nuclear family environment was strife-ridden), but observing a stable, well-functioning remarriage can help teach children how to have satisfying interpersonal relationships as well.

Having a stepparent also provides children with an additional model of what a "mother" or "father" can be. It even provides them with new models of how to be a "man" or a "woman." Children often imitate their parents, and having intimate knowledge of more than one model can be very helpful to them in deciding how they want to be as adults.

3. A child's development is often considered to be enriched by variety. When stepparents and other steprelations (e.g., stepsiblings, stepgrandparents) enter their lives, they are often introduced to new ways of doing things. This may include hobbies they had not been exposed to previously, different family rituals, new ideas about vacations, new skills, and new ways of thinking. Children learn that there is more than one way to do things—an important lesson for life.

4. Parental remarriage frequently results in an increase in household income. Thus, children may be better provided for in terms of health care, clothing, housing, and other financial necessities if a stepparent is in the home. The effects of poverty on children have been well-documented, and single-parent households, particularly those led by women, are especially likely to be poor. The added benefit of more income may be an advantage for stepchildren and may contribute to their well-being, even if the stepparent provides them with little else (Coleman and Ganong, 1989).

5. It has been suggested that a stable, well-functioning stepfamily environment is less stressful for children than an unhappy nuclear family or a single-parent household in which the parent is unhappy. This certainly can be true. One adolescent that we interviewed preferred his stepfamily to the chaos of his original nuclear family, because "my real dad was always in jail or with his girlfriends. . . ." Children who lived in families where there was alcoholism, drug abuse by parents, or other self-destructive and antisocial behavior may find that a new, stable household situation can provide an arena in which they can feel safe and loved. Clinicians sometimes warn stepparents about the dangers of trying to "rescue" their new spouse and stepchildren; these cautions are valid ones, but stepparents nonetheless potentially can provide a needed sense of stability for chaotic situations.

6. An expanded kin network has been mentioned as a valuable resource for stepchildren. They may add stepsiblings, stepgrandparents, and other steprelatives to the group of people who care about them. The addition of steprelatives was one of the most commonly mentioned "good" things about being in a stepfamily by the 71 adolescents we recently interviewed. Only-children usually appreciated having siblings for the first time, and many indicated particular fondness for stepgrandparents. Steprelatives can be an important source of social support for stepfamilies (Visher and Visher, 1988), a resource that is especially important when the community as a whole fails to offer institutionalized support (Cherlin, 1978).

Mutually rewarding friendships often develop between stepsiblings. This gives children in stepfamilies an additional support group. When older stepsiblings are added to the family, an additional model is provided for the stepchild. Older stepsiblings can serve as valuable resources for younger children, teaching them how to interpret the stepparent's behaviors, giving advice, and sharing possessions.

7. Since stepparent roles are generally less-well-defined than parental roles (Cherlin, 1978), stepparents and stepchildren potentially can create a role for the stepparent that helps the child fulfill his or her needs. For instance, since stepparents may interact with stepchildren with less emotional intensity than parents do, they can be useful advisors for children who are facing difficult personal decisions. Stepparents can serve the function of being a relatively objective adult who cares about the child and has their best interest at heart but who may not be personally invested in specific decisions the child might make.

The lack of clear guidelines related to the stepparent role can have the unintended effect of making the stepparent try harder to meet the child's needs. There is evidence that stepfathers in particular are very critical of their performance as stepparents, far more critical than their spouses or stepchildren are (Bohannon and Yahraes, 1979).

Contributions Made by the Child

It is well known that children are not simply passive recipients of external forces that "shape them," but are also active creators of their own development (Bell, 1968). The second major area of influences on stepchildren's successful development identified by clinicians, therefore, concerns the contributions that children make to their own positive outcomes. In general, children who are outgoing and relate well to others, who welcome new experiences and adapt easily to change, who have high tolerance for ambiguity, and who enjoy solving problems, will make the best adjustment to stepfamily living.

1. Stepfamily living may provide opportunities for children to learn cooperation and sharing skills. They may have to share their parents with stepparents and stepsiblings, they may have to share possessions and space with new stepfamily members, and they may have to cooperate in learning and developing a set of mutual household rules. Children who are outgoing and enjoy interacting with others may be at an advantage.

2. Some children seem to do well because they are comfortable with ambiguity. They are flexible, and change does not especially bother them. For example, they are able to deal with more than one person in a parenting role and can establish roles and parameters for each. Children with high tolerance for ambiguity can often see advantages in having multiple "parents." Similarly, some stepparents do well also because they see the ambiguous role of the stepparent as an interesting opportunity rather than an overwhelming challenge. Living in a stepfamily may actually increase the child's capacity to be flexible by providing opportunities to learn how to cope with change and with ambiguous situations.

3. Being a child of divorced parents often means that children learn negotiation skills they would not necessarily have learned otherwise. That is, in dealing with their divorced parents, children can learn how to deal with people who may not get along well and who seldom agree with each other. Traditionally viewed as a handicap (i.e., "the poor child has to deal with all this hostility, etc."), this can be reframed as an opportunity for children to learn new skills. Someone has said stepchildren should be outstanding at middle management!

4. Learning to adapt to change may facilitate the development of self-confidence. If problems in family living are not so severe that they are overwhelming, children can gain self-esteem from being able to deal with them. Novelist Paula Danzigor (1982, p. 51) expresses this well, via a character who is an adolescent stepchild, "I feel grown up . . . like I can handle anything. I think that kids who have gone through divorces are more used to handling problems."

Because of the theoretical focus of empirical research on stepfamilies, comparisons of well-functioning and poorly functioning groups have not been made, nor have efforts been expended in determining the correlates of adaptive functioning in stepchildren. In this chapter, we have emphasized societal myths and biases regarding stepchildren because they appear to be widely held, in spite of considerable evidence indicating that, as a group, stepchildren function similarly to other children.

However, Brody, Newbaum, and Forehand (1988) have expressed concern about the effect of serial remarriage on children. There is increasing evidence that a growing number of children are being exposed to multiple "family" disruptions. About half of those whose parents remarry are likely to experience a second divorce (Bumpass, 1984). An unknown number are exposed to disruptions of more cohabiting relationships. Is there a negative cumulative effect of experiencing *multiple* periods of marital hostility, disrupted parenting, and reduced income? Are serial marriers and/or cohabiters less psychologically stable; more likely to abuse drugs or alcohol? Are these children more at risk than those whose parents remarry only once? Investigations of the children of multiple marriers should be emphasized in future research.

What Can Be Done to Enhance Opportunities for Stepchildren?

Even though researchers' findings show that stepchildren, on average, fare comparably to children who have not experienced parental remarriage, there is also some evidence that there is a greater variation in how stepchildren function. There appears to be a bipolar effect of living in a stepfamily, at least for women (Spanier and Furstenberg, 1982). Remarriage enhances well-being for some while reducing it for others. Global generalizations about the effects of remarriage on children must be tempered by the knowledge that there is great variety in stepfamilies. Some stepchildren may find their lives enhanced by parental remarriage; others may be put at risk. A number of societal changes could potentially reduce the risk and enhance the possibilities for all stepchildren.

1. Better employment opportunities and higher pay for women would indirectly improve the lot of a significant number of stepchildren. Single women with children sometimes make poor marriage choices in their search for financial security. Fewer unhappy remarriages would ensue if women could financially provide better for their children.

2. The increased use of divorce mediation rather than litigation may help parents to better maintain their mutual parenting roles. When parents plan for their children's future together, rather than adversarially battling it out through their lawyers, there is a better chance that they will be able to make compromises and continue to jointly parent the

child. This greater ability to work together may have positive effects on children after their parents remarry.

3. Increased societal support for stepfamilies would help reduce negative effects and facilitate positive consequences for children (Cherlin, 1978). Several studies in the past decade found support for the "incomplete institution" hypothesis that stepfamilies are more at risk because they lack societal sanctions, guidelines for behavior, and well-developed norms (Coleman and Ganong, in press). There are several areas needing change.

Language. Avoidance of terms with negative connotations may help to reduce negative attitudes and expectations. The term "stepchild" used as a metaphor for something that is unwanted or abused should be considered as inappropriate to use to illustrate a point as a racial or ethnic slur would be. Descriptors such as "real" or "natural" to refer to biological parents should also be avoided, since this implies that stepparents are unreal and unnatural.

Education. Education about stepfamilies could enhance societal support for stepchildren. Schoolchildren should learn about stepfamilies, because a significant proportion of them may eventually become stepchildren and/or become the next generation of stepparents. If they learn more about stepfamilies, stepchildren of the future may benefit.

School policies should be examined for possible biases toward nuclear families. Biased policies put a strain on stepchildren and their families and send implicit messages about how families should be. For example, official forms should include information about stepparents as well as biological parents, and school activities (e.g., father-son banquets) that assume all children come from nuclear families should be modified or discontinued.

The education of teachers and helping professionals should include training about stepfamilies. This training should be balanced, with strengths presented along with potential problems. Teachers and helping professionals should be sensitized to the needs of stepchildren and to their own biases regarding stepfamilies.

Legal Issues. Increasing legal rights for stepparents would represent societal support for that difficult role. In many states stepparents have no right to visitation with a stepchild in the event of the biological parent's death or in case the remarried couple divorce, even though the stepparent may have raised the child from infancy (Fine, 1989). Although stepparents often are not aware of how few rights they have regarding their stepchildren, legal recognition of what is often an important psychological relationship may help add stability to the lives of stepchildren.

Media. A more balanced emphasis by the media on the positive and negative aspects of stepfamilies would be helpful in setting expectations and attitudes. The darker side of stepfamilies seems to be the primary focus and is not typically offset by positive examples of stepfamily life. It is not too farfetched, considering how stepfamily life is often portrayed, for stepchildren to *assume* they will be abused and unloved by their stepparent.

When children do not see stepfamilies presented as "normal" families in their storybooks and on television, the subtle message is that stepfamilies do not measure up in some way. Fiction for children featuring stepfamily members should be in every school library. These stories could be helpful to stepchildren in their attempts to problem solve and they can also present information that will help children who do not live in stepfamilies develop understanding of them. The media are powerful forces in enhancing or downgrading a child's sense of self.

SUMMARY

Speculations about the contributors to successful outcomes for stepchildren far exceed what is clearly documented and known through empirical research. We can conclude that stepchildren are not generally at risk, but we are not yet able to explain why some stepchildren adjust better than others. The gradual emergence of a normative-adaptive perspective in studying stepchildren and their families promises to provide answers to these questions. Researchers would do well to read clinical writers and subject their speculations to empirical examination. The past decade has seen a tremendous increase in the quantity and quality of research on stepchildren. The next decade will likely be even more productive. Stepfamilies and stepchildren represent a substantial proportion of our society. A focus in the future on understanding and facilitating the growth of well-functioning stepchildren is an endeavor in which all of us has a stake.

REFERENCES

Ahrons, C. and Wallisch, L. (1987). Parenting in the binuclear family: Relationships between biological and stepparents. In K. Pasley and M. Ihinger-Tallman (Eds.), *Remarriage and stepparenting: Current research and theory* (pp. 225-256). New York: Guilford.

Amato, P. (1987). Family processes in one-parent, stepparent, and intact families: The child's point of view. *Journal of Marriage and the Family, 49,* 327-337.

Baydar, N. (1988). Effects of parental separation and reentry into union on the emotional well-being of children. *Journal of Marriage and the Family, 50,* 967-981.

Bell, R. W. (1968). A reinterpretation of the direction of effects in studies of socialization. *Psychological Review, 75,* 81-95.

Bohannan, P., and Yahraes, H. (1979). Stepfathers as parents. In E. Corfamn

(Ed.), *Families today: A research sampler on families and children* (pp. 347-362). NIMH Science Monograph. Washington, DC: U.S. Government Printing Office.

Bray, J. (1988). Children's development during early remarriage. In M. Hetherington and J. Arasteh (Eds.), *Impact of divorce, single parenting and stepparenting on children* (pp. 279-298). Hillsdale, NJ: Lawrence Erlbaum.

Brody, G., Newbaum, E., and Forehand, R. (1988). Serial marriage: A heuristic analysis of an emerging family form. *Psychological Bulletin, 103,* 211-222.

Bumpass, L. (1984). Demographic aspects of children's second-family experience. *American Journal of Sociology, 90* (3), 608-623.

Cherlin, A. (1978). Remarriage as an incomplete institution. *American Journal of Sociology, 86,* 634-650.

Clingempeel, G. and Segal, S. (1986). Stepparent-stepchild relationships and the psychological adjustment of children in stepmother and stepfather families. *Child Development, 57,* 474-484.

Coleman, M. and Ganong, L. (1984). Effect of family structure on family attitudes and expectations. *Family Relations, 33,* 425-432.

______. (1986), November). Stepchildren: Empirical examination of some clinical assumptions. Paper presented at the NCFR Annual Conference, Detroit.

______. (1987). The cultural stereotyping of stepfamilies. In K. Pasley and M. Ihinger-Tallman (Eds.), *Remarriage and stepparenting: Current research and theory* (pp. 19-41). New York: Guilford.

______. (1989). Financial management in stepfamilies. *Lifestyles: Family and economic issues, 10,* 217-232.

______. (in press). Remarriage and stepfamily research in the '80's: Increased interest in an old family form. *Journal of Marriage and the Family.*

Danzigor, P. (1982). *The divorce express.* New York: Delacorte.

Duberman, L. (1973). Step-kin relationships. *Journal of Marriage and the Family, 35,* 283-292.

Ferri, E. (1984). *Stepchildren: A national study.* Windsor, UK: NFER-NELSON Publishing Co., Ltd.

Fine, M. (1989). A social science perspective on stepfamily law: Suggestions for legal reform. *Family Relations, 38*(1), 53-58.

Flinn, M. (1988). Step- and genetic parent/offspring relationships in a Caribbean village. *Ethnology and Sociobiology, 9,* 335-369.

Furstenberg, F., and Nord, C. (1985). Parenting apart: Patterns of childbearing after marital disruption. *Journal of Marriage and the Family, 47,* 893-904.

Ganong, L. and Coleman, M. (1984). Effects of remarriage on children: A review of the empirical literature. *Family Relations, 33,* 389-406.

______. (1986). A comparison of clinical and empirical literature on children in stepfamilies. *Journal of Marriage and the Family, 48,* 309-318.

Ganong, L., Coleman, M. and Mapes, D. (in press). A meta-analytic review of family structure stereotypes. *Journal of Marriage and the Family.*

Glick, P. (1989). Remarried families, stepfamilies, and stepchildren: A brief demographic analysis. *Family Relations, 38,* 24-27.

Guttman, J. and Broudo, M. (1989). The effect of child's family type on teachers' stereotypes. *Journal of Divorce, 12,* 315-328.

Hetherington, M., Cox, M., and Cox, R. (1985). Long-term effects of divorce and remarriage on the adjustment of children. *Journal of the American Academy of Child Psychiatry, 24,* 518-530.

Hobart, C., and Brown, D. (1988). Effects of prior marriage children on adjustment in remarriage: A Canadian study. *Journal of Comparative Family Studies, 19,* 382-396.

Isaacs, M. and Leon, G. (1988). Remarriage and its alternatives following divorce: Mother and child adjustment. *Journal of Marital and Family Therapy, 14*(2), 163-173.

Kinnaird, K. and Gerrard, M. (1986). Premarital sexual behavior and attitudes toward marriage and divorce among young women as a function of their mother's marital status. *Journal of Marriage and the Family, 48,* 757-765.

Lightcap, J., Kurland, J., and Burgess, R. (1982). Child abuse: A test of some predictions from evolutionary theory. *Ethology and Sociobiology, 3,* 61-67.

Needle, R., Su, S., and Doherty, W. (1990). Divorce, remarriage, and adolescent substance use: A prospective longitudinal study. *Journal of Marriage and the Family, 52*(1), 157-169.

Peterson, J. and Zill, N. (1986). Marital disruption, parent-child relationships, and behavior problems in children. *Journal of Marriage and the Family, 48,* 295-307.

Seltzer, J. and Bianchi, S. (1988). Children's contact with absent parents. *Journal of Marriage and the Family, 50*(3), 663-677.

Spanier, G. and Furstenberg, F. (1982). Remarriage after divorce: A longitudinal analysis of well-being. *Journal of Marriage and the Family, 44,* 709-720.

Steinberg, L. (1987). Single parents, stepparents, and the susceptibility of adolescents to antisocial peer pressure, *Child Development, 58,* 269-275.

Visher, E. B. and Visher, H. S. (1988). *Old loyalties, new ties: Therapeutic strategies with stepfamilies.* New York: Brunner/Mazel.

Zill, N. (1988). Behavior, achievement, and health problems among children in stepfamilies: Findings from a national survey of child health. In E. Mavis Hetherington and J. D. Arasteh (Eds.), *Impact of divorce, single parenting, and stepparenting on children* (pp. 325-368). Hillsdale, NJ: Lawrence Erlbaum.

Chapter 5

Foster Family Care: Solution or Problem?

Edith Fein and Anthony N. Maluccio

Foster care has always had a place in the story of the human family. From the time of Moses, perhaps our first known foster child, some youngsters have been unable to live with their biological families. The families' inability to rear their children may be due to poverty, natural or family disaster, shame for the child's or parent's condition, hope for a better life for the child, or indifference to the child's well-being. Up to the end of the middle ages, these reasons led to the physical abandonment of children, literally by the wayside (Boswell, 1988). That such abandonment did not produce a high death rate is surprising, until other aspects of the phenomenon are appreciated. As Boswell points out, in those years, because the labor of children was valued, the "kindness of strangers" came to the rescue and abandoned children were able to take their place in new households with no unusual increase in child death rates. By the end of the middle ages, however, the church became stronger in its intervention in sexual and domestic affairs; by the thirteenth century, foundling homes were established as an institutional alternative for parents unable or unwilling to care for their children. In these cases, the children went into the oblivion of the institution, where they died in great numbers or were reared by strangers and subsequently entered society as strangers to the norms of the everyday world.

In intervening years, up to the present, youngsters not reared by their own families have been cared for in poorhouses, almshouses, orphanages, as indentured laborers or apprentices, in boarding or foster homes, and in a variety of institutions according to the fashion of the times. In all cases, the children have been dependent on the altruism or self-interest of unrelated adults for physical care, nurturance, and emotional well-being. Our current adoption and foster care systems spring from this lineage. This chapter will review one modern-day response to children whose families cannot care for them—foster family care—and assess the impact on youngsters growing up in such circumstances. An underlying issue to be considered is whether foster family care is a solution or a problem. The adverse aspects of the system will be examined, but factors contributing to successful outcomes, often ignored in our commendable zeal to improve conditions for children, will be the focus of discussion. The research evidence will be considered and implications drawn for policy and practice in child welfare.

BACKGROUND

Modern child welfare practices can be traced to the middle of the nineteenth century, when the movement "to seek out and to rescue" children who were neglected or cruelly treated had its origins (Anderson, 1989, p. 223). Agencies devoted to the rescue of children proliferated from the model of animal rescue, and the common outcome from the investigation of complaints was placement in an institution. From these institutions, and from almshouses and orphanges, children were often placed with surrogate families who could use their labor or to whom they were indentured. The first choice for placement was a rural, preferably farm, family, which provided free care for the children (Jones, 1989). In 1867, the Commonwealth of Massachusetts engaged its first visiting agent to check on the care and treatment given to the over 800 children it had indentured or placed in free foster homes (Leavey, 1987).

By the 1920s, however, with changing social and economic conditions (the relative decrease in farm families, an increasing divorce rate, and larger numbers of women working outside the home), the use of paid "boarding homes" was replacing the free foster family care that had previously existed. By the time of the great depression of the early 1930s, free foster family care was a thing of the past, and orphanages and similar institutions now had to pay board for the youngsters in their care if they were to be placed with a family. The Social Security Act of 1935, with its support to families with dependent children, weakened the economic grounds for taking children from their parents, and thus helped narrow the concept of child protection as pertaining to abused and neglected children. By that time, the growth of social casework pointed to the rehabilitation of parents as a reasonable outcome, and the perception of foster care as child-rearing by a substitute family on a temporary basis gradually evolved.

With the advent of the permanency planning movement in the 1980s and the consequent emphasis on maintaining children in their own families or in another permanent family through adoption, the use of foster family care came into dispute. It was no longer viewed as a viable long-term alternative for children who were removed from their biological families, although in the early years of the decade, up to 40 percent of the children in care had been there two years or more (Federal Register, 1983). At present, efforts to prevent placement and reunify removed children with their biological families have been successful enough to result in a foster care system in which the most "difficult" youngsters remain, typically those who come from disorganized and poorly functioning families and display multiple behavioral, developmental, and other problems and needs. As a consequence, administrators, practitioners, and others are increasingly underscoring the need for specialized or therapeutic foster family-based treatment homes (Hawkins and Breiling, 1989; Hudson and Galaway, 1989), improved services to all children in care (Ryan, 1990), and the professionalization of foster parenting (Fein, Maluccio, and Kluger 1990). In addition, there is growing recognition that service systems should be responsive to the special needs and qualities of minority children and families, who are disproportionately represented in the child welfare system.

DOES FOSTER FAMILY CARE WORK?

In recent decades, a pervasive concern in the field of child welfare has been whether the system achieved its primary goal of returning children to their own families following a temporary placement and rehabilitation of child and family. Much of the early evidence about the temporariness of foster care is negative. Although definitive data are not available, from the 1950s through the 1970s many children entering foster care remained there until maturity or spent a substantial proportion of their formative years in out-of-home placement (Gruber, 1978; Fanshel and Shinn, 1978; Wiltse and Gambrill, 1974). Lutsk and Parish (1977) found, for example, that 46 percent of all children placed in one region in Connecticut had been in care six years or more, and Fanshel and Shinn (1978) reported that 36 percent of the children in their New York sample remained in care at the end of a five-year study period.

More recent studies indicate that foster care has become a two-tiered system with a large number of children entering and leaving care within a year or two, but with a sizable-minority—between 30 and 40 percent—remaining in care over two years (Gershenson, 1987). Many children, moreover, are repeaters; almost one in three coming into care in 1985 had been in care earlier (Mech, 1988). What does this constant movement from home to home, or, on the other hand, long-term removal from the biological family, mean for children?

The pain of separation and loss has been the hallmark of foster care for children, their families, and their foster caretakers. The trauma exists regardless of the fact that most children come into care because they were neglected or abused; it is exacerbated when youngsters are forced to move from foster home to foster home or other placement such as residential care; and it is further increased when young people are adrift in the system and there are no plans for rehabilitating their parents so the family can be reunited, or of freeing the children for the stability of an adoptive placement. There is thus a widespread perception that placement in foster care has short-term as well as long-term adverse effects on children in areas such as identity formation, sense of trust, interpersonal relationships, and adult development and functioning (Bryce and Ehlert, 1971; Frank, 1980).

Recent efforts to examine the short- as well as long-term effects of placement in foster care on the children's development have been hampered by various methodological limitations. For example, it has not been possible to control for the children's preplacement experiences, a crucial variable, since children placed in foster homes typically are reported to have developmental and other problems prior to entering the system. "Thus, even if placement in foster care had *no effect* on these children, their early developmental problems might be expected to adversely affect their later adjustment and behavior" (Polit, 1989, p. 21).

The prevailing empirical evidence, however, does not support a negative view of foster care. One of the earliest evaluations of foster care was the 1867 report of the Massachusetts Visiting Agent, who collected statistics, visited placed children, filled out data forms, and chronicled "hardships and wrongs." He concluded: "But these cases of injustice and abuse are the exceptions, not the general rule. Aside from slight neglects, which are not being corrected, the majority of children are doing well and (in) pretty good homes. Some of them take the names of the families in which they live, and are treated in all respects as children of these families" (Leavey, 1987, p. 66).

In contrast to expectations, studies have consistently reported that many foster care graduates function well, or that no marked negative effect of foster care on the child's adjustment is detected. Current research indicates minimal effect of child abuse, a prime reason for entry into care, on subsequent adult criminality (Widom, 1989). Further, in the most sophisticated longitudinal study of foster care carried out to date, Fanshel and Shinn (1978) examined the patterns of children's emotional adjustment through a variety of psychological tests, on three occasions over a five-year period, and reported that "consistently normal ratings were obtained for 52 percent of the subjects. Another 25 percent progressed to normal over the course of the study" (p. 323), whereas less than 24 percent shifted toward "abnormal" ratings. On the basis of these and other related data, Fanshel and Shinn concluded that "our findings do not show that children who remained in foster care fared less well with respect to intellectual abilities, school performance, and personal and social adjustment, compared to those who returned to their own homes" (p. 479).

Similar results have been reported in follow-up studies of adults who had been placed in foster care. In one such study Festinger (1983) examined the views, experiences, and functioning of 277 young adults who had grown up in foster care in New York City. She concluded that they "were not so different from others their age in what they were doing, in the feelings they expressed, and in their hopes about the future" (p. 294).

> The assumptions and expectations that abound concerning the dire fate of foster care children seem to have little validity. The products of foster care—the young adults whom we followed in this study—did not measure down to such dire predictions. They were not what might be described as problem ridden when they were discharged nor did they become so in subsequent years; there was no support for the generational repetition of foster care; there was no evidence of undue economic dependence on public support; and their records of arrest were not excessive (Festinger, 1983, pp. 293-294).

Triseloitis (1980) reported similar findings in a British follow-up study of 49 young adults who were born in the mid-1950s, placed in foster care at different ages, and had each spent from 7 to 15 years in a single foster home prior to age 16:

> Twenty-four (or 60 percent) of the former foster children enjoyed their fostering experiences and were generally coping well at the age of twenty or twenty-one. For another six (or 15 percent) the experience had many satisfactions but also some identifiable difficulties. . . . Finally ten (or 25 percent) of the subjects had mostly negative feelings about their fostering experience, and their current level of functioning gave cause for some concern (p. 156).

The results of the Festinger and Triseliotis studies should be examined in the context of the considerable stability in the placement history of the subjects. Festinger indicates that her research was "based on a highly selected, particular group of young adults, most of whom were in placement for a very long time, much of which was spent in a stable placement" (p. 295). Forty-four percent of her subjects had been in one or two placements (Festinger, 1983, p. 55). As for the Triseliotis study, the subjects spent from 7 to 15 years in their final foster family placement. This degree of stability is not believed to be typical of children who entered foster care more recently. Although definitive data are not available, it is reported that a sizable group of children tend to experience multiple placements. Lutsk and Parish (1977) found that 40 percent of the children in their sample had three or more placements, with 14 percent experiencing six or more moves. More than ten years later, a comparable percentage (33 percent) had experienced more than two placements in their foster care careers, which at the time of the study had lasted two years or more (Fein, Maluccio, and Kluger, 1990).

More recently, one of the most thorough retrospective studies of foster care examined the experiences of 585 children in placement from 1966 to 1984 in six divisions of the Casey Family Program. A follow-up study was conducted on 106 of the children on average seven years after they left foster care (Fanshel, Finch, and Grundy 1989). The findings support the conclusion that there is a considerable group of children who can do well when the permanent plan for their growing-up years is long-term foster care. These were youngsters who could not be reunified with biological parents because the adults were unavailable or incompetent, and whose prospects for adoption were dim, because of age or psychological condition. The youngsters generally presented more difficult problems than other foster children when coming into care; they had many previous placements, had been in institutional care, and were troubled and insecure about their relationships with adults. Yet, Fanshel et al. (1989, p. 470) concluded:

> Despite the evidence in the data that this agency has taken into its care a highly distressed group of children with unstable life histories and associated problematic behaviors, almost three in five were successfully sustained in the program, some after many agency replacements, until emancipation. In addition, one in five were returned to their parents. A majority of those who achieved emancipation status were showing good ajustment at departure.

The data from the young adults who were interviewed in the same study indicated that adjustment as an adult was related to the youth's condition at exit from care. Thus, children who were relatively well-adjusted when they came into foster care did well during care, and were adjusted when they were emancipated, were also functioning well as adults. Moreover, youngsters who were distressed when they entered care, but were able to respond well enough during their care years to exit care relatively well-adjusted, also did well as adults. The most potent variable was the child's hostile and oppositional behavior coming into care. Program services that had an impact on this negative behavior led to better outcomes during and after the foster care years. As a corollary, physically abused boys who might be expected to display difficult behaviors did not do as well in foster care and afterward as boys who were not abused. The results of the study are a strong indication that intensive services to troubled children, such as the Casey Family Program provides, can have impressive effects on the adjustment and functioning of foster youth after they leave care.

A complementary study of approximately 100 children, from the Montana and Idaho divisions of the Casey Family Program, found that it was possible to predict the outcome and stability of foster placements from such factors as the child's previous placement history, current maladaptive behaviors, characteristics of the biological parents, and qualities of the foster home (Walsh and Walsh, 1987). Positive outcomes were associated with the child's older age at first placement and avoidance of passive aggressive behavior; the foster mother's "emotional coherence"; the foster father's emotional involvement with the child; and the child-centeredness of the home (Walsh and Walsh, 1990). The study demonstrated that the Casey Family Program was doing an effective job of serving these "underachievers of the child welfare system" (p. 207). Their placements were stable and the foster families were considered to be functioning at "acceptable to good" (p. 207) levels.

Similar findings were obtained in another study involving a statewide sample of 779 children and youth who had been placed in foster care at least two years in Connecticut (Fein et al., 1990). The functioning of the youngsters was assessed, on the basis of reports from foster parents, in the areas of school functioning, behavioral functioning, emotional and developmental functioning, and family adjustment. The results showed that, according to the foster parents, most children functioned positively. Among the factors that apparently contributed to this outcome were:

- the stability of foster care placements for most children and youth;
- the establishment of a permanent plan for most children, with at least one-fourth of the foster parents planning to adopt the children in their care; and
- the foster parents' expectation that most youngsters would remain with their foster families until emancipation (p. 69).

In sum, the findings of these and other studies reviewed elsewhere (Maluccio and Fein, 1985) "do not support prevailing wisdom regarding the widespread negative impact of growing up in foster care" (Maluccio and Fein, 1985, pp. 130-131). While these findings should be viewed with caution, because of the methodological limitations inherent in research on foster care outcomes, the evidence points to positive post-discharge functioning of foster care graduates. Such evidence, however, continues to be questioned in the field, as exemplified by Fanshel and Shinn's conclusion (1978, p. 479) upon completion of the longitudinal study mentioned earlier:

> We are not completely sure that continued tenure in foster care over extended periods of time is not in itself harmful to children. On the level at which we are able to measure the adjustment of the children we could find no such negative effect. However, we feel that our measures of adjustment are not without problems, and we are not sure that our procedures have captured the potential

feelings of pain and impaired self-image that can be created by impermanent status in foster care.

Further research is vital, especially since the characteristics of the recipients of care, their families, and the child welfare system are always changing. As suggested by Fanshel and Shinn, there is no simple or clear-cut answer to the question of whether foster family care "works." A major reason for this is that, as indicated by the studies cited previously as well as others (Rowe, et al., 1984; Rowe, Hundleby, and Garnett, 1989), the outcome of foster care placement depends on an extensive and complex set of factors that are interactive, rather than a series of casual relationships between discrete factors. As we have noted elsewhere, "it would be satisfying to discover simple guidelines that would enable practitioners to apply specific interventions to achieve successful outcomes of permanency, adequate functioning, and coping after emancipation. Like the search for such guidelines in clinical services, there are no easy answers" (Fein et al., 1990, p. 76).

WHY SOME CHILDREN SUCCEED

Despite the lack of clear-cut answers or specific practice prescriptions, the studies that have been reviewed in this chapter indicate that at least some youngsters do "succeed" after spending time, essentially growing up, in foster care. There *are* youngsters who overcome the odds and develop into competent adults who lead productive lives. The studies, moreover, allude to some of the reasons for such success, and thus point to a number of implications that must be taken into account if child welfare and related services are to be effective in overcoming the potentially negative aspects of foster care placement and its antecedents.

First, policies and practices in child welfare must support the child's sense of security, stability, and permanency in the foster family. This can be accomplished, for example, through some form of legal guardianship or custodianship. If long-term foster care is the plan, intensive work with children, foster parents, and biological parents will reduce the children's uncertainty and increase the perception of permanence on their part and that of the caretakers. Clinical intervention, when parents continue to be involved with their children in foster care, will help the children cope with their confusion, ambivalence toward the parents, and conflict in loyalties. Planned, therapeutic use of parent-child visiting and, where appropriate, consistent work with biological parents will enhance the quality of their continuing relationship with their children and the placement itself, and ultimately will free the parents sufficiently to give their children permission to form lasting attachments to the foster parents or other substitute parental figures (Jackson and Dunne, 1981;

Hess and Proch, 1988; Maluccio and Whittaker, 1989; Bryce and Lloyd 1981; Horejsi et al. 1981; Maluccio and Sinanoglu 1981; Maluccio, Fein, and Olmstead, 1986). Such intensive work with children and adults calls for funding adequate to the seriousness and importance of the undertaking, rather than the fragmented and inconsistent service currently provided in many agencies because of insufficient resources.

Second, ways must be found to make goals and expectations, roles and responsibilities, and tasks as explicit as possible for all participants in the drama of foster care, including children, biological parents, foster parents, social workers, and other service providers. There is evidence that such clarification counteracts the ambiguity and confusion inherent in foster care placement and helps promote the child's development and well-being (Aldgate, Maluccio, and Reeves, 1989; Maluccio, Krieger, and Pine, 1990; Rowe et al., 1989). Supporting this work, service provision to the child and family must be carefuly monitored through the use of case managers and periodic reviews (Maluccio et al., 1986).

Third, it should be acknowledged that foster parents play an essential role in the efforts to help children in their care "overcome the odds." This means that, in policy as in practice, foster parents need to have appropriate rewards, adequate training, ongoing supports, and explicit recognition as members of the service team and partners in the helping process.

Fourth, children growing up in foster care need extensive help to prepare for life after foster care, for independent living. In particular, such preparation should incorporate the development of satisfying, potentially life-long relationships that can help compensate for the loss of the biological family; the building of a variety of supportive social networks; the availability of a family with which the young person can identify and return to—as he or she faces life crises; and training in a variety of skill areas essential for independent living (Stein and Carey, 1986; Stone, 1987; Maluccio et al., 1990).

Underlying these considerations, social policy needs to address the systemic difficulties that predispose children's entry into care, to keep them languishing there when a return home is possible, and subject them to the revolving door of entering and exiting care. The positive effects, in recent years, of the Adoption Assistance and Child Welfare Act of 1980 (in which the federal government provided financial incentives to the states to support permanency for children, preferably by keeping them in their families or quickly returning them) are being reduced by the current growth of poverty and homelessness and the epidemic of crack cocaine use. Some writers feel that the single-parent family is now giving way to the no-parent child, and that our response as a society must be creative, dramatic, and immediate (Brennenman 1989; Moynihan 1990).

Although outcomes of foster care continue to be a controversial issue, there is some movement in the field toward recognition of permanent foster family care as a sound plan for some youngsters, such as older children with significant ties to their biological parents. The follow-up studies suggest that the initially negative effects of separation and placement in foster care can be counteracted or reduced through the influence of stable foster home placements and strong services to the children and their foster and biological parents. Every child needs affection, stability, and continuity to develop. There is no reason to believe that biology is destiny, and that foster parents cannot provide the nurturance to youngsters if foster care is condoned by society and properly supported.

REFERENCES

Aldgate, J., Maluccio, A. N., and Reeves, C. (Eds.) (1989). *Adolescents in foster families.* London: B. T. Batsford, and Chicago: Lyceum Books.

Anderson, P. G. (1989). The origin, emergence, and professional recognition of child protection. *Social Service Review, 63*(2), 222-224.

Boswell, J. (1988). *The kindness of strangers.* New York: Pantheon Books.

Brenneman, F. S. (1989). Legislative change for a different ballgame. Paper presented at the Conference on Chemically Dependent Parents (Child Protection Council of Northeastern Connecticut), Mansfield, CT.

Bryce, M. and Ehlert, C. (1971). 144 foster children. *Child Welfare, 50,* 499-503.

Bryce, M. and Lloyd, J. D. (Eds.) (1981). *Treating children in the home.* Springfield, IL: Charles C. Thomas.

Fanshel, D., Finch, S. J., and Grundy, J. F. (1989). Foster children in life-course perspective: The Casey Family Program Experience. *Child Welfare, 68*(5), 467-478.

Fanshel, D. and Shinn, E. B. (1978). *Children in foster care—A longitudinal investigation.* New York: Columbia University Press.

Federal Register (1983, October 18). *Fiscal year 1984 coordinated discretionary funds programs.* Washington, DC: Department of Health & Human Services, Office of Human Development Services.

Fein, E., Maluccio, A. N., and Kluger, M. (1990). *No more partings: An examination of long-term foster care.* Washington, DC: Child Welfare League of America.

Festinger, T. (1983). *No one ever asked us . . . A postscript to foster care.* New York: Columbia University Press.

Frank, G. (1980). Treatment needs of children in foster care. *American Journal of Orthopsychiatry, 50,* 256-263.

Gershenson, C. (1987). *Child welfare research notes #19.* Washington, DC: Administration for Children, Youth and Families, Department of Health and Human Services.

Gruber, A. R. (1978). *Children in foster care.* New York: Human Sciences Press.

Hawkins, R. P. and Breiling, J. (Eds.) (1989). *Therapeutic foster care—Critical issues.* Washington, DC: Child Welfare League of America.

Hess, P. M. and Proch, K. P. (1988). *Family visiting in out-of-home care: A guide to practice:* Washington, DC: Child Welfare League of America.

Horejsi, C. R., Bertsche, A. V., and Clark, F. W. (1981). *Social work practice with parents of children in foster care.* Springfield, IL: Charles C. Thomas.

Hudson, J. and Galaway, B. (Eds.) (1989). *Specialist foster family care—A normalizing experience.* New York: Haworth Press.

Jackson, A. D. and Dunne, M. J. (1981). Permanency planning in foster care with the ambivalent parent. In A. N. Maluccio and P. A. Sinanoglu (Eds.), *The challenge of partnership—Working with parents of children in foster care* (pp. 151-164). New York: Child Welfare League of America.

Jones, M. B. (1989). Crisis of the American orphanage, 1931-1940. *Social Service Review, 63*(4), 613-629.

Leavey, J. M. (1987). *Special commission on foster care. A final report.* Boston: Communities for People, Inc.

Lutsk, B. and Parish, E. (1977). *Foster children: Does custody insure security?* Hartford, CT: Junior League of Hartford.

Maluccio, A. N. and Fein, E. (1985). Growing up in foster care. *Children and Youth Services Review, 7,* 123-134.

Maluccio, A. N., Fein, E., and Olmstead, K. (1986). *Permanency planning for children.* London: Tavistock Publications.

Maluccio, A. N., Krieger, R., and Pine, B. A. (Eds.) (1990). *Preparing adolescents for life after foster care: The central role of foster parents.* Washington, DC: Child Welfare League of America.

Maluccio, A. N. and Sinanoglu, P. A. (Eds.) (1981). *The challenge of partnership: Working with parents of children in foster care.* New York: Child Welfare League of America.

Maluccio, A. N. and Whittaker, J. K. (1989). Therapeutic foster care: implications for parental involvement. In R. P. Hawkins and J. Breiling (Eds.), *Therapeutic foster care—Critical Issues* (pp. 161-182). Washington, DC: Child Welfare League of America.

Mech, E. V. (1988). Out-of-home placement rates. *Social Service Review, 57*(4), 659-667.

Moynihan, D. P. (1990). Toward a post-industrial social policy. *Families in Society, 71*(1), 51-56.

Polit, D. (1989). National longitudinal study child welfare: planning phase. Washington, DC: Department of Health and Human Services, Office of Human Development Services.

Rowe, J., Cain, H., Hundleby, M., and Keane, A. (1984). *Long-term foster care.* London: Baatsford Academic and Educational, in association with British Agencies for Adoption and Fostering.

Rowe, J., Hundleby, M., and Garnett, L., (1989). *Child care now—A survey of placement patterns.* London: British Agencies for Adoption and Fostering.

Ryan, P. (1990). Increased federal funding for foster parent education. *Fostering Ideas, 4,* p. 1.

Stein, M. and Carey, K. (1986). *Leaving care.* Oxford: Basil Blackwell.

Stone, H. D. (1987). *Ready, set, go—An agency guide to independent living.* Washington, DC: Child Welfare League of America.

Triseliotis, J. (1980). Growing up in foster care and after. In J. Triseliotis (Ed.), *New developments in foster care and adoption.* London: Routledge and Kegan Paul.

Walsh, J. A. and Walsh, R. A. (1987). *Quality care for tough kids.* Missoula: University of Montana.

______. (1990). Studies of the maintenance of subsidized foster placements in the Casey Family Program. *Child Welfare, 69*(2), 99-114.

Widom, C. S. (1989). Child abuse, neglect and adult behavior: Research design and findings on criminality, violence, and child abuse. *American Journal of Orthopsychiatry, 59*(3), 355-367.

Wiltse, K. T. and Gambrill, E. (1974). Foster care, 1973: A reappraisal. *Public Welfare, 32*(1), 7-14.

Chapter 6

Children Who Lose a Sibling

Helen Rosen

Our knowledge of children's reactions to loss, and the ways in which they attempt to cope with the death of a close family member, is still in its infancy. We contradict ourselves in the assumptions we make about children and death. On the one hand, common understanding holds that children are too young to understand death, and that their youth provides them with a natural resilience and ability to bounce back from an experience that we often acknowledge to have potentially devastating consequences for an adult. We hold that their immaturity protects them from experiencing deep grief and despair when a significant loss occurs. Yet, paradoxically, we also look for relationships between early loss and depression, schizophrenia, or drug abuse. We study maternal deprivation, abandonment, and the effects of divorce on children, building on the assumption that some early losses have the potential for catastrophic effects on the development of the child, effects that are possibly immutable.

Much of the speculation concerning children and loss has focused specifically upon the impact of parental loss on the child, maintaining, as we traditionally have, an emphasis on the unique importance of the parent/child relationship, and especially the mother/child relationship. Research and clinical observation focusing on the loss of a sibling have been rare, as has any attention to the impact of the loss of extended family members on a child. Our awareness of the importance of the mother/child relationship has unfortunately resulted in a body of knowledge that almost entirely fails to take into account the impact of the loss of any other close family member during the preadult years.

As part of our efforts to understand the relationship between children and death, we have of necessity explored the question of how and when children understand the meaning of death. Beginning with Nagy's (1948) seminal work with Hungarian children in the late 1940s, we have investigated when and how children understand the basic concepts of death, its finality and universality. Even here, however, our present-day thinking is beset by opposites—that is, while a majority of investigators believe that knowledge of death is an important factor influencing how a child copes with loss, there are others who propose that, regardless of a child's intellectual understanding, the *experience* of loss (that is, of no longer having the person available as an object) will be a potent and powerful challenge for the child to overcome. Between these two points of view are those emphasizing the range of experiences, interacting with cognition, that determine how and when a child understands death, and how that understanding influences the child's ability to cope with experiences of loss.

A further characteristic of our interest in the effects of loss on children has been the tendency to focus our investigative efforts on the traumatic effects of loss. We have concentrated our efforts on attempts to understand loss as a developmental interference (see, for example, Nagera, 1970), on pathological mourning responses (Elizur and Kaufman, 1983), or on the ill effects of losses of various kinds on both the short-term and long-term mental health of bereaved children (Markusen and Fulton, 1971; Tennant, Bebbington, and Hurry, 1980). Much less frequently have our efforts been directed toward developing an understanding of the positive outcomes that might be associated with the mastery of the death of a significant other. A noteworthy exception to this trend has been the work of Pollock and others on mourning and creativity. Pollock (1978) has been creating a body of knowledge concerning object loss and mourning, and their relation to creativity. Through his investigations into the mourning process and the meaning of object losses in the lives of creative individuals, Pollock has developed a convincing argument for the influence of the mourning process on creativity. He writes: "The creative genius is not a direct result of the mourning process, but the creative product may be strongly influenced by this process and may show evidence of its presence in theme, content, style, or purpose" (p. 444). In the same vein, Szekely (1983) examined the relationship between the creative activity of a theoretical physicist and object loss and mourning. He found that while "motivational elements in the unconscious core of a theoretical physicist's psyche may also be a source of the creative product . . . the final product . . . does not exhibit these same marks" (p. 156).

These limited forays aside, the majority of research into object loss and mourning has *not* examined ways in which loss and mourning may contribute to and enrich the personality of the bereaved, nor have they elucidated to any great extent the factors associated with those who are able to use loss and mourning in these ways. And yet, "researchers who study children at risk have repeatedly observed that, despite the burdens of stress in their everyday lives, there are many children who manifest competency and autonomy in their behavior, compared to others who, exposed to similar stresses, develop serious coping problems" (Hauser et al., 1989, p. 110-111). Understanding how this comes about, what factors are associated with coping and "resilience" in children, has become increasingly important for us to understand. We have begun to realize the one-sidedness of approaches that focus only on pathology, and thus the need for broader research approaches that attempt to take into account factors that can explain why some children cope better than others. We are beginning to look for those factors in a wider range of circumstances than ever before, including, for example, such adversities as poverty, parental alcoholism, and chronic illness.

RESILIENCE IN CHILDREN

Garmezy and Rutter (1983, p. 73) describe resilience in children and adolescents as "associated with a heightened probability of present or future maladaptive outcomes but which are not actualized in some children whose behavior instead is marked by patterns of behavioral adaptation and manifest competence." In the same vein, Werner and Smith (1982, p. 4) define resilience as "the capacity to cope effectively with the internal stress of vulnerabilities (such as labile patterns of autonomic activity, developmental imbalances, unusual sensitivies) and external stresses (such as illness, major losses and dissolution of the family)." Abend (1986, pp. 96-97), for example, in discussing potential trauma (prior to presenting case material on childhood sibling loss) states:

> What a given experience means in the psychological life of an individual, from an analytic standpoint, is affected by many factors, including (1) his unconsciously determined predispositions; (2) subsequent developments in his psychology which favor attributing certain meanings to past events and experiences; and (3) the impact of the traumatic events on other people in the patient's life, and therefore on a host of significant emotional interactions with those people which are indirectly determined by the trauma as well.

The first two of these factors really lend themselves only to psychoanalytic investigation, depending as they do on an intimate knowledge of an individual's unconscious as well as conscious thought processes. The third factor has been noted as well by others, such as, Hauser et al. (1989), who write that variables related to coping and resiliency include family characteristics and properties of the surrounding community, as well as personality characteristics or dispositions in the child.

Those researchers whose interest has focused on resilience in children have tried to identify those factors that could account for the capacity to adapt "despite the odds." Werner and Smith (1982) found that resilient adolescents have better verbal communication skills than those who succumb to stress. Along similar lines, Wynne, Jones, and Al-Khayyal (1982, p. 4) suggest that "there is 'healthy communication' in families that may provide the high-risk child with the resources and coping strategies underlying resiliency and healthy functioning."

Presenting a less conventional point of view, Dugan (1989, p. 157) suggests that "acting-out" in adolescence can be related to resilience—that is, "while the concept of acting-out is often used in a pejorative manner and seen as psychopathological, acting-out behavior may also be an indicator of hope and potential for success in the face of adversity."

COPING WITH CHILDHOOD SIBLING LOSS

Before beginning an examination of factors associated with sibling loss and children's successful mastery of that loss, it will be helpful to review what we know about the risks involved in the childhood death of a sibling. When a brother or sister dies in childhood, surviving siblings are presented with a myriad of problematic issues and potential psychological conflicts. Guilt as a consequence of the loss of a loved one has been documented in the literature in innumerable writings, including Freud's classic essay *Mourning and Melancholia* (1952). For the child whose brother or sister has died, guilt toward the deceased, as a result of the ambivalence that we all experience in human relationships, is heightened by the ubiquitous rivalry and death wishes that we know are commonplace among siblings, toward the competitive sibling. In addition, the parents of the surviving sibling are typically struggling to endure an enormous loss of their own, which often makes it difficult, or even impossible, for them to assist the remaining children with their grief and loss.

As the immediate impact of the loss of a sibling recedes, surviving siblings often find themselves struggling with issues of protectiveness toward the grief-stricken parents, desires to make up for, in some way, the loss the parents have sustained (as well as their own), and conflict over their own needs and their wish not to see their parents hurt again. In adolescence, this frequently results in difficulties negotiating the developmental path toward autonomy and separation from the family of origin. Attempts to become a "replacement" child may derail a surviving sibling from his or her own developing sense of identity.

Finally, in adulthood, in addition to carrying forward any of the conflicts just described, surviving siblings may find themselves experiencing difficulties in intimate relationships, fearful of the loss of a loved one, or overly protective and anxious regarding the welfare of their children. It is not uncommon for these adult manifestations connected to the loss of a sibling to impel the adult survivor into psychotherapy or counseling, often with no conscious awareness of the way in which these difficulties relate to the death of their sibling.

In my own research on childhood sibling loss (Rosen, 1986), I was able to shed some light on how children cope with the death of a sibling and these possible psychological and developmental consequences of the loss. Although my research did not look at the role of personality or intrapsychic factors in coping with loss, the findings did point to several external factors that appear to help children cope. By far the most important of these was the family's ability to communicate among themselves about the loss. Lack of communication about the loss was experienced as an isolating factor, making it difficult or even impossible for the bereaved sibling to express feelings of grief, anger, or anxiety, and preventing bereaved siblings from having an opportunity to correct distortions in their perceptions of how their sibling had died and its implications for them. In families that were able to talk about the loss, on the other hand, there was shared mourning as well as shared movement within the family toward reconstituting as a new, different, but still functional family unit.

Not only did the ability to communicate about the loss seem to help in the immediate coping with the loss, but it also appeared to play a positive role in the continuing long-term relationships among family members. As adults, "expressive" survivors of childhood sibling loss continued to have more frequent contact with their mothers and remaining siblings (at a statistically significant level) than did "nonexpressive" survivors. While there was also more frequent contact between the "expressive" adult surviving siblings and their fathers, it was not at a statistically significant level.

In addition to the above, the sibling loss study illuminated some behaviors that surviving siblings reported as being helpful to them in their attempts to cope with the loss. The most frequently reported of these behaviors included concentrated focus on school activities, retaining personal objects that belonged to the deceased, engaging in religious activity, and attending the services for the deceased. Bereaved siblings seemed to engage in activities that I classified as being helpful in maintaining a sense of continuity and safety, in contrast to their parents, who reportedly tried to cope with grief and loss through behaviors that assisted them in breaking the emotional ties to the deceased—that is, removing the belongings of the deceased from the house. For children, loss and grief always contain the fear of the loss of their security (Jackson, 1965). We would thus expect that bereaved children whose needs for continuity and safety were met within their environment would cope better with sibling loss than children whose needs in this regard were unfulfilled.

In keeping with the research trends noted earlier, the sibling loss study was initiated with the expectation that the findings would primarily indicate difficulties associated with adaptation to the death of a brother or sister. However, in an unforeseen outcome to sibling loss in this study, it was also found that for some children, *mastery* of the death of their brother or sister, in addition to the challenges to coping that one would expect, also altered the study participants' view of themselves and their world in an unanticipated and, from their perspective, positive way. In this study, some survivors of childhood sibling loss reported that the experience of the loss and their adaptation to it had made them more compassionate, altruistic, and mature. They believed that the experience made them more aware of the fragility of life and the need to live each day to the fullest. They reported being drawn to charitable causes through the desire to help others cope with those problems that can be solved (in contrast to those problems associated with losses that are out of one's control). They felt that the experience made them more caring and loving individuals, more able to appreciate and value their loved ones. As an intrinsic part of these attitudes, they reported a heightened awareness of the reality of death.[1]

As a final factor associated with children's successful coping with the death of a sibling, this reseach indicated that even the community at large, what I termed the "bereaved community" (those that interact with the bereaved family at the time of the loss), can have an effect on how children experience sibling loss. The failure of those around the bereaved child—friends, extended family members, teachers, neighbors—to *acknowledge* the child's loss was experienced by the surviving siblings as further evidence of the need for them to keep their feelings hidden and minimize their communications about the loss. On the other hand, when their loss *was* recognized and openly acknowledged, surviving siblings felt more empowered to validate their own feelings and grieve. Some siblings felt that they had been abandoned and betrayed when those around them failed to speak with them about the loss, while even awkward and incomplete expressions of interest helped them to experience their feelings.

CASE REPORT

Betty D., a white girl, was 15 when she was referred for psychotherapy following a suicide attempt in which she had ingested various medications that she found in the medicine cabinet at her home. She stated that the suicide attempt was necessary in order to draw attention to her need for help, as she had been asking her parents for some time to take her for professional counseling or therapy. They had responded by arranging for her to see the school counselor—a step that Betty felt had not been sufficient.

Betty attended the first session accompanied by her mother and stepfather. Her mother was clearly depressed, had difficulty making eye contact, and cried easily during the session. Mr. D. was fairly uncommunicative, although he did occasionally participate, and supported the effort to get help for his stepdaughter. Betty herself was highly verbal, articulate, and anxious. She was happy to be getting help and was eager to cooperate.

Betty reported a progression of difficulties coping with her life since the death of her brother three years earlier. Joseph, five years her senior, had been hit by a car one evening as he walked down a dark country road. He had died instantly. Betty described the difficulties that she and her mother had encountered in coming to terms with his death (Mrs. D. and Betty's father were divorced at the time; there were no other siblings). She felt that many of her present difficulties originated in the experience of his death and in the changed relationship with her mother that resulted. She stated that since her brother's death, she had felt a responsibility toward her mother to protect her from any further pain. As a result, she found it difficult to talk with her mother about any problems she was having in her daily life. Mrs. D. also acknowledged that the relationship with her daughter had changed, that she no longer felt that she could rely on her own judgment as a mother and that she had, to a large extent, withdrawn from her daughter. Both mother and daughter were interested in working on their problems, and both were seen for a period of one year, first in sessions together and eventually in individual psychotherapy.

Work with Betty focused initially on her reactions to the death of her brother. She described her relationship with Joseph as a close one, and her reliance on him as a protector and confidante. She had experienced a tremendous loss at his death but had been careful not to exhibit her feelings, as she felt her mother was too grief-stricken to help Betty with her loss. At the same time, she experienced a wish to try and be like her brother, to "fill his shoes." This was understood to be a way of mitigating the loss of both her and her mother. She adopted a more rebellious, antisocial stance toward authority, as she perceived her brother to have demonstrated. She became somewhat promiscuous and began experimenting with drugs. Her school performance also deteriorated at this time.

During this period, following the death of her brother, Betty read extensively and kept both a journal and a notebook of original short stories, maintaining pride in her creative writing ability. She continued to enjoy a close relationship with her biological father, and worked at babysitting jobs during the summer. She was popular at school, and had a few close girlfriends who sympathized with her plight. At the time of the referral for psychotherapy, Betty had become increasingly aware of the self-defeating nature of her attempts to be like her brother, and how she had somehow gotten "off course" in her own life. She responded with enthusiasm to our work together, and her behavior gradually became more age-appropriate and less self-destructive.

DISCUSSION

Betty's resilience was evidenced in various ways following the death of her brother. Her suicide attempt, while a multidetermined acting-out behavior, had as at least one of its motivations the wish for help. Previous, more appropriate ways of communicating that need had failed. Her family responded to the suicide attempt by bringing her for treatment.

Like many other survivors of childhood sibling loss, Betty felt loyalty to her bereaved mother, and therefore had to truncate her own response to the loss. She was protective of her mother, both for her mother's sake and to protect her mother for her own survival. However, unlike many survivors of sibling loss, Betty became aware of her efforts to replace Joseph, and of the difficulties developing out of her inabiilty to communicate with her mother about any unpleasant or difficult subjects. She was unusually articulate and insightful concerning the ways in which her life had changed since her brother's death. She became the spokesman for change in the family.

Betty continued to experience pride and a sense of accomplishment in her creative writing. In addition to writing in her journal and notebook, Betty became unusually adept at letter writing, frequently using that medium to express her feelings toward others. Betty also took great pride in her collection of bottles, which had been started by her brother and which she had maintained, and made additions to, after her brother died.

In speculating on the sources of Betty's resilience, one would have to look at a number of factors, including her style of coping, personality attributes, and properties of her family and the surrounding community. Betty engaged in an activity, after the death of her brother, which enabled her to maintain a tie to the deceased—namely continuing her brother's bottle collection. This activity belongs to the category of coping behaviors (behaviors that assist in maintaining continuity and safety) that has been found to be helpful to bereaved siblings in their attempts to cope with the loss (Rosen, 1986). In addition, Betty was endowed with intelligence and social skills surpassing those of either parent. Garmezy (1981) and others have noted that competent children are generally friendly and well-liked, have good peer relationships, and are interpersonally sensitive and socially responsive—attributes that aptly characterize this young woman. A supportive peer group, and one that can acknowledge the bereaved sibling loss and grief, has also been found to be an important factor in coping with loss in childhood and adolescence (Rosen, 1986). For both these reasons, then, Betty's social skills and social relationships probably contributed to her ability to respond adaptively to the loss she experienced.

Intelligence as a predeterminant of resilience in adolescence has been cited by numerous researchers, including Anthony (1974). Betty was an unusually bright, attractive teenager who appeared to have the capacity to utilize to the fullest whatever resources were available in her environment. Her capacity for self-observation and self-awareness (formidable ego strengths) were developed to a degree not generally encountered in adolescent psychotherapy patients.

While Betty's ability to cope with the loss of her sibling appears largely related to her own disposition and personality attributes, there was one particular family characteristic that stood out as having likely played a part in her resiliency. In their discussion of resilience in adolescence, Hauser et al. (1989) discuss the role of the family in promoting or discouraging autonomy as a factor predictive of coping. Contrasting "enabling" behaviors from parent to child facilitates coping in the child. This lack of interference with autonomy and independent behavior was very much a characteristic of Betty's family and had facilitated her coping in many areas of her life. Betty's mother had consistently viewed Betty as a competent young woman with significant ability to master life events on her own. Similarly, Betty had from late childhood been expected to contribute in age-appropriate ways to the functioning of the family—that is, being responsible for cleaning her room, sharing in general household duties, and such. As Betty became adolescent, these capacities were expanded to include functioning in the outside world in after-school and weekend jobs.

We also see in Betty the kind of "acting-out" described by Dugan (1989) in which the behavior, while certainly containing the potential for a severely self-destructive outcome, was used as a method of self-advancement and growth. While clearly not the sole motivation, the suicide attempt was at least in part an adaptive effort to make clear to her family Betty's urgent need for more sophisticated and serious attention to her psychological situation. Her behavior was highly successful in this regard.

Lastly, in Betty's creative writing I believe that we can see, on an everyday scale, an example of the kind of creativity Pollock (1978) and others describe in association with mourning and loss. "In talented individuals, the death of a sibling can stimulate or direct creativity" (p. 481). In her writing, Betty was able to explore the depth of feeling that she was unable to express through verbal communication.

CONCLUSION

The purpose of this chapter has been to examine, in however preliminary a fashion, the factor of resilience in children, and how that resilience may be observed in relation to childhood sibling loss. We have begun to acquire a growing body of knowledge concerning the role of siblings in development, and the potential consequences of sibling loss, especially when those consequences are conceptualized in terms of potential damage and predisposition to psychopathology. It is essential for a more complete understanding of the impact of childhood sibling loss on bereaved siblings that we consider the possible outcomes related to mastery of sibling loss as well. There are usually few unexpected findings today in studies that focus on the development of psychopathology in childhood, but when we look to the reasons for survival among those who have lived difficult or traumatic lives, there is much cause for surprise, and much that we can learn that will have implications for all those who struggle against the odds.

NOTE

1. Supportive of this last statement were research findings as part of the study that indicated that survivors of childhood sibling loss score higher on a measure of death anxiety than any other group that has been tested with this instrument, including junior and senior high school students and a controlled comparison group.

REFERENCES

Abend, S. (1986). Sibling loss. In A. Rothstein (Ed.), *The Reconstruction of trauma* (pp. 95-104). Madison, CT: International Universities Press.

Anthony, E. (1974). The syndrome of the psychologically vulnerable child. In E. Anthony and C. Koupernik (Eds.), *The child in his family,* vol. 3: *Children at psychiatric risk* (pp. 529-544). New York: Wiley.

Dugan, T. (1989). Action and acting out: Variables in the development of resiliency in adolescence. In T. Dugan and R. Coles (Eds.), *The child in our times: Studies in the development of resiliency* (pp. 157-178). New York: Brunner/Mazel.

Elizur, E. and Kaufman, M. (1983). Factors influencing the severity of childhood bereavement reactions. *American Journal of Orthopsychiatry, 53*(4), 668-676.

Freud, S. (1952). *Mourning and melancholia.* New York: Standard Edition.

Garmezy, N. (1981). Children under stress: Perspectives on antecedents and correlates of vulnerability and resistance to psychopathology. In A. I. Robin, J. Aronoff, A. M. Barclay, and R. A. Zucker (Eds.), *Further exploration in personality* (pp. 196-269). New York: Wiley.

Garmezy, N. and Rutter, M. (1983). *Stress, coping and development in children.* New York: McGraw-Hill.

Hauser, S., Vieyra, M. A., Jacobson, A. and Wertlieb, D. (1989). Family aspects of vulnerability and resilience in adolescence: A theoretical perspective. In T. Dugan and R. Coles (Eds.), *The child in our times: Studies in the development of resiliency.* New York: Brunner/Mazel.

Jackson, E. (1965). *Telling a child about death.* New York: Channel Press.

Markusen, E. and Fulton, R. (1971). Childhood bereavement and behavior disorders: A critical review. *Omega: Journal of Death and Dying, 2,* 107-117.

Nagera, H. (1970). Children's reactions to the death of important objects: A developmental approach. *Psychoanalytic Study of the Child, 25,* 360-400.

Nagy, M. (1948). The child's theories concerning death. *Journal of Genetic Psychology, 73,* 3-27.

Pollock, G. (1978). On siblings, childhood sibling loss, and creativity. *The Annuals of Psychoanalysis, 6,* 443-481.

Rosen, H. (1986). *Unspoken grief: Coping with childhood sibling loss.* Lexington, MA: Lexington Books.

Szekely, L. (1983). Some observations on the creative process and its relation to mourning and various forms of understanding. *International Journal of Psychoanalysis, 64,* 149-157.

Tennant, C., Bebbington, P., and Hurry, J. (1980). Parental death in childhood and risk of adult depressive disorders: A review. *Psychological Medicine,* 10(2), 289-299.

Werner, E. and Smith, R. (1982). *Vulnerable but invincible: A study of resilient children.* New York: McGraw-Hill.

Wynne, L., Jones, J., and Al-Khayyal, M. (1982). Healthy family communications patterns: Observations in families "at risk" for psychopathology. In F. Walsh (Ed.), *Normal family processes.* New York: Guilford Press.

Chapter 7

Risk and Resilience in Teenagers Who Avoid Pregnancy

Howard Stevenson and Warren A. Rhodes

Adolescent sexuality and pregnancy have been the subject of much controversy over the last two decades (Chilman, 1983). This was especially true after the dramatic increase in teenage sexual experimentation between 1971 and 1976 (Kantner and Zelnik; 1972, Zelnik and Kantner, 1977), as well as the subsequent increase in recent years (Zelnik and Shah, 1983). Researchers have acknowledged the potential negative impact of teen pregnancy on future generations and on the quality of life of the children born to these adolescents (Baldwin and Cain, 1980; Belmont et al., 1981; Broman, 1980; Hardy et al., 1978; DeLissovoy, 1973; Ladner, 1988; Oppel and Royston, 1971). Many studies suggest that there are an overwhelming number of possible negative outcomes of teenage pregnancy, including increased potential for child abuse (DeLissovoy, 1973; Svobodny, 1988), increased academic difficulties (Oppel and Royston, 1971), lower IQ scores (Broman, 1980), increased potential for low-birth-weight infants, and infant mortality (Green and Potteiger, 1977).

While the long- and short-term problems of teenage sexuality and subsequent pregnancy have been debated for decades, this negative focus overshadows the lives of high-risk persons who have not become pregnant during their teen years (Jones and Philliber, 1983). Rhodes (1986, p. 4) states,

> Instead of looking at why adolescents become pregnant and generating primary prevention efforts based on the logic obtained (negative outcomes), it may be more useful to look at why these adolescents who were theoretically supposed to

become pregnant (high risk) did not become pregnant (positive outcome). In other words, where did the adolescent go *right*?

This question is the subject of this chapter. It is proposed that helpful methods leading to the decrease of teenage pregnancy or its deleterious results can be gathered and implemented by investigating the strengths of resilient and invulnerable teenagers.

TEENAGERS AT RISK FOR THE INITIATION OF SEXUAL ACTIVITY AND PREGNANCY

Determining high risk is a difficult and complex process at best, as there are many different reasons why children initiate sexual activity (Walters, Walters, and McKenry, 1987). For some, the idea of getting pregnant never entered their minds, since the desire to have intercourse was the primary goal. For others, pregnancy is intended. Yet, before one reaches the far-reaching conclusion that one is at high risk for pregnancy simply because he or she is adolescent (Walters et al., 1987), factors that have been empirically shown to increase one's chances for pregnancy must be identified. Adolescents at risk for pregnancy can be described a number of ways. Jorgensen and Alexander (1983, p. 126) have defined adolescent pregnancy-risk as "the probability that an adolescent or adolescent couple will engage in sexual intercourse without the use of effective contraception." For the most part, research defines risk as a cluster of factors that have been empirically determined to be associated with the initiation of unprotected sexual intercourse and/or teen pregnancy.

Initiation of Sexual Activity

The initiation of sexual activity pushes adolescents toward transition into adulthood earlier than they are ready (Forste and Heaton, 1988). Teen pregnancy presents an even greater challenge to the transition process. Factors influencing the initiation of sexual activity are germane to the topic of teen pregnancy as they may be the same reasons pregnancies "just happen." While most pregnancies continue to be unintended (Presser, 1974), intended pregnancies are becoming a concern of behavioral scientists (Scott, 1983; Zelnik and Kantner, 1980). For those youth who "do not care" what happens as a result of their sexual activity, teen pregnancy becomes a greater risk.

Explanations behind youth's initiation of sexual activity include experiences influenced by family and community environments, socialization settings, and sex education instruction (Forste and Heaton, 1988). Family and community influences that tend to be negatively correlated with early sexual activity include parental education, both parents living at home, moderate parental strictness, higher socioeconomic status, and living in rural areas (Coles and Stokes, 1985; Flick, 1986; Miller et al., 1986; Zelnik and Shah, 1983; Zelnik, Kantner, and Ford, 1981). Extremely conservative and extremely liberal home environments are more likely to be related to a higher incidence of adolescent sexual involvement (Miller et al., 1986).

Major socialization experiences that tend to be associated with low levels of premarital intercourse are religious affiliation and church attendance (Brown, 1985; Coles and Stokes, 1985; Flick, 1986; Zelnik et al., 1981). The salient issues here are the degree to which church environments openly express values against premarital sex and that there tends to be consistent reinforcement of these values as a form of "social control" (Scott, 1983).

Sex education has been shown to increase adolescents' use of contraceptives, although those who receive sex education are no more or less likely to engage in sex (Flick, 1986). The context of sexual informaiton is also crucial. Premarital sexual behavior tends to be less prevalent if sex education takes place at school *and* at home (Furstenberg, Moore, and Peterson, 1985). Generally, the more accurately sex education is integrated into the daily lives of adolescents and is being taught by knowledgeable and capable adults (as opposed to promiscuous peers), in environments familiar to them, the more teenagers tend to engage in protected sex (Coles and Stokes, 1985).

It is not necessarily true that all of the reasons that teens are engaging in sex explain both the initiation of sexual activity *and* the increased risk of pregnancy. Scott (1983) interviewed 123 school-age mothers (SAMs) in an effort to ascertain the relationship between initiating sexual activity and love sentiments. It was found that love was more related to pregnancy than initiating sexual intercourse. Over 80 percent of the respondents acknowledged being in love with their partner when they became pregnant, while less than 50 percent of white and black school-age mothers stated love was the reason for their initiating sexual activities. Therefore, another example of an adolescent at risk for pregnancy may be the one who experiences sentiments of love, or is led to believe the unprotected sexual act will end in future marriage (Scott, 1983). This interaction could effectively decrease cognitive dissonance for the adolescents involved and nullify (for the moment) the "social stigmatization" associated with premarital sexual relations.

The question must be raised, however, whether it is possible to differentiate between teenage girls who become pregnant and those who do not. That is, is it true that the one who is at risk and does not get pregnant is psychologically and/or socially more well-adjusted than the one who is at risk and does become pregnant? What about those who abort? First, what are the risk factors for teen pregnancy?

Teen Pregnancy Risk

The literature suggests a number of high-risk factors for teen pregnancy, none of which can be considered in isolation. Gottschalk et al. (1964) found that absence of parental supervision, less church attendance, and earlier sexual maturation were associated with adolescent pregnancy. In a study of a psychiatric inpatient population, Abernathy and Abernathy (1974) found that alienation from mother, low self-esteem, an overidealization of the relationship with the father, and an isolation from relationships with females were significant variables that placed adolescents at risk for pregnancy.

Goldfarb et al. (1977) controlled for social class and other intervening variables and found the risk of adolescent pregnancy to be correlated with poorer academic achievement, larger family size, more unmarried sisters with children, later sex education, and initial sex education taught by a peer rather than adult.

Adolescent pregnancy risk has also been ascertained by investigating the psychosocial and psychological characteristics of those teens who are currently pregnant and comparing them to those who have never become pregnant (Brunswick, 1971; Kaplan, Smith, and Pokorny, 1974; Ralph, Lochman, and Thomas, 1984). Kaplan et al. (1974) found that, compared to controls, the pregnant adolescents were less able to handle threats to their self-esteem, more likely to view their relationships to school, family, and peers as not contributing to self-esteem, less apt to demonstrate attitudes of positive self-imaging, and more likely to develop problematic and antisocial behaviors. Other studies show little to no differences between pregnant and never-pregnant adolescents on measures of psychological and psychosocial adjustment such as self-esteem, mood, life aspirations, family structure, and educational attainment (Brunswick, 1971; Ralph et al., 1984).

Ralph et al. (1984) studied the personal and family histories, locus of control, and self-image perceptions of 19 pregnant and 20 never-pregnant adolescents with average ages of 15.8 and 16.2 years, respectively. They found some differences, but overall results showed there was no variable or relationship found to be statistically significant to distinguish between pregnant and never-pregnant adolescents. Some general hypotheses were suggested by the authors. Members of the pregnant group tended to have later sex education, more brothers, poorer vocational and educational aspirations, and a mother with a lower educational level as compared to the nulliparous group.

In an attempt to compare teenagers who risk pregnancy with those who plan, Jones and Philliber (1983) found similarities—not differences—between them. They found the groups similar in their motivations for not becoming pregnant and in their social network support for those motivations. In contrast to other studies where pregnant and nonpregnant teens or contraceptive users versus nonusers were compared, the authors chose a group of teenagers who had never been pregnant but were sexually active and found that only 36 percent of them were consistent contraceptive users (i.e., planners).

The relationship of pregnancy risk and personality organization was studied by Hart and Hilton (1988) and differences were found between experimental groups. They compared four groups of older teenage girls, including those who were sexually inactive and had never had intercourse (Inactive), those who were sexually active and always used reliable birth control devices (Birth Control), those who were sexually active but did not use birth control consistently or at all (Nonbirth Control), and those who were pregnant and planning to give birth (Pregnant). Results indicated that the Inactive group struggled with developing personal autonomy and wanted to keep life from passing too quickly. They were described as often complacent and morally righteous. Most of the members of the Inactive group tended to be unclear about futuristic issues, while there were some in this group who were more psychologically mature. The Birth Control group showed a higher sense of personal autonomy, respect for the autonomy of others, and an ability to relate in an emotionally mature manner to others. The girls in the Nonbirth control group were at highest risk for pregnancy and were in conflict with their personal values and the values of their parents.

The Pregnant group was described primarily as either "oblivious to or given to defiance of social sanction" (Hart and Hilton, 1988, p. 129). While emotional development tended to be limited and there were some internal fears about developing selfhood, they tended to be connected to people. Some caution must be used in interpreting these interesting findings, as the authors used nontraditional research assessment instruments in the gathering of their data. They utilized a Sentence Completion Test, the Rorschach (Friedman Developmental Level Scoring System), the Thematic Apperception Test, and the Urist Mutuality of Autonomy Scale. The authors raise some important concerns with respect to counseling, however. They suggested that, in addition to contraceptive counseling, "education in self-awareness, understanding of one's personal values and goals, self-regulation, and awareness of the needs, feelings, differences, and separateness of others" (p. 131) might also be included.

In an attempt to isolate factors that are crucial in determining contraception, abortion, or bringing a pregnancy to term, Landry et al. (1986) found living with parents to be important in the decisionmaking process. Adolescents who chose to carry their pregnancy to term "were less likely to be living with their parent(s) than other nonpregnant teens" (p. 273). Those who terminated pregnancy were more likely to have educational aspirations and more involvement with at least one parent. It was in this study that the authors sought to answer the question, "Why do some high-risk, sexually active teenagers avoid teenage pregnancy?" Their answer to this question, albeit limited, was that motivation to act on one's contraceptive beliefs plays a major role. They too challenge general conceptions about how teens who become pregnant are different from those who do not. They found similarity between terminators, contraceptors, and deliverers in their attitudes toward school, self-reports of grades achieved, plans to graduate from high school, and level of promiscuous behavior.

Walters et al. (1987) discovered that there is no easy formula that will distinguish between girls who become pregnant and those who do not. In an attack on the current view of adolescent sexuality and pregnancy, they state:

> Historically, it has been thought that there must be something wrong with young girls who become pregnant. The assumption has not been that only their circumstances in life have been different, for we are a nation with a deep belief in the ability of an individual to rise above a deprived environment. The implication has been that young girls who become pregnant are intrinsically different from those who do not (p. 26).

In their study, they did not find any differences between the two groups along psychological characteristics. Only race and socioeconomic status differentiated these groups and they proposed that environmental issues ought to be looked at more carefully. In fact, they go further to propose that perhaps all adolescents are at risk and nontraditional educational settings and methods (e.g., schools, religious institutions, and peers) ought to be included in the education process.

The lack of cognitive capacity of adolescents to actually make reasonable decisions about sexual activity or contraceptive protection has been proposed (Pestrak and Martin, 1985). Risk may be a function of this limited developmental capacity to apply values, grasp long-term consequences, delay immediate gratification, and/or meet birth control demands (Pestrak and Martin, 1985).

In sum, research on the initiation of unprotected sexual activity is important in identifying teenagers at risk for pregnancy. Reasons for initiating sexual activity are associated with reasons for not planning for the consequences of sexual activity, and thus pregnancy is that much more likely to occur. In the case of love sentiments and marriage aspirations toward one's partner, this motivation for engaging in sexual intercourse is more related to pregnancy than sex initiation in that one is more intentional in engaging in unprotected sex (Scott, 1983). It is not true that all who initiate sexual activity early in adolescence are destined to become pregnant, but this group would clearly be at higher risk than those who initiate sexual activity later in adolescence.

The work on protective factors by Garmezy (1985) suggests that issues of self-esteem, family support and lack of family discord, and presence and accessiblity of extended support systems are all influential in the development of coping abilities in children. If high-risk teenagers have access to these elements, then the likelihood for family stability increases and the occurrence of first intercourse decreases (Forste and Heaton, 1988).

Second, while there are clusters of risk factors associated with persons who have become pregnant or have avoided pregnancy, research is mixed in distinguishing between these two groups. One might be inclined to agree with Walters et al. (1987) that all adolescents are at risk, given limited cognitive capacity, stressful social demands, and intimidating future aspirations. In fact, except for a few instances, there seems to be more research support for similarity than differences between those who get pregnant and those who do not, between contraceptors and nonusers, and between terminators, contraceptors, and deliverers. Instead of viewing risk as a function of the presence or absence of factors, the Bingo approach, it may be more helpful to view risk and resilience within an interactional and systemic framework. That is, risk may be a function of the interaction of both risk and resilience in the individual and in his or her environment.

BROADENING THE VIEWS OF RESILIENCE AND RISK

The research on resilience and risk has generated some interesting ideas on how children and adolescents become or avoid being trapped into difficult life circumstances (Garmezy, 1985; Rutter, 1987). Rutter has identified four processes that underlie the notion of protective mechanisms that counter the risks of adverse social and psychiatric situations. In fact, he argues against the use of the word "variables" as it presupposes an artifact that can capture one's being at risk or not. Such a notion is not possible in our world, where complexity of relationships and happenings determine outcome. The protective processes identified by Rutter are reduction of the impact of risk, reduction of negative chain reactions, the development and enhancement of self-esteem and self-efficacy, and the creation of opportunities. Each of these mediating mechanisms is important in understanding how some teenagers may avoid pregnancy and others do not. One very interesting point made by Rutter (1987) is that different children will be at risk for psychiatric or interpersonal disturbances for different reasons. To suggest that an individual will become pregnant because she is at high risk would be erroneous because of the differential responses to risk situations that various adolescents present.

The protective mechanism of reduction of risk impact involves alteration of the risk itself and alteration of the child's exposure to the risk situation. Here, Rutter (1987) makes the crucial point that successful interaction with risk situations may in fact lead to resilience from these situations. This successful reaction or coping can be isolated and investigated for further use in high-risk situations. Could resilient high-risk teens actually benefit from their exposure to varied social demands to become pregnant? Conversely, Rutter points out that distractions or distancing from risk situations may include effective coping strategies that decrease the risk effect, as in the example of the teenager who runs away from an incestuous home situation.

It appears that a relationship with a family member or close friend plays a significant role in the teenage female's decision to have sex, use contraceptives, abort, and/or bear the child (Brown, 1985; Landry et al., 1986). The old adage of many families, "You are what your friends are," is true. Thus, the fear that many parents have regarding the "kind of crowd" that their children socialize in, is well-founded. Encouraging information generated from this research is that the earlier parents can involve their children in peer groups that foster values and ideas that are inconsistent with early sexual experimentation and isolated decision-making, then the higher the likelihood that these children will be influenced positively in choices about their sexual behavior. This strategy represents an alteration of the risk or exposure to the risk. Additionally, an adolescent who is involved in a peer network that meets the basic needs of self-esteem, belongingness, individuation in peer pressure situations, gradual sexual and intellectual maturity, career aspirations, and self- and other-caring is more likely to avoid "falling" into early sexual experimentation as a function of unmet emotional needs.

The reduction of negative chain reactions represents the second category of protective mechanisms, which implies that exposure to risk will not automatically end in the risk effect (e.g., pregnancy). It is the concomitant and subsequent reactions and interactions that continue to happen within the individual and his or her environment that can solidify or prevent the risk effect. An adolescent who begins to struggle with sexuality at 15 because her mother gave birth to her at 15 may find this struggle more cumbersome if her relationship with her mother is tumultuous, if 80 percent of her close friends are pregnant or have children, if she does not find school appealing, and if she feels she is in love with her boyfriend. The question to ask is, "What are the possible interventions or changes that could reduce the negative chain reactions for this person?" Changes in relationship with her mother, or boyfriend, or friendships could be the beginning of a spiraling into or a climbing out of difficult circumstances.

Self-efficacy represents the third group of protective mechanisms proposed by Rutter (1987) and it is developed through personal relationships, through the successful accomplishment of tasks, and serendipitous turning points. Taking our example used earlier, one might consider this teenager at a different level of risk if she felt confident about her worth as a person, was involved in an intimate relationship with friends who encouraged her to use contraceptives, or was gaining social praise for her talents in sports or some other hobby.

For teenagers whose initiation of sexual activity and subsequent pregnancy occurs as a function of overwhelming peer pressure, romantic love notions, having to prove one's prowess, or unmet need satisfactions, the enhancement of self-esteem may serve as a protective mechanism. Conversely, these teens may be more at risk in social situations where peer pressure and individual low self-esteem are compounded.

Turning points can be applied to this example as well. What happens if the teenager in our example is sent to live with relatives who live in another geographical location (e.g., "the country") in order to "save" her from herself and her varied influences. This is a common practice in some families who have migrated from the South. You might begin to see the logic in this decision if you take into account the notion of adolescent cognitive development and how responsible decisionmaking may be an advanced developmental task.

At 15, a sexually active teenager may be less inclined to think of the risk of pregnancy as compared to the age of 17, when career and life goals may be at the forefront of her mind. A turning point, however, may represent that event or series of events that allows the teen at risk to move from blind submission to reasoned planning without becoming pregnant. Sending a child to relatives in another geographical surrounding accomplishes many things. It may buy time until reasoned planning can begin. The adolescent has to make new friends, realign with family, and gradually get her footing. This may be just enough time for the adolescent to "get her head together." A breakup in the relationship with a boyfriend may be a turning point, also. The notion of turning point seems to be something many intruding parents and loved ones misapply by their varied attempts to disrupt the lives of teenagers for the sake of "saving them from themselves."

The last protective mechanism group is the opening up of opportunities; this has special significance for teen pregnancy in that there is research to suggest that lack of future or career opportunities can be crucial in the decision to risk pregnancy (Ladner, 1988).

DISCUSSION AND IMPLICATIONS

What can we learn from the literature on adolescent pregnancy-risk? A wealth of information has been gathered and treatment and research directions can be suggested. First, one must speak in broad terms when discussing those adolescents who do not become pregnant. Why some succeed despite the odds tends to be a function of the interaction of individual and environmental vulnerabilities and protective mechanisms (Rutter, 1987). There do not seem to be radical differences in areas of personality, environment, and family and social relations between girls who avoid pregnancy and those who do not. There are general statements that can be made, however.

Teenage pregnancy may be one of many reactions high-risk youth have toward life trauma and transitions, and thus resolution of the problem may need to come from comprehensive models of early intervention and prevention (Mills, Dunham, and Alpert, 1988). That is, if an adolescent is troubled by school failure, negative interpersonal relationships, and perceived lack of social competence, he or she is more prone to engage in high-risk behaviors (e.g., delinquency, substance abuse, etc.), of which one may be unprotected sexual activity, which can lead to pregnancy (Mills et al., 1988).

Second, investigating the lives of adolescents who do not become pregnant is helpful, but it is limited by cursory data-gathering methods. The case study approach could provide more in-depth information and is better suited for identifying protective mechanisms, such as turning points, alteration of exposure to risk, and reduction of negative chain reactions, all of which can lead to the avoidance of pregnancy. Conducting case studies on a number of high-risk adolescents from various backgrounds and asking about protective mechanisms and vulnerabilities is encouraged. It is further suggested that future research efforts avoid deficit-ridden assumptions that seek to interpret adolescent sexuality from a negative rather than from a positive outcome framework (Rhodes, 1986). Given a deeper level of research investigation, the positive outcome approach can be a helpful process to identify programmatic and therapeutic prevention strategies.

Third, in addition to asking why some adolescents at risk for pregnancy succeed despite the odds, we should investigate how various social environments initiate or maximize the development of protective mechanisms. For example, what is it about religious affiliation that might be related to lower premarital sexual relations, as has been suggested (Brown, 1985; Coles and Stokes, 1985; Flick, 1986; Forste and Heaton, 1988)? Brown (1985) investigated the sexual permissiveness of black adolescent females and found that the perception of permissiveness of close friends may play a major role in sexual behavior. In addition, it was found that church participation may significantly influence how sexually liberal a teenager may behave. This influence may lead to inhibition of sexual experimentation and, in the least, the supportive role of the church in teenage pregnancy prevention may need to be reevaluated (Stevenson, 1990). The church and its varied organizations can serve as external support systems or kinship networks that have been identified as protective (Garmezy, 1985). There are numerous opportunities for developing self-esteem and intervening in negative chain reactions.

What kind of therapeutic situations can be established that will counteract the risk effect? Some teens get involved with sexuality because of a host of reasons. From a clinical standpoint, however, it is crucial that the reasons are identified, if they are specific, as this may be crucial information in identifying the specific risk situation that increases the teenager's vulnerability or promotes protective mechanisms.

One implication from the research reviewed is that counselors would do well not to trust simply the stated motivations that teenagers (male and female) give that suggest they do not want to get pregnant (Jones and Philliber, 1983). The inconsistency between statement and behavior for this age group might be expected, since cognitive consistency for adolescents is still developing (Pestrak and Martin, 1985). Social skills training and sex education may be very helpful deterrents to early pregnancy if they help to alter the risk by changing the teenagers' lack of heterosocial skills and cognitive perceptions regarding impinging social demands.

More study is required to look at the avoidance of teen pregnancy within the broader context of individual, social, and community systems. Resilience, as broadly defined by Rutter (1987) as being an interactional process that can be found in a variety of networks, will need to be defined and harnessed more readily than it is at present. Prevention programs can then be developed based upon an underlying principle of resilience. Given this shift in program development, however, prevention programs will most assuredly require the collaboration of traditional and nontraditional community institutions if avoidance of teen pregnancy is to become a planned rather than a serendipitous event.

REFERENCES

Abernathy, V. and Abernathy, G. (1974). Risk for unwanted pregnancy among mentally ill adolescent girls. *American Journal of Orthopsychiatry, 44,* 442-450.

Baldwin, W. and Cain, V. (1980). The children of teenage parents. *Family Planning Perspectives, 12,* 1, 34-43.

Belmont, L., Cohen, P., Dryfoos, J., Stein, Z., and Zayac, S. (1981). Maternal age and children's intelligence. In K. G. Scott, T. Field, and E. Robertson (Eds.), *Teenager parenting and their offspring.* New York: Grune and Stratton.

Broman, S. H. (1980). Longterm development of children born to teenagers. In K. G. Scott, T. Field, and E. Robertson (Eds.), *Teenager parenting and their offspring.* New York: Grune and Stratton.

Brown, S. V. (1985). Premarital sexual permissiveness among black adolescent females. *Social Psychology Quarterly, 48*(4), 381-387.

Brunswick, A. F. (1971). Adolescent health, sex and fertility. *American Journal of Public Health, 61*(4), 711-729.

Chilman, C. S. (1983). *Adolescent sexuality in a changing society.* New York: Wiley.

Coles, R. and Stokes, G. (1985). *Sex and the American Teenager.* New York: Harper and Row.

DeLissovoy, V. (1973). Child care by adolescent parents. *Children Today, 35,* 22-25.

Flick, L. M. (1986). Paths to adolescent parenthood: Implications for prevention. *Public Health Reports, 101,* 132-147.

Forste, R. T. and Heaton, T. B. (1988). Initiation of sexual activity among female adolescents. *Youth and Society, 19,* 250-268.

Furstenberg, F. F., Jr., Moore, K. A., and Peterson, J. L. (1985). Sex education and sexual experience among adolescents. *American Journal of Public Health, 75,* 1331-1332.

Garmezy, N. (1985). Stress resistant children: The search for protective factors. In J. Stevenson (Ed.), *Recent research in developmental psychopathology.* Oxford: Pergamon Press.

Goldfarb, J. L. Mumford, D. M., Shurn, D. A., Smith, P. B., Flowers, C., and Shum, C. (1977). An attempt to detect "pregnancy susceptibility" in indigent adolescent girls. *Journal of Youth and Adolescence, 6,* 127-144.

Gottschalk, L. A., Titchener, J. L., Piker, H. N., and Stewart, S. S. (1964). Psychosocial factors associated with pregnancy in adolescent girls: A preliminary report. *Journal of Nervous and Mental Diseases, 138,* 524-534.

Green, C. P. and Potteiger, K. (1977). *Teenage pregnancy: A major problem for minors.* Washington, DC: Zero Population Growth.

Hardy, J. B., Welcher, D. W., Stanley, J., and Dallas, J. R. (1978). Long-range outcome of adolescent pregnancy. *Clinical Obstetrics and Gynecology, 21,* 4.

Hart, B. and Hilton, I. (1988). Dimensions of personality organization as predictors of teenage pregnancy risk. *Journal of Personality Assessment, 52,* 116-132.

Jones, J. B. and Philliber, S. G. (1983). Sexually active but not pregnant: A comparison of teens who risk and teens who plan. *Journal of Youth and Adolescence, 12,* 235-251.

Jorgenson, S. R. and Alexander, S. J. (1983). Research on adolescent pregnancy-risk: Implications for sex education programs. *Theory into Practice, 22,* 125-133.

Kantner, J. G. and Zelnik, M. (1972). Sexual experimentation of young unmarried women in the United States. *Family Planning Perspective, 4,* 9-18.

Kaplan, H. B., Smith, P. B., and Pokorny, A. D. (1974). Psychosocial antecedents of unwed motherhood among indigent adolescents. *Journal of Youth and Adolescence, 3,* 181-207.

Ladner, J. A. (1988). The impact of teenage pregnancy on the Black family: Policy directions. In H. P. McAdoo (Ed.), *Black families.* Newbury Park, CA: Sage.

Landry, E., Bertrand, J. T., Cherry, F., and Rice, J. (1986). Teen pregnancy in New Orleans: Factors that differentiate teens who deliver, abort, and successfully contracept. *Journal of Youth and Adolescence, 15*(3), 259-274.

Miller, B. C., McCoy, J. K., Olson, T. D., and Wallace, C. M. (1986). Parental discipline and control attempts in relation to adolescent sexual attitudes and behavior. *Journal of Marriage and the Family, 48,* 503-512.

Mills, R. C., Dunham, R. G., and Alpert, G. P. (1988). Working with high-risk youth in prevention and early intervention programs: Toward a comprehensive wellness model. *Adolescence, 23,* 643-660.

Oppel, W. C. and Royston, A. B. (1971). Teenage births: Some social, psychological, and physical sequelae. *American Journal of Public Health, 61,* 4.

Pestrak, V. A. and Martin, D. (1985). Cognitive development and aspects of adolescent sexuality. *Adolescence, 20,* 981-987.

Presser, H. (1974). Early motherhood: Ignorance or bliss? *Family Planning Perspectives, 6,* 8-14.

Ralph, N., Lochman, J., and Thomas, T. (1984). Psychosocial characteristics of pregnant and nulliparous adolescents. *Adolescence, 19,* 283-294.

Rhodes, W. A. (1986). A new perspective on teenage pregnancy. Unpublished manuscript. Delaware State College.

Rutter, M. (1987). Psychosocial resilience and protective mechanisms. *American Journal of Orthopsychiatry, 57* (July), 316-331.

Scott, J. W. (1983). The sentiments of love and aspirations for marriage and their association with teenage sexual activity and pregnancy. *Adolescence, 18,* 889-897.

Stevenson, H. C. (1990). The role of the African-American church in the education about teenage pregnancy. *Counseling and Values, 34,* 130-133.

Svobodny, L. A. (1988). Adolescents with moderate learning difficulties: Are they "at risk" for exhibiting abusive parenting interactions? *Maladjustment and Therapeutic Education, 6*(1), 14-22.

Walters, L. H., Walters, J., and McKenry, P. C. (1987). Differentiation of girls at risk of early pregnancy from the general population of adolescents. *Journal of Genetic Psychology, 148,* 19-29.

Zelnik, M. and Kantner, J. (1977). Sexual and contraceptive experience of young unmarried women in the United States, 1966-1971. *Family Planning Perspectives, 9,* 55-71.

______. (1980). Sexual activity, contraceptive use and pregnancy among metropolitan-area teenagers: 1971-1979. *Family Planning Perspectives, 12,* 230-237.

Zelnik, M., Kantner, J. F., and Ford, K. (1981). *Sex and pregnancy in adolescence.* Beverly Hills, CA: Sage.

Zelnik, M. and Shah, F. K. (1983). First intercourse among young Americans. *Family Planning Perspectives, 15,* 64-70.

Chapter 8

Factors Affecting Positive Long-Term Outcome in Attention Deficit Hyperactive Disorder

Lily Hechtman

Following children with a particular disorder into adolescence and adulthood provides one with a view of the natural history and prognosis of the condition, as well as how the condition may affect adolescent and adult outcome. Most importantly, it can provide clues as to what factors may influence this outcome in a positive or negative direction.

ADOLESCENT OUTCOME OF ATTENTION DEFICIT HYPERACTIVE DISORDER

A number of studies have prospectively followed children with attention deficit hyperactive disorder (ADHD) into adolescence. The first of these, conducted by Weiss and her colleagues (Weiss et al., 1971) was a comprehensive five-year prospective, controlled follow-up study of 91 subjects, aged 10 to 18 (mean 13.3) years. Weiss found that, compared to a control group matched for age, sex, IQ, and social class, hyperactive adolescents had poorer self-esteem and more academic problems. In addition, 25 percent had significant delinquent behavior and most continued to be distractible, impulsive, and emotionally immature, although less hyperactive.

In another prospective, controlled study of hyperactive adolescents, Akerman, Dykman, and Peters (1977) compared a normal control group (N=31), a learning disabled group (N=39) and a third group of hyperactive and learning disabled adolescents (N=23). All subjects had IQs of at least 80 and were 14 years of age at follow-up. The hyperactive learning disabled group had significantly more oppositional or delinquent behavior, as well as lower self-esteem. They were also more fidgety, impulsive, inattentive, and immature. This group had poorer academic performance when compared to controls, but not in comparison to the other learning disabled group.

Satterfield, Hoppe, and Schell (1982) conducted a prospective, controlled study involving 110 hyperactive adolescents (mean age 17.3 years) and 88 matched control subjects. Fifty percent of the hyperactives had had a felony arrest (for burglary, grand theft, or assault with a weapon), compared to less than 10 percent of the controls. Nineteen percent of the hyperactives and none of the controls had been institutionalized. Surprisingly, neither social class nor stimulant treatment in childhood influenced these results. Satterfield, Satterfield, and Cantwell (1981), however, suggested that long-term multimodal treatment may positively affect outcome in a three-year prospective, uncontrolled study of 100 hyperactive boys. Treatment was individualized to the needs of each child and family, and included stimulant medication and remedial education, in addition to individual and/or group therapy for the child and parents. The group receiving longer treatment seemed to have better academic and social outcome.

Recently, Lambert et al. (1987) reassessed 59 pervasively hyperactive boys, age 12 (originally seen in childhood) and 59 control subjects matched for age, race, and parental occupation. Comprehensive evaluations involved parents, teachers, and children. Hyperactives performed significantly worse than controls on IQ tests, academic achievement, cognitive development, and cognitive style. Hyperactives also had significantly more antisocial behavior, as shown by increased school suspensions (14 versus 2 percent), problems with law enforcement agencies (19 versus 3 percent) and admission to juvenile facilities (5 versus 0 percent).

Lambert et al. concluded that 20 percent of the hyperactives had no problems at follow-up. Thirty-seven percent had persistent learning, behavior, or emotional difficulties, but were no longer receiving medical intervention (residual group). Forty-three percent of the hyperactive subjects were still in treatment for hyperactivity and had learning, behavior, and/or emotional difficulties (still hyperactive group).

All hyperactives had received multiple treatments, including medication and educational and psychological intervention. The residual and still hyperactive groups required more treatment (i.e., more interventions for longer periods of time). Furthermore, no early correlates that might predict outcome could be identified. However, the nonproblem group showed cognitive and behavioral maturity; the residual group exhibited cognitive immaturity but behavioral maturity, while the still-hyperactive group showed both cognitive and behavioral immaturity.

Generally, these studies suggest that 70 to 80 percent of adolescents who had attention deficit hyperactive disorder in childhood continue to have significant problems. Often, they have symptoms meriting the diagnosis—for example, restlessness, overactivity, impulsivity, attentional problems, and cognitive difficulties. Educational problems with poor academic performance are frequent. Personality difficulties include immaturity and impulsivity with social problems involving peers, teachers, and parents. Low self-esteem is common. Significant antisocial behavior in adolescents is seen in about 25 percent of subjects, particularly if they also had unsocialized aggression or conduct disorder when first referred.

Recent reviews on adolescent outcome by Hechtman (1985) and Thorley (1988) generally support the above picture, but make the added point that stimulant treatment in childhood does not seem to significantly affect the outcome outlined above.

ADULT OUTCOME IN ATTENTION DEFICIT HYPERACTIVE DISORDER

There are few studies that have prospectively followed children with ADHD into adulthood. Weiss and Hechtman (1986) conducted a controlled, prospective 10-, 12-, and 15-year follow-up study of 75 young adults and 45 normal controls matched initially on age, sex, IQ, and socioeconomic status. Subjects had a mean age of 19 at 10-year follow-up and a mean age of 25 at 15-year follow-up. The evaluations were comprehensive and included demographic, academic, work, psychiatric, social (including antisocial behavior and drug and alcohol abuse), as well as physiological and psychological parameters. In addition to interviews with subjects and parents, reports were obtained from school, employers, and the court system.

Results of the 10- to 12-year follow-up (Hechtman et al., 1981) indicated that, compared to matched controls, hyperactives moved more frequently and fewer of them still lived with their parents. Hyperactives also had more car accidents. Their academic histories (Weiss et al., 1979) suggested that they had completed less education, had failed more grades, and had achieved lower marks. Work histories (Hechtman, Weiss, and Perlman, 1978) were not significantly different at 10-year follow-up, but became so at 15-year follow-up. Hyperactives had more court referrals (Hechtman, Weiss, and Perlman, 1984) and tried nonmedical drugs more often; however, drug abuse was not significantly greater in the hyperactive group. Weiss et al. (1979) indicated that psychiatrically, as adults, hyperactives had more impulsive and immature personality traits, were more restless, and rated their childhoods more negatively. Hyperactives also did worse in areas of social skills, self-esteem (Hechtman, Weiss, and Perlman, 1980) and various cognitive tests (Hopkins et al., 1979).

The two groups showed no significant differences in physiological measures of height, weight, blood pressure, pulse (Hechtman, Weiss, and Metrakos, 1978), or electroencephalography (EEG) (Hechtman, Weiss, and Perlman, 1978). A comparison of EEGs of hyperactive subjects over time (i.e., initially, 5- and 10-year follow-up) indicated that normalization of EEG tended to take place in adolescence. Initial EEG patterns were not predictive of outcome in adolescence or adulthood.

At 15-year follow-up (Weiss et al., 1985), more than half of the hyperactive subjects (66 percent) still had at least one disabling symptom of the syndrome. Hechtman and Weiss (1986) showed that 23 percent had an antisocial personality disorder. There were also more suicide attempts in the hyperactive group. Generally, problems persist in adulthood in many, though not all, hyperactive subjects.

Gittelman et al. (1985) also conducted a prospective, controlled study of hyperactives as young adults. The study involved 101 hyperactive subjects and 100 matched normal controls, aged 16 to 23 years (mean 18.3 years). Comprehensive evaluation included interviews with subjects and parents and various rating scales. Thirty-one percent of the hyperactives had full ADHD. Another 9 percent had two of the three key symptoms (attention deficit, hyperactivity and impulsivity, as outlined in DSM-III). In addition, 20 percent of hyperactives had conduct disorder and 12 percent had substance abuse disorder. Other conditions did not differ significantly between the two groups. It also appears that the likelihood of developing conduct disorder is greater if ADHD persists, and that substance abuse is often linked with or follows the conduct disorder.

In a related paper involving the same follow-up subjects, Mannuzza et al. (1988) showed that hyperactive subjects who did not receive a DSM-III diagnosis at follow-up did worse than controls in school adjustment, but no differences were seen in occupational adjustment, temperament, alcohol abuse, or antisocial activities.

We have focused mainly on prospective studies because, as Hechtman (1989) has pointed out, retrospective studies have significant methodological flaws and tend to give very divergent pictures. Some paint a fairly negative picture (e.g. Milman, 1979; Menkes and Menkes, 1967) while others suggest a more positive outcome (Borland and Heckman, 1987; and Feldman, Denhoff, and Denhoff, 1979).

In summary, the adult outcome of ADHD can be extremely varied. Hechtman et al. (1981) characterized this outcome as falling roughly into three categories. The first includes ADHD subjects who, in adulthood, function fairly normally compared to matched controls. The second category includes those patients who, as adults, continue to have significant concentration, social, emotional, and impulsive problems. The problems often result in difficulties with work, interpersonal relationships, poor self-esteem, impulsivity, irritability, anxiety, and emotional liability. The vast majority of young adults fall into this group. Finally, the third group includes those who have serious psychiatric and/or antisocial pathology. These subjects may be extremely depressed, even suicidal, heavily involved in drug/alcohol abuse, or guilty of significant antisocial behavior (e.g., assault, armed robbery, breaking and entering, or drug dealing). It thus becomes important to try to identify factors that may influence positive versus negative outcome.

PREDICTORS OF OUTCOME

Only a few follow-up studies on children with hyperactivity have focused on which factors are most important in predicting outcome. Most of these studies have focused on initial factors affecting adolescent outcome. Thus, Weiss et al. (1971) showed that children with initial higher IQs and lower initial scores of hyperactivity and distractibility fared better academically in adolescence. In addition, the 25 percent of hyperactive adolescents who showed significant antisocial behavior had higher initial ratings of aggressivity and more pathological family scores.

Loney, Kramer, and Milich (1981), using stepwise multiple regression statistics, showed that initial measures of aggressivity, socioeconomic class, familial measures, and response to treatment were all important in various aspects of adolescent outcome—for example, adolescent aggression, hyperactivity, delinquency, and scholastic achievement. For example, Loney and colleagues (1981) noted that, in addition to other measures, the initial aggressive factor was a predictor for adolescent aggression and antisocial behavior. Socioeconomic status (SES) (with other factors) predicted high adolescent hyperactivity.

Hechtman, Weiss, Perlman, and Amsel (1984) looked at which initial factors may affect adult outcome.

Predictor Measures from Initial Assessment

I. *Personal Characteristics*
   1. IQ
   2. Hyperactivity
   3. Aggressivity
   4. Emotional stability or instability
   5. Low frustration tolerance

II. *Social-Academic Measures*
   1. Academic performance
   2. Peer relationships
   3. Adult relationships
   4. Antisocial behavior

III. *Family Parameters*
   1. Socioeconomic status (SES)
   2. Mental health of family members
   3. Emotional climate of the home
   4. Child-rearing practices
   5. Overall family rating

Outcome Measures

I. *Emotional Adjustment,* comprising
   1. Brief psychiatric rating scale
   2. Personality trait disorder
   3. Peer relationships—friends

II. *Academic Achievement,* measured via
   1. Grades completed
   2. Academic standing
   3. Number of grades failed

III. *Work Record,* reflected by
   1. Number of full-time jobs
   2. Percentage of jobs fired from
   3. Percentage of jobs laid off from
   4. Longest full-time job

IV. *Police Involvement,* included
   1. Number of offenses
   2. Severity of offenses

V. *Car Accidents,* included
   1. Number of accidents
   2. Accidents with bodily injury
   3. Cost of damage

VI. *Nonmedical Drug or Alcohol Use,* measured via
   1. Present use
   2. Past use
   3. Extent of current use
   4. Extent of maximum use
   5. Number of drugs used

For each set of outcome measures, a selection of the theoretically most relevant predictor measures was made for analysis. These measures were analyzed both singly and in multiples—for example, via univariate correlation (or analysis of variance) and multivariate stepwise cumulative regression techniques (or discriminant analysis). This provided us with a view of the power of any initial individual variable predicting adult outcome, as well as the group of initial variables that together may predict outcome. Detailed results are presented and discussed by Hechtman, Weiss, Perlman, and Amsel (1984).

In summary, the most important initial predictors include:

I. *Adult Emotional Adjustment*
Initial family parameters
- Family rating (global rating on family assessment scale)
- Mental health of family members
- Emotional climate of the home

II. *Adult Academic Achievement*
Initial measures of:
- personal characteristics—e.g., IQ
- family parameters—e.g., SES, child rearing practices

III. *Work Record*
Initial social measures—e.g., relationships with adults
Family parameters—e.g., SES

IV. *Police Involvement*
Initial personal characteristics of emotional instability
Family parameters
- SES
- mental health of family members
- child rearing practices

V. *Car Accidents*
Initial personal characteristics
- low frustration tolerance

Family parameters
- emotional climate of the home

VI. *Nonmedical Drug Use*
Initial personal characteristics
- IQ

Social parameters
- initial antisocial behavior

Family parameters
- mental health of family members

We thus see that for many adult outcome variables, a combination of initial measures of *individual personal characteristics* (e.g., IQ, emotional instability, low frustration tolerance), *family parameters* (e.g., SES, mental health of family members, emotional climate of the home, and child rearing practices), and *social environmental measures* (e.g., relationships with adults, antisocial behavior) influence the adult picture.

These findings are very similar to those described by researchers exploring factors contributing to resilience in children at risk due to a variety of circumstances (e.g., Werner and Smith, 1982; Garmezy, 1985; Rutter, 1985; and Anthony, 1987). These authors have all stressed that the factors influencing resilience involve three interrelated areas—that is, factors pertaining to the child, the family, and the larger social and physical environment.

FACTORS PERTAINING TO THE CHILD

Health

Children with fewer health problems, either during pregnancy, perinatally, or in infancy, are more likely to fall into the more resilient group (Werner and Smith, 1982).

Temperament

Several authors in this area (Rutter, 1979; Cohler, 1987; Werner and Smith, 1982; Anthony, 1987) have stressed the importance of temperament attributes in developing resilience and positive outcome. Thus, less vulnerable children tend to be more active, adaptable, and socially responsive. They are able to elicit positive responses from their environments and have the capacity for finding solace and satisfaction. They often have more reflective versus impulsive cognitive styles and are able to control their feelings appropriately.

Intelligence

Countless studies have shown that children with greater intelligence fare better in difficult circumstances than children with lower IQs. Intelligence is often reflected in more advanced self-help abilities as well as more adequate problem-solving capacities. Sensorimotor integration and perceptual motor development are often more advanced, as are language development and communication skills. Thus, intellectual development may pave the road to other social and/or academic success.

Psychological Factors

The resilient children appear to have a greater sense of autonomy and internal locus of control and more positive self-esteem. They have better ego strengths as reflected in their positive coping skills, responsibility and achievement orientation. Their better social skills are seen in their positive orientation toward themselves and others, their empathy, good peer relationships, and sense of humor. Resilient children can ask help of others and are generally optimistic about themselves and their futures. It is needless to say that children with ADHD with some of the above attributes will fare better than those without them.

Factors Pertaining to the Family's Socioeconomic Status

Many studies have demonstrated the importance of socioeconomic status on the outcome of children with a variety of conditions and in diverse circumstances. Higher social status gives children access to physical, social, and educational advantages, as well as a variety of services (medical and educational), perhaps not readily available to others. Furthermore, poverty itself presents significant risks for children that higher social status children need not endure. Thus, social status has a strong influence on outcome in attention deficit hyperactive disorder and other conditions.

Emotional-Psychological Factors in the Family

Many authors (Rutter, 1979; Werner and Smith, 1982; Garmezy, 1985; and Anthony, 1987) have stressed the importance of warm, affectionate, cohesive, supportive family environments in influencing positive outcome for children. The negative effects of discord have been well documented by Rutter (1979) and others.

The presence or absence of such a positive supportive atmosphere is often linked to the mental and/or physical health of family members, particularly the primary caregiver. Resilient children often grow up in such positive family environments where warmth and support are amply displayed and where emotional expressiveness is encouraged, as are open communication and independence. Such families often have supportive networks of a father, grandparents, and/or older siblings to help out when the mother is overburdened or absent.

Family Composition and Structure

As Werner and Smith (1982) have pointed out, resilient children seemed to come from two-parent families with fewer children and with greater spacing between children. This allowed the primary caregiver to have time to devote to the care of the infant without feeling overwhelmed. Furthermore, households of resilient children tended to have more structure, regularity, more clearly defined rules and roles, and generally more supervision. There also tended to be clear-cut, realistic expectations of the child and his responsibilities.

In the predictive study by Hechtman, Weiss, Perlman, and Amsel (1984), family parameters such as socioeconomic status, emotional climate of the home, mental health of family members, and child rearing practices were all related to various aspects of adult outcome in ADHD.

Larger Social and Physical Environment

Werner and Smith (1982), Rutter (1979), and others have pointed out the importance and role of extrafamilial supports in positive outcomes of children at risk. Extended family members, friends, school or church personnel have all been cited as potentially providing the care and support lacking at home. Rutter (1979) particularly drew attention to the positive impact of certain schools that were concerned with the growth of the child and his well-being. Such schools made realistic demands of the students and fostered social, athletic, musical, and scholastic success. Success in any of these areas was an important factor in influencing more positive adult outcome for the children at risk. Religious affiliation and/or beliefs have also played an important role in providing a sense of meaning, purpose, acceptance, and belonging for children at risk.

In the long-term prospective follow-up of children with ADHD (Weiss and Hechtman, 1986), young adults were asked what, if anything, was most helpful to them while they were growing up. The most frequent response was that there was someone—a parent, a teacher, or a coach—who believed in them. This person gave them the feeling that they were worthwhile and that there was optimism about their futures. Furthermore, some of the best outcomes were from people with special skills or abilities. One such person was a professional athlete with a major national team. Thus, the importance and influence of the larger environment in providing opportunities for support and success should not be overlooked.

All the factors influencing positive outcome can perhaps be better illustrated by a case vignette that clearly underlines the interrelationship of the various factors, as well as pure chance circumstances in the adult outcome picture of attention deficit hyperactive disorder.

CASE VIGNETTE

Anthony was first referred to the Child Psychiatry Department at age 7. The presenting complaints at that time were:

- Severe hyperactivity and restlessness since he began to walk
- Poor concentration and a very short attention span
- Poor speech articulation
- Disobedient, does not listen
- Repeating Grade 1
- Enuresis and occasional encopresis
- Very untidy

Anthony's birth history was normal as were his neurological examination and EEG. However, he had body-image and visual motor problems. Anthony's WISC IQ full-scale was 115 with marked scatter. Psychiatric evaluation revealed a friendly, charming, very attractive 7-year-old boy with articulation problems and marked restlessness.

The family consisted of two biological parents and two older sisters. The father was an executive and the family was clearly middle class. Father traveled a fair amount for work and mother stayed home to look after the children. The parents described themselves as being happily married and the two older girls were doing well.

Short-term intervention included a consultation to the school and some parental counseling to help the family deal more effectively with the child, his hyperactivity, his enuresis and encopresis.

At adolescent follow-up, when Anthony was 14 years old, he was sent to a boarding school because his behavior and learning difficulties made succeeding in a regular class almost impossible. However, Anthony found school work boring. He was poor at spelling and behind in reading. There was no evidence of any antisocial behavior (e.g., stealing) or drug or alcohol abuse. However, Anthony had no close friends, no strong sense of responsibility, nor any plans or goals for the future. Nonetheless, he was friendly, charming, and happy-go-lucky, with a wonderful sense of humor and very likeable.

At 10-year follow-up, when Anthony was 20 years old, we discovered that the family had moved overseas some years previously. We wrote to Anthony there, sending him numerous self-rating scales and a history for him to complete. One of these forms was the California Personality Inventory (CPI), which has some 450 self-rating items. We did not hear from Anthony for two years after the forms were mailed, and gave him up as a lost subject. One day, Anthony knocked on Dr. Gabrielle Weiss's office door and announced himself and his girlfriend, Sally. He had come from New Zealand to let us know that the CPI was a "truly crazy test" and there was no way he would complete "500 dumb questions."

It seems that while living with his parents overseas, Anthony had refused to continue in school (he had only completed Grade 9). He worked intermittently at various jobs and lived with his parents. His last job was collecting stray cats and dogs for the local SPCA. Anthony felt his father looked down on this job even though he was told that any honest work was OK. "He obviously didn't mean it. Anyway, I got laid off and since I have ants in my pants, I went to New Zealand." There, he met Sally. They were soon living together and she helped Anthony settle down.

Sally suggested that he could mow people's lawns for some income. She helped him save some money, secured a small loan, and Anthony bought a few secondhand lawn mowers and employed a younger boy to mow lawns. A year later, they had repaid their debts and saved $5,500. "I gave up the lawn mowing business because one day I just found it tense and boring and I wanted to quit and travel. I also wanted to tell you about this crazy test."

Anthony appeared happy and as impulsive, though charming and likeable, as ever. For example, he succeeded in getting Sally a work permit by telling the immigration official that if the permit were refused, he would marry Sally and the official would have to give them a permit anyway. The official would then be sorry because he made them get married so young. Sally was a bright, stable, delightful young woman who appreciated Anthony's qualities and had a strong influence on him.

At 15-year follow-up, Anthony was 25 years old. We could not interview him in New Zealand, but we met with his parents who had visited him and Sally recently. Anthony and Sally were still together and planned to be married soon. Anthony was at university studying communications; he had entered as a mature student. He was interested in the area though he was having some difficulties with his courses because of concentration problems, but he was managing to pass. Sally had a malignant lump removed from her breast. Anthony and Sally dealt well with their grief and anxiety over her diagnosis, and Anthony's parents stated that he and Sally had an excellent relationship. Sally organized their finances and family life and took much of the initiative regarding friends. Anthony was described as still impulsive and very restless. He still talked too much and lost some part-time jobs because of his "big mouth." The parents felt that Anthony had matured a great deal since Sally's medical problems. The couple had no debts and Anthony planned to start an advertising business when he received his university degree.

Anthony's parents were asked what they felt contributed to his good outcome. His father stated that "even while Anthony was hyperactive and a discipline problem as a child, he was very loveable. Sally was the turning point for Anthony. She gave him what we couldn't: confidence in himself and a source of direction. She had always loved him and believed in his future when we frankly did not."

This case clearly illustrates that Anthony had severe hyperactivity and attentional problems. In addition, significant learning disabilities made it very difficult for him to succeed in school. He had given up scholastically while still young and his family was not optimistic about his future. However, several factors contributed to his positive outcome. Anthony's personal characteristics included a high IQ, a good sense of humor, great charm, likeability, and adventurousness. His family was middle class, stable, loving, and generally supportive. However, chance circumstances linked him with Sally, whose love and belief in him, combined with her support and encouragement, turned things around. Again, one sees the interplay of personal characteristics, family factors, and larger environmental circumstances all influencing positive long-term outcome.

REFERENCES

Akerman, P., Dykman, R., and Peters, J. (1977). Teenage status of hyperactive and nonhyperactive learning disabled boys. *American Journal of Orthopsychiatry, 47,* 577-596.

Anthony, E. J. (1987). Children at high risk for psychosis growing up successfully. In E. J. Anthony and B. J. Cohler (Eds.), *The invulnerable child.* New York: Guilford Press.

Borland, B. and Heckman, H. (1987). Hyperactive boys and their brothers: A 25-year follow-up study. *Archives of General Psychiatry, 33,* 669-676.

Cohler, B. J. (1987). Adversity resilience and the study of lives. In E. J. Anthony and B. J. Cohler (Eds.),. *The Invulnerable child.* New York: Guilford Press.

Feldman, S., Denhoff, E., and Denhoff, E. (1979). The attention disorders and related syndromes: Outcome in adolescence and young adult life. In E. Denhoff and L. Stern (Eds.), *Minimal brain dysfunction: A developmental approach* (pp. 133-148). New York: Masson Publishers.

Garmezy, N. (1985). Broadening research on developmental risk implications from studies of vulnerable and stress-resistant children. In W. F. Frankenburg, R. N. Emde, and J. W. Sullivan (Eds.), *Early identification of children at risk* (pp. 45-58). New York: Plenum Press.

Gittelman, R., Mannuzza, S., Shenker, R., and Bonagura, N. (1985). Hyperactive boys almost grown up, I: Psychiatric status. *Archives of General Psychiatry, 42,* 937-947.

Hechtman, L. (1985). Adolescent outcome of hyperactive children treated with stimulants in childhood: A review. *Psychopharmacology Bulletin, 21,* 178-191

______. (1989). Attention-deficit hyperactivity disorder in adolescence and adulthood: An updated follow-up. *Psychiatric Annals, 19,* 597-603.

Hechtman, L. and Weiss, G. (1986). Controlled prospective 15-year follow-up of hyperactive adults: Non-medical drug and alcohol use and antisocial behavior. *Canadian Journal of Psychiatry, 31,* 557-567.

Hechtman, L., Weiss, G., and Metrakos, K. (1978). Hyperactives as young adults: Current and longitudinal electroencephalographic evaluation and its relation to outcome. *Canadian Medical Association Journal, 118,* 912-923.

Hechtman, L., Weiss, G., and Perlman, T. (1978). Growth and cardiovascular measures in hyperactive individuals as young adults and in matched normal controls. *Canadian Medical Association Journal, 118,* 1247-1250.

______. (1980). Hyperactives as young adults: Self-esteem and social skills. *Canadian Journal of Psychiatry, 25,* 478-483.

______. (1984). Hyperactives as young adults: Past and current antisocial behavior (stealing, drug abuse) and moral development. *American Journal of Orthopsychiatry, 54,* 415-425.

Hechtman, L., Weiss, G., Perlman, T., and Amsel, R. (1984). Hyperactives as young adults: Initial predictors of adult outcome. *Journal of the American Academy of Child Psychiatry, 25,* 250-260.

Hechtman, L., Weiss, G., Perlman, T., and Tuck, D. (1981). Hyperactives as young adults: Various clinical outcomes. *Adolescent Psychiatry, 9,* 295-306.

Hopkins, J., Perlman, T., Hechtman, L., and Weiss, G. (1979). Cognitive style in adults originally diagnosed as hyperactives. *Journal of Child Psychology and Psychiatry, 20,* 209-216.

Lambert, N., Hartsaugh, C., Sassone, D., and Sandoval, J. (1987). Persistence of hyperactivity symptoms from childhood to adolescence and associated outcomes. *American Journal of Orthopsychiatry, 57,* 22-31.

Loney, J., Kramer, J., and Milich, R. (1981). The hyperkinetic child grows up: Predictors of symptoms, delinquency and achievement at follow-up. In K. Gadow and J. Loney (Eds.), *Psychosocial aspects of drug treatment for hyperactivity.* AAAS Selected Symposium.

Mannuzza, S., Gittelman-Klein, R., Bonagura, N., Konig, P. H., and Shenker, R. (1988). Hyperactive boys almost grown up: States of subjects without a mental disorder. *Archives of General Psychiatry, 45,* 13-18.

Menkes, M., Row, J., and Menkes, J. (1967). A twenty-five year follow-up study on the hyperactive child with minimal brain dysfunction. *Pediatrics, 39,* 393-399.

Milman, D. H. (1979). Minimal brain dysfunction in childhood: Outcome in late adolescence and early adult years. *Journal of Clinical Psychiatry, 40,* 371-380.

Rutter, M. (1979). Protective factors in children's responses to stress and disadvantage. In M. W. Kent and J. E. Rolf (Eds.), *Primary prevention of psychopathology,* Vol. 3. Hanover, N.H.: University Press of New England.

Rutter, M. (1985). Resilience in the face of adversity: Protective factors and resistance to psychiatric disorder. *British Journal of Psychiatry, 147,* 598-611.

Satterfield, J., Hoppe, C. and Schell, A. (1982). Prospective study of delinquency in 110 adolescent boys with attention deficit disorder and 88 normal adolescent boys. *American Journal of Psychiatry, 139,* 797-798.

Satterfield, J., Satterfield, B., and Cantwell, D. (1981). Three-year multimodality treatment study of 100 hyperactive boys. *Journal of Pediatrics, 98,* 650-655.

Thorley, G. (1988). Adolescent outcome for hyperactive children. *Archives of Disabled Children, 63,* 1181-1183.

Weiss, G. and Hechtman, L. (1986). *Hyperactive children grown up.* New York: Guilford Press.

Weiss, G., Hechtman, L., Milroy, T., and Perlman, T. (1985). Psychiatric status of hyperactives as adults: A controlled prospective 15-year follow-up of 63 hyperactive children. *Journal of the American Academy of Child Psychiatry, 23,* 211-220.

Weiss, G., Hechtman, L., Perlman, T., Hopkins, J., and Wener, A. (1979). Hyperactives as young adults: A controlled prospective ten-year follow-up of 75 children. *Archives of General Psychiatry, 36,* 675-681.

Weiss, G., Minde, K., Werry, J., Douglas, V., and Nemeth, E. (1971). The hyperactive child, VIII: Five-year follow-up. *Archives of General Psychiatry, 24,* 409-414.

Werner, E. E. and Smith, R. S. (1982). *Vulnerable but invincible: A study of resilient children.* New York: McGraw-Hill.

Chapter 9

Forging Competence in Developmentally Delayed Children: Grounds for Optimism, Directions for Intervention

Kofi Marfo

INTRODUCTION

Defining the Population

The term "developmental delay" tends to be used much less precisely in the literature than other labels used to describe various exceptional child populations. It is often used as a substitute for more precise diagnosis, and in the United States it has more of a clinical than a legislative meaning (Bernheimer and Keogh, 1986). In other circles, especially in the service sector, it is increasingly being used as a less pejorative replacement for all degrees and etiological classes of mental retardation. These varied uses of the term diminish its diagnostic value and reduce the degree of specificity with which research findings regarding developmentally delayed children can be generalized. Because of the above reasons, I begin this chapter with a definitional framework. Central to this framework is the concept of delay as a *discrepancy* between observed level of functioning and chronological age-determined expected level of functioning in the domains of cognition and language/communication. During the first six years of life it is not always possible to ascertain whether this discrepancy is a temporary delay (with the connotation that the child could potentially catch up, even in the absence of intervention) or represents a more enduring delay.

In this chapter, the term developmentally delayed (DD) is applied exclusively to the following two categories of children: (1) children with apparently intact intellectual function who nevertheless manifest, albeit temporarily, varying degrees of delay in the acquisition and use of cognitive, social, language, and communication skills; and (2) children with a relatively more enduring *mild* cognitive delay resulting from polygenic inheritance, adverse early experiential environments, or the interaction of both. The children included in this second category are essentially those who fall into Class II (familial retardation) and Class III (polygenic isolates) of Zigler's system of classifying mental retardation (Zigler, Balla, and Hodapp, 1984; Zigler and Hodapp, 1986). Both classes of children are deemed to have no known organic pathology and manifest IQ levels between about 50 and 70. While Class II children tend to have at least one parent whose IQ is below 70, Class III children are also polygenically retarded but are the offspring of nonretarded parents.

There is one significant way in which developmentally delayed children differ from many of the other risk populations who are the subject of research and discussions on resilience. Let us call these other children *vulnerable children.* They include many of the groups covered in this volume: delinquent children, runaways, foster children, children from chronic poverty backgrounds, war-uprooted children, children of psychotic parents, and children who have survived traumatic human atrocities, such as the Holocaust. The risk condition for these vulnerable children *resides outside* the child, and it is usually defined as an attribute of the child's experiential, socioeconomic, or political environment that has the potential to affect him or her in many significant ways. On the other hand, developmental delay has traditionally connoted an established risk that is inherently tied to the child's person; regardless of whether the delay is caused by polygenic inheritance factors or by environmental deprivation in the infancy and early childhood years, it is an attribute—an effect—that literally resides in the child and is responsible for the difficulty in behaving or performing in age-appropriate ways.

To clarify the distinction further, let us consider some of the common attributes that researchers have ascribed to vulnerable children who manifest remarkable resilience. Citing the work of O'Connel-Higgins, Werner (1984, p. 69) identifies the following characteristics that resilient children have in common:

1. an active, evocative approach toward solving life's problems, enabling them to negotiate successfully an abundance of emotionally hazardous experiences;
2. a tendency to perceive their experiences constructively, even if they caused pain or suffering;
3. the ability, from infancy, to gain other people's positive attention;
4. a strong ability to use faith in order to maintain a positive vision of a meaningful life.

With the exception of 3—which is a definite requirement, if a developmentally delayed child is to attain positive developmental outcomes—each of the above personal resources that, according to Werner and others, are the ingredients for resilience, would seem to be constrained by lowered intellectual ability. It seems to me, then, that the notion of resilience takes on a slightly different meaning and perhaps calls for a different focus and different strategies when the population of concern is developmentally delayed children. While the DD child is faced with the additional challenge of dealing with or overcoming psychological roadblocks, such as negative attitudes, low expectations, and learned helplessness—a challenge that other vulnerable children must also face to varying degrees—the DD child's ability to succeed in this regard hinges on how well he or she is helped to harness his or her cognitive potential to its uppermost limits.

Focus of the Chapter

Consistent with the optimistic thrust of this volume, the discussion in this chapter will center on mechanisms that have the potential to promote positive developmental outcomes for DD infants and young children. I have chosen to focus on mechanisms related to early intervention because of my firm belief that one major reason why some DD children succeed, despite the incredible biological and sociocultural odds, is sustained and intensive exposure to developmentally enhancing early intervention activities.

Of course the controversy as to whether early intervention makes a relatively durable positive impact on the development of socially disadvantaged, handicapped, or developmentally delayed children has continued to rage since the Westinghouse evaluation of Head Start programs for disadvantaged children (Westinghouse Learning Corporation, 1969). The most prolonged, and perhaps most intriguing, debate has revolved around Head Start-type early intervention programs for disadvantaged children. Severe criticisms of efficacy claims, especially those criticisms focusing on the washout of IQ gains (e.g., Jensen, 1969), have produced extensive conceptual defenses in which alternative outcome measures—such as social competence—have been emphasized (Zigler and Berman, 1983; Zigler and Seitz, 1980; Zigler and Trickett, 1978), and have spurred empirical analyses of longitudinal data in which a broad range of outcome variables beside IQ-type indices have been examined (e.g., Consortium for Longitudinal Studies, 1978, 1983; Darlington et al., 1980; Lazar and Darlington, 1982; Schweinhart and Weikart, 1980, 1985). The composite picture that is emerging from these longitudinal studies is that well-planned early intervention programs could and do have lasting positive effects on the developmental and learning potential of disadvantaged children (see Woodhead, 1988, for an incisive review and critique of the policy implications of early intervention for disadvantaged children).

Although the subfield of early intervention for handicapped and developmentally delayed children cannot boast of the kinds of widely acclaimed longitudinal efficacy research that exist for socially disadvantaged children, the efficacy debate in this area has been equally intense. Analyses of this field have generally produced a mixed bag of conclusions. Reviews that essentially synthesize the findings of individual empirical reports without questioning the soundness of the research methodology tend to find overwhelming evidence in support of efficacy. However, critical methodological reviews, such as Dunst and Rheingrover's (1981), have revealed how very little scientifically rigorous and valid empirical research exists to warrant judgements in one direction or another. Nevertheless, it appears that even when judgments are based only on the smaller subset of studies utilizing scientifically acceptable methods, there is sufficient evidence in support of the effectiveness of early intervention (see Simeonsson, Cooper, and Scheiner, 1982).

In a recent paper, my colleagues and I (Marfo et al., 1989) have cautioned against interpreting the absence of overwhelming scientific evidence in support of efficacy as an indication that early intervention with handicapped and developmentally delayed children is ineffective. The absence of overwhelming evidence, as we point out, "merely reflects the complexity of the conceptual and methodological issues associated with early intervention evaluation research" and is "more an indictment of the quality of evaluation research . . . than of the value of early intervention per se" (p. 1). Thus, notwithstanding the shaky status of evaluation research in this field, the notion of early intervention per se has a great deal of intuitive value. For this and other reasons (such as the fact that early intervention programs have now become an integral part of publicly funded human service delivery systems), the next generation of early intervention evaluation researchers needs to look beyond the traditional efficacy question ("Does early intervention work?") in search of insights into how the complex welter of mechanisms associated with child, program, and family ecology interact to determine the outcomes—positive or otherwise—of early intervention services.

As I thought through my assigned topic, it occurred to me that I could approach this chapter from at least two perspectives. One approach would be to chronicle and discuss factors that have emerged from existing research as variables responsible for successful outcomes for this population of young children. A second approach would be to integrate theoretical perspectives and specific concepts that provide a basis for and suggest potentially viable ways of enhancing the developmental adjustment potential of developmentally delayed children. I chose to devote most of the chapter to the second approach for two reasons:

1. While an appreciably large empirical research base on the effects of early intervention with developmentally delayed children has accumu-

lated over the past two decades (for reviews and summaries of aspects of this literature see Dunst and Rheingrover, 1981; Farran, 1990; Marfo and Kysela, 1985; Meisels and Shonkoff, 1990; Simeonsson et al., 1982), the findings of this research have been rather too general. This situation is itself largely because greater attention has been paid to the question of whether early intervention works than to identifying specific dimensions of the intervention process or aspects of the child's environment that are more closely tied to intervention outcomes (Marfo et al., 1989; Marfo and Cook, in press). In most reports of efficacy research, the intervention programs tend to be so globally decribed that it is often impossible to ascertain which specific components of the intervention are more closely associated with successful outcomes.

2. It has often been remarked that much of early intervention work is *atheoretical*. Beyond specially funded model programs and university-affiliated demonstration projects or research initiatives, intervention activities and procedures are often not based on clearly articulated theoretical models about the nature of development, the nature of developmental change, and the mechanisms of effecting change. The approach taken in this chapter is thus intended to stimulate further thinking on the need to embed intervention activities in explicit theoretical frameworks. More importantly, however, I felt the need to depart from the traditional accomplishments-of-the-field review and instead, to highlight several specific theoretical perspectives that have significant relevance for intervention work with developmentally delayed children and their families but that remain to be harnessed fully and effectively in the early intervention field.

THE BASIS FOR INTERVENTION WITH DD CHILDREN

The foundations of an optimistic or *positive outcomes* approach to the problem of developmental delay can be found in several theoretical formulations in the developmental literature that have focused on the nature of development and developmental change. In this section I review two classes of work. The first class focuses on transactional models of development and developmental outcomes. Under this class, I examine some of the central elements of formulations proposed by Urie Bronfenbrenner (1979, 1989) and Arnold Sameroff and his associates (Sameroff, 1975, 1980; Sameroff and Chandler, 1975; Sameroff and Fiese, 1990). The second class focuses on explicit theories of cognitive modifiability. While the work of Carl Haywood and his associates (e.g., Haywood and Switzky, 1986; Switzky and Haywood, 1984) has relevance under this class, the primary emphasis will be on Reuven Feuerstein's theory of structural cognitive modifiability (Feuerstein et al.,

1980). Finally, I examine the contributions of Vygotsky's notion of the zone of proximal development (Rogoff, Malkin, and Gilbride, 1984; Wertsch, 1984; Wertsch and Rogoff, 1984) to reiterate the importance of the social context of development.

Development as a Transactional Process

The common thread in the two frameworks considered in this section is the proposition that neither biological/constitutional factors nor experiential/environmental factors are the sole determinants of developmental outcomes. For years, the prominence of Bronfenbrenner's work has been tied almost exclusively to his overwhelming emphasis on the role of the environment in shaping developmental outcomes. However, both the original and more recent formulations of his ecological systems theory (Bronfenbrenner, 1979, 1989) specify clearly that the processes and outcomes of development occur as a joint function of factors pertaining to the person and the environment. This sounds like the traditional interactionist position in the age-old *nature-versus-nurture* debate, but Bronfenbrenner's position is more than that. He goes beyond a static, additive model of person-environment interaction to emphasize the dynamic nature of person-environment transactions, such that at any given time, specific characteristics of the person and the environment are deemed to be both "products and producers of development" (Bronfenbrenner, 1989, p. 191).

In Bronfenbrenner's scheme, environments do not affect the person independently of the latter's characteristics; depending upon the individual characteristics of the person, particular environmental conditions produce different developmental outcomes. In the same vein, characteristics of the person do not produce developmental outcomes independently of the environment. In his extensive analysis of a 30-year-old Scottish study of developmental sequelae associated with prematurity (Drillien, 1957, 1964), Bronfenbrenner (1989) highlighted the following observations:

1. Responsive maternal care can substantially reduce the severity of psychological problems associated with low birth weight among socioeconomically deprived families, and can subsequently reduce the number of low-birth-weight children experiencing any serious difficulty (p. 199).
2. Living organisms have the capacity, and indeed the active disposition, to heal themselves over time. . . . In sum, significant resources for counteracting effects of prenatal handicaps exist both on the side of the environment and of the organism itself (p. 198).

The first of the observations bears a great deal of semblance to conclusions drawn by Sameroff and Chandler (1975) from their analysis of models for predicting developmental outcomes for biologically at-risk children. At the time they published their now-classic paper, "Reproductive Risk and the Continuum of Caretaking Casualty" (Sameroff and Chandler, 1975), one of the dominant models for predicting developmental outcomes for children was what they referred to as the *main-effect* model. In research depicting the main-effect model, constitutional and environmental forces were construed to exert unilateral influences on human development. That is, regardless of the nature and quality of the environment, aberrations in constitutional development would produce poor or negative developmental outcomes, while a deprived environment would necessarily lead to poor outcomes regardless of the intactness of constitution.

The limitations of the main-effect model of predicting long-term developmental outcomes have been discussed extensively by Sameroff and his associates (Sameroff, 1975, 1980; Sameroff and Chandler, 1975; Sameroff and Fiese, 1990). From an empirical point of view, support for this model tended to come only from retrospective studies, such as those synthesized by Passamanick and Knobloch (1966), in which most of the children with the biological risk conditions studied appeared also to have come from poorer socioeconomic backgrounds. A totally different picture emerged from prospective studies of children with such *reproductive casualties* as anoxia, prematurity, and perinatal complications. As Sameroff (1980, p. 344) observed,

> whenever a perinatal risk factor was hypothesized to be related to later dysfunction, prospective studies found no greater incidence of disorder in the risk population than in control populations without the risk factor. Whether the risk was related to preterm birth, low birthweight, anoxia, or neurological signs, few causal chains were found when appropriate control populations were studied.

This observation led Sameroff and Chandler (1975, p. 238) to conclude that "even if one continues to believe that a continuum of reproductive casualty exists, its importance pales in comparison to the massive influences of socio-economic factors on both prenatal and postnatal development."

The *transactional model* that both Bronfenbrenner (1979, 1989) and Sameroff and Chandler (1975) have proposed as a more valid framework for understanding developmental outcomes perhaps provides one of the strongest bases for a positive-outcomes perspective on developmental delay. According to the transactional model, "although reproductive casualties may play an initiating role in the production of later problems, it is the caretaking environment that will determine the ultimate outcome" (Sameroff, 1975, p. 274). Thus, the long-term developmental outcomes of problems with biological or constitutional roots can only be understood in relation to a "continuum of caretaking casualty." At the extreme positive end of this continuum, it is deemed conceivable that a supportive and ameliorative caretaking environment can even eliminate the effects of biological insult, whereas on the extreme negative end, a deficient caretaking environment can indeed aggravate the effects of early biological insult (Sameroff, 1975, 1980; Sameroff and Chandler, 1975).

Bronfenbrenner has applied the label *vicious or benign circles* to the phenomenon whereby the synergistic action of two or more forces produces an effect that is greater than the sum of the individual effects. For example, in reviewing Drillien's findings, Bronfenbrenner (1989, p. 199) found that "the combination of low birthweight and disadvantaged socioeconomic status had greater negative impact than would have been expected from the separate effects of each."

Also noteworthy is the transactional view that the manner in which characteristics of the child and the nature of the caretaking environment interact is dynamic rather than static. That is, as both the child and the caretaking environment mutually affect each other, each is constantly changing as a result of that ongoing mutuality of effect.

Does the work summarized above have any relevance for children with established developmental delay? The answer to this question is affirmative, to the extent that developmental delay, as defined in this chapter, is considered to be as malleable as the perinatal conditions upon which empirical evidence in support of transactional models of developmental outcomes have been based. As will be seen in the section on cognitive modifiability, the extrapolation is not an unreasonable one; consequently, we can proceed to examine some of the implications that transactional models have for intervention with DD children.

The most profound limitation of a main-effect view of developmental outcomes is that it does not permit a theory of psychosocial or psychoeducational intervention that can challenge DD children, especially those with polygenic etiology, to reach significantly beyond their assessed level of functioning. The traditional special educational practice of offering watered-down versions of the school curriculum to developmentally delayed children is perhaps a good illustrative example of one manifestation of the main-effect view. While adjusting both content and method of instruction to the functional level of the student is a sound pedagogical practice, when it is carried to the extreme of subjecting the student permanently to watered down tasks—as often tends to be the case—this practice can potentially deny DD students the opportunity to develop and demonstrate competencies beyond their assessed level of functioning.

Applied developmental psychologists are interested in understanding the factors that are associated with the regulation of human development, to the extent that such understanding provides us with the tools for designing potentially effective intervention models. The transactional model provides significant impetus for designing interventions to foster resilience or enhance developmental outcomes for DD children. It sheds significant light on the mechanisms by which human development is regulated, and suggests that some of the problems of development in early life may be reversible or can at least be minimized. Logically, the single most significant general mechanism for reversing or minimizing problems of development is the enrichment of the experiential environment. Not only does the model provide optimism, but it also provides a framework for conceptualizing the intervention process. For example, the view of the caretaking environment-child relationship as a "continual interplay between a changing child and a changing environment" (Sameroff, 1980, p. 345) suggests that intervention activities need to be constantly modulated to reflect the progressions of change occurring within the child, within the caretaking environment, and within the caretaking environment-child relationship.

Cognitive Modifiability

While the foregoing discussion on transactional models of development underscores the prominent role of the environment in shaping developmental outcomes, neither of the two perspectives presented specifically addresses the issue of cognitive modifiability in DD children as a function of particular approaches to manipulating the child's experiential environment. At best, the potential for cognitive modifiability in this population of children is only implied. For DD children, however, theories that make explicit propositions on the malleability of intellectual functioning provide even a stronger basis for hope and intervention. In this section, I review some theoretical viewpoints regarding cognitive modifiability.

Let me begin by suggesting that even the best evidence presented by some of the most ardent proponents of the *immutability of intelligence* view fails to demonstrate that intellectual functioning is controlled completely by genetic inheritance. Consider the following statement from one of Jensen's (1985, p. 557) recent writings:

> I suspect that a substantial part of the individual variance in I.Q. and scholastic achievement—probably somewhere between 50 percent and 70 percent, according to the best evidence on the heritability of I.Q.—is not subject to manipulation by any strictly psychological or educational treatment. The reason for this, I assume, is that the main locus of that unyielding source of variance is more biological than psychological or behavioral.

Applied researchers in the environmentalist tradition may not have succeeded in producing universally acclaimed evidence in support of their *plasticity of human intelligence* position. But how critical is the need to produce such evidence if the best evidence in support of the immutability position suggests—albeit implicitly, as the above quotation illustrates—that anywhere from 30 to 50 percent of the variance in intellectual functioning may be subject to psychoeducational manipulation?

One explicit view of cognitive modifiability is found in Haywood and Switzky's *biosocial ecological* perspective on mental retardation (see Haywood and Brooks, in press; Haywood, Brooks, and Burns, 1986; Haywood and Switzky, 1986; Switzky and Haywood, 1984). There are two interrelated dimensions to this perspective, both of which have significant implications for applied developmental work with DD children. First, cognition is deemed to be composed of many kinds of abilities, which can be classified into at least two distinct categories: *native abilities,* which are the product of polygenic inheritance, and *cognitive functions,* which are largely acquired and include "learned cognitive operations, principles, processes, and strategies," and such nonintellective variables as "attitudes toward learning, work habits, and motives" (Haywood and Switzky, 1986, p. 249). The implication here is that one of the components of intelligent behavior, by virtue of its being an acquired capability, can be fostered through planned interventions.

The second dimension of Haywood and Switzky's perspective pertains to the manner in which genetic and experiential forces interact to determine the expression of native intelligence. This dimension is explained in transactional terms. Aligning their views with those of Waddington (1962), Switzky and Haywood (1984, p. 860) wrote:

> In a transactional model of development one must stress the plastic character of the environment and the "self-righting" tendencies of the organism to maintain its growth. The responses of children to their environment reflect the attempts not only to organize and structure their psychological world but also to maintain their growth trajectory.

A closer scrutiny of Haywood and Switzky's theory reveals, however, that the degree of modifiability is hypothesized to vary as a function of whether the cause of low intellectual functioning is genetic or experiential. In other words, modifiability is not necessarily an unconditional attribute of intellectual ability. According to the theory, the prospect for modifiability should be stronger if the basis for low intellect is experiential and weaker if low intellect is genetically based:

> In cases of experientially deprived persons, substantial modification of the phenotype can be achieved through carefully structured positive developmental

experiences. It would be much more difficult to bring about such substantial changes either when (a) there has been no appreciable deprivation of growth-enhancing experiences and circumstances, or (b) the genetically-determined level of intelligence is extremely low (Haywood & Switzky, 1986. p. 246).

The cautious optimism reflected by the above quotation is worth emphasizing. The prospect for intervention-induced enhancements in the cognitive competence of DD children is generally good, because of the mildness of DD children's intellectual deficit; however, professionals and parents alike need to be reminded that intervention would produce differential outcomes as a function of whether the delay is experientially or polygenically determined.

Reuven Feuerstein's theory presents an even bolder view of cognitive modifiability. The *theory of structural cognitive modifiability* (Feuerstein et al., 1980, p. 9) states that "changes of a structural nature that can alter the course and direction of cognitive development" can be effected through systematic and consistent mediation. Feuerstein contrasts structural changes with specific changes in an individual's repertoire of skills (such as the acquisition of a particular strategy for encoding the essential features of narrative passages) that result from exposure to a given set of experiences. "Structural changes . . . refer not to isolated events but to the organism's manner of interacting with, acting on, and responding to, sources of information" (p. 9). The ultimate manifestation of structural cognitive change is receptivity and sensitivity to internal and external sources of stimulation.

Are DD children susceptible to structural cognitive modifiability? Are there genetic and other constitutional barriers to cognitive modifiability? The answer to these two questions can be found in Feuerstein's characterization of the determinants of retarded cognitive performance. He distinguishes between two determinants: *distal* and *proximal.* Factors that are traditionally considered as the causes of developmental delay—such as polygenic inheritance, biological insult associated with teratogenic and other noxious agents, and early environmental deprivation—are classified by Feuerstein as *distal* etiologic factors. These factors are labeled distal because, in the words of Feuerstein and his associates, they "neither directly nor inevitably cause" retarded performance (p. 17). The immediate or *proximal* determinant of retarded performance, instead, is a lack of or reduced exposure to mediated learning experience (MLE).[1] MLE is defined as the process by which environmentally emitted stimuli "are transformed by a 'mediating' agent, usually a parent, sibling, or other caregiver," who, "guided by his (her) intentions, culture, and emotional investment, selects and organizes the world of stimuli for the child" (p. 16).

According to this framework DD children, like nonhandicapped and culturally disadvantaged children, are highly susceptible to structural cognitive modifiability. The so-called distal factors, traditionally considered to be the primary cause of mild mental retardation or developmental delay, are not deemed to constitute a significant hindrance or limit to modifiability (1) as long as the quality of MLE is high and (2) "except in the most severe instance of genetic and organic impairment" (p. 9).

An analytical comment on the relative role of distal and proximal factors in retarded performance is necessary at this point in the discussion. At face value, the claim that those factors which Feuerstein and his associates label as distal "neither directly nor inevitably cause retardation" appears to be a radical departure from conventional wisdom and may even sound untenable. It is possible, however, to reconcile conventional wisdom and Feuerstein's perspective by viewing MLE as moderating the *expression* of polygenic inheritance or the developmental manifestations of biological insult. In other words, polygenic inheritance and biological insults of a pre-, peri-, and postnatal environmental nature can be a necessary and sufficient cause of retarded cognitive performance, if these forces are not countered effectively through high-quality MLE. In a sense, then, as radical as Feuerstein's theory may sound, it really represents a more focused variant (more focused because it deals with cognition or intellectual functioning per se) of the transactional model of development.

Recast in transactional terms, the theory states that the long-term developmental manifestations of either polygenic predisposition to low cognitive functioning or biological insult can only be understood in relation to a continuum of MLE. In the best of scenarios, an extremely high-quality MLE can conceivably nullify the effects of these "distal" factors, and in the worst situation, a deficient MLE can aggravate the effects of these determinants. Bronfenbrenner's (1989) notion of *vicious or benign circles* applies here too. That is, the combined effects of the distal etiologic factors and poor-quality MLE are likely to be more deleterious than the sum of the individual effects.

Beside the theory's general optimistic approach to the problems of child development and learning, two specific elements that have profound significance for intervention work with developmentally delayed children are (1) the notions of *mediation* and *mediated learning experience* and (2) the theory's inherent *active modification approach* to intervention.

MLE Revisited. According to Feuerstein, the development of cognitive structures and cognitive functions occurs as a function of two forms of organism-environment interaction: (1) direct exposure to sources of stimuli and (2) mediated learning. Without doubt, more of the developing child's experiences comes from direct exposure to sources of stimuli than from mediation. It is not surprising, therefore, that traditional developmental theorists, such as Piaget, place greater emphasis on this particular determinant of development than on mediated experience. However, Feuerstein argues that the "sets of strategies and repertoires" that are made available to the developing child through mediated learning experience significantly enhance the efficiency with which children make use of direct exposure to sources of stimuli. Consequently Feuerstein has formally expressed the relationship between the two forms of organism-environment interaction in the following way: high-quality MLE provided very early in the child's life increases his or her capacity to efficiently use and be affected by direct exposure to stimuli; on the other hand, low-quality MLE will have the tendency to reduce the child's capacity to become affected and modified by direct exposure to stimuli. For this reason, Feuerstein views MLE as "*the ingredient* (my emphasis) that determines differential cognitive development in otherwise similarly endowed individuals" (p. 16) living under the same conditions of stimulation.

What are some of the key characteristics of MLE that make it such a highly acknowledged, crucial determinant of differential development? Although Feuerstein and his associates identify as many as ten defining characteristics of MLE, perhaps the two most important attributes of MLE are *intentionality* and *transcendence:* "An interaction that provides mediated learning must include an intention, on the part of the mediator, to transcend the immediate needs or concerns of the recipient of the mediation by venturing beyond the here and now, in space and time" (Feuerstein et al., 1980, p. 20).

In mediated learning, the mediator consciously (i.e., intentionally) sets out to employ elements of the interaction to stimulate or effect cognitive change in the child. For this reason, the mediator always tries to take the interaction beyond the content of the immediate experience (i.e., transcendence), through such "instructional" tools as elaborations, analogies, and comparisons. Transcendence seeks to link related events, concepts, and experiences across time, and is thus a major tool for promoting generalization and application. Other, more specific, features of mediation include (1) the explicit communciation of the meaning and purpose of shared activities and (2) the promotion of a feeling of competence through acknowledgment and discussion of good performance on the part of the child (see Haywood and Brooks, in press).

Active Modification Approach to Intervention. The thrust of the active modification approach is that intervention activities should be aimed at changing the DD child through the training and nurturing of essential cognitive functions that will enable the child to adapt successfully to his or her environment. Underlying this approach is the presupposition that an "individual's manifest level of functioning at any given point in his (her) development cannot be regarded as fixed or immutable, much less a reliable indicator of future performance" (Feuerstein et al., 1980, p. 2). The antithesis of the active-modification approach is what Feuerstein characterizes as the passive-acceptant approach, in which the focus of intervention tends to be on the altering of aspects of the child's environment to accommodate the child's low level of functioning. Without doubt, while enabling the child with special needs to cope with his or her limitations, the passive-acceptant approach only serves to perpetuate those limitations.

Significant Parallels between MLE and the Mediational Implications of Vygotsky's Notion of the Zone of Proximal Development

Another theoretical framework with potential implications for intervention work with DD children, but that remains to be explored fully in this field, is that of the Soviet psychologist L. S. Vygotsky. One significant commonality between the works of Feuerstein and Vygotsky is their strong emphasis on the social and cultural context of development. Both theorists view social interaction between adult and child as a crucial propellant of children's development. We have seen how the concept of *mediation* (the process whereby an adult selects and organizes the world of stimuli for the child so as to maximize the latter's adaptation and learning) is pivotal in Feuerstein's theory of the development of cognitive competence.

Mediation is similarly pivotal in Vygotsky's theorizing about children's development of higher mental functions. All higher mental functioning, according to Vygotsky, has its origins in social life—appearing first on the social or interpersonal plane and then within the child (see Wertsch, 1989; Wertsch and Rogoff, 1984). Stated more directly, children's higher mental functions—including thinking, reasoning, memory, and problem solving—not only develop in a social milieu (Wertsch and Rogoff, 1984) but are internalizations of processes that are transmitted from adult to child through social interaction. Consequently, as Wertsch and Rogoff note, close examination of the patterns of social interactions in which the child participates is necessary to understand the child's cognitive growth.

Vygotsky introduced the notion of the *zone of proximal development* (ZPD) to illustrate the practical applications of the general principle that all higher mental functioning in the individual has its origins in social interaction (Wertsch and Rogoff, 1984). He defined it as "the distance between the actual developmental level as determined by independent problem solving and the level of potential development as determined through problem solving under adult guidance or in collaboration with more capable peers." (Vygotsky, 1978; cited in Wertsch, 1984, p. 8).

In simple terms, ZPD describes the region (*zone*) between the two levels of performance (a lower level and a higher level) that children manifest at any given point in development. The lower level represents the child's independent performance (i.e., without adult assistance), while the higher level represents performance after mediation by an adult has resulted in better clarification and representation of the problem or in a better comprehension of the context of the problem. The former is seen as reflecting the child's *actual level of development,* while the latter reflects the *level of potential development.* How does this conceptualization inform intervention? The following quotation from Wertsch and Rogoff (1984, p. 3) sums up the answer to the question: "For a child to profit from joint cognitive activity, such activity must be geared appropriately to the child's level of potential development, thereby advancing the child's level of actual development."

There is an important convergence between Feuersteinian and Vygotskian theory that I want to underscore, because of its profound implications for working with DD children, indeed with all children—that is, the spontaneous level of performance a child manifests in any given context does not represent the child's best level of performance. This has implications, first, for assessment; indeed, it calls for a rethinking of current assessment practices. It suggests that knowing how much mediation it takes for a child to accomplish at the upper limits of his or her potential is a much more useful index of competence and performance, from the standpoint of intervention, than knowledge of the spontaneous level of performance.

Its implications for developmental intervention are equally profound. Intervention becomes a process whereby the adult is continually seeking to reduce the discrepancy between the child's typical spontaneous level of performance and his or her potential level of performance (Haywood, Brooks, and Burns, 1986). Intervening within the zone of proximal development, as we may call this process, requires skills on the part of both adult and child. The child's skills in any given activity constitute the beginning point for intervention, but the adult needs the relevant skills to nurture and extend those entry-level skills of the child to a higher level of competence. These include: (1) observational skills necessary for identifying critical child actions that can be capitalized upon for mediation; (2) assessment skills for ascertaining the quality and complexity of the child's knowledge and skills relative to the requirements of the task or event at hand; and (3) scaffolding process skills, such as (a) identifying and sharing alternative solution strategies, (b) determining what kinds of guidance to provide, (c) selecting appropriate points in the interaction to provide guidance, and (d) determining when to adjust the scaffolding process itself (see Rogoff, Malkin, and Gilbride, 1984, for a more detailed look at parent-child interaction in the zone of proximal development).[2]

IMPLICATIONS FOR INTERVENTION

From the combined contributions of transactional models of development, theories of cognitive modifiability, and Vygotskian theory, the following principles, assumptions, and statements of rationale can be derived to guide the conceptualization and design of intervention for DD children.

1. Children play an active role in their own development through the resources and skills with which they pursue a variety of learning experiences and opportunities. One effect of developmental delay is the potential reduction of the child's active role in his or her own development. Consequently, one purpose of systematic mediation is to nurture, refine, and sustain the kinds of cognitive functions, competencies, skills, and dispositions that enable the child to interact effectively with his or her environment and thus contribute to his or her own development.
2. Each child is a unique individual who influences his or her environment in unique ways; consequently, different children may require different mediational input.
3. DD children are not condemned for life to the level of competence and performance that they manifest at the earliest stages of life; developmental mechanisms internal to the child interact with developmental mechanisms in the inanimate and caretaking environment to determine the level of functioning at any given point in time.
4. Because one ingredient of intellectual competence consists of *learnable* strategies, operations, and dispositions, it is possible to boost cognitive competence through mediation that has as its goal the cultivation of essential cognitive functions.
5. The extent to which the manifest level of competence and performance can be altered depends upon the quality of the developmental and caretaking environment to which children are exposed.
6. A key element of the developmental and caretaking environment is systematic mediation (planned or unplanned) provided by a primary caregiver or a significant other adult in the child's life.
7. The primary vehicle for mediation is the day-to-day social interactions between adults and the child. Concepts such as intentionality, transcendence, and scaffolding may be drawn upon to develop specific intervention strategies for enriching interactions between parents/caregivers and children.
8. Center- or school-based programs that emphasize basic skills and/or subject matter content can be further enriched through the incorporation of social interaction-based mediational strategies. In this case, direct instructional strategies would be replaced by social interaction-based mediational strategies that utilize some of the core concepts introduced in this chapter.
9. Quality mediation seeks to change the child, rather than his or her environ-

ment, by nurturing the essential cognitive functions that will enable the child to adapt effectively to the environment.

10. It is axiomatic, from the nature of the foregoing principles, that the family environment and the earliest years be seen as the foremost contexts for intervention. Consequently, parents and other primary caregivers—the child's first teachers—need support and guidance in the development of the kind of quality interactional skills/styles which form the basis of sound mediation.
11. Development and learning are life-long processes that take place in multiple contexts across time. Sound mediation should therefore not be conceptualized in relation to the home environment or the early years alone. For this reason, child care workers, teachers, and other professionals who share the joint responsibility of providing care and education for the child need professional assistance and training to develop effective mediation skills so they can provide continuity and extension to the mediation the child receives at home.

Current Status of Applications with Preschool Children

Some of the principles summarized above only serve the purpose of strengthening the theoretical rationale for interventions with DD children, while others provide new and potentially viable directions for conceptualizing intervention. So far, Haywood and his associates at Vanderbilt University are perhaps the first to draw upon the body of theoretical work surveyed in this chapter to develop a comprehensive intervention program for preschool handicapped and developmentally delayed children. The Cognitive Curriculum for Young Children (CCYC) is currently being evaluated in a number of centers in the United States and Canada (Haywood, personal communication), but a preliminary report based on 27 handicapped and 48 high-risk children who had received one academic year of CCYC has already been published (Haywood, Brooks, and Burns, 1986). A comparison of the high-risk children in CCYC with 44 high-risk children receiving other types of preschool programs showed that CCYC children made significantly stronger gains on cognitive performance as measured on the McCarthy Scales. While there was no contrast group for the 27 handicapped children receiving CCYC, the authors reported significant pretest to posttest changes not only on the General Cognitive Index of the McCarthy but on each of the four subscales as well.

Dale and his associates (Dale, 1990; Dale and Cole, 1988) at the Experimental Education Unit of the University of Washington are utilizing a randomized design to assess the effectiveness of the mediated learning approach to preschool education in relation to the traditional direct instructional technique. The mediated learning program in this investigation is based on the Vanderbilt program, although it is not clear from the reports the extent of match between the two programs. The earlier report from this project (Dale and Cole, 1988) indicated that both programs produced gains, with the programs having differential effects on specific measures. For example, while direct instruction led to greater gains on two measures of language development, mediated learning produced greater gains on the McCarthy verbal and memory subscales. The more recent report from this project (Dale, 1990), with a sample almost double the sample size in the earlier report, failed to find the differential effects reported earlier but confirmed that generally neither of the two approaches was superior in terms of intellectual and scholastic achievement outcomes.

Obviously, my recommendation that early interventionists give serious consideration to the social interaction-based mediational approach to intervention with DD children is not offered on empirical grounds, but solely on the intuitive soundness of the underlying concepts and principles of the approach.

Implications for Home-Based Interaction-Focused Early Intervention in the Infancy and Early Childhood Years

Although the guiding principles and assumptions outlined above set the stage for conceptualizing intervention in a variety of contexts across the life span, they are of especial relevance for home-based early intervention with DD infants and young children, given the current zeitgeist in the early intervention field. With very few exceptions, the typical early intervention program for developmentally delayed children employs a skills-based curriculum with an early intervention worker or the parent as the instructor. Intervention targets are determined on the basis of assessments in one or more domains of development (e.g.., cognitive, motor, social, communication, and self-help). In home-based, parent-as-instructor programs, parents are taught observational, assessment, recording, and didactic instructional techniques. While this approach to early intervention has produced positive results vis-a-vis children's acquisition of developmentally appropriate skills, it is increasingly being seen as reflecting a rather oversimplified view of the contexts and mechanisms of early development.

During the course of the past decade, however, a gradual shift from the *infant curriculum model* toward an *interaction-focused model* has been occurring in early intervention work with handicapped, developmentally delayed, and at-risk children (see Bromwich, 1981; Mahoney, 1988; Mahoney and Powell, 1988; Marfo, 1988a, 1990; McCollum, in press). As I have indicated elsewhere (Marfo, 1988b), this new direction is a very important development that needs to be nurtured. However, as an approach that is still in its infancy (perhaps even neonatal stage), interaction-focused early intervention (IFEI) currently lacks a unifying set of concepts, principles, and techniques. This situation is largely because the impetus for the few existing IFEI programs and investigations comes from a variety of disciplines and theoretical orientations (see Marfo 1990; McCollum, in press) and reflects interest in a variety of developmental domains.

It appears from the discussion of Feuerstein's theory of mediated learning experience and Vygotsky's theory on the development of higher mental functioning that these two theoretical frameworks may very well provide at least some of the unifying concepts and principles that the fledgling IFEI approach so desperately needs at this stage in its evolution. The concepts of *intentionality, transcendence* (from Feuerstein's theory), *reduction of discrepancy,* and *scaffolding* (from applications of Vygotskian theory) have particular appeal as organizing principles for developing specific interactional strategies.

Admittedly, the work presented in this chapter is still far away from specifying exactly how these concepts might be employed to design specific interaction-focused intervention strategies. It can only be hoped that it will spawn interest and a quest for further refinement so that we may move more closely to operationalizing these concepts and principles in more elaborate models of intervention. In this regard, two beginning efforts known to me are worth mentioning. Over the past several years, Ruth Kahn of the Family Development Resource Center at St. Joseph College, West Hartford, Connecticut, has been developing an intervention curriculum and related assessment instruments based on this framework (Kahn, 1990). During the same period, Carol Lidz of Temple University and her associates have been studying parent-child interactions, using the Mediated Learning Experience Rating Scale (MLERS) (Lidz, Bond, & Dissinger, in press). Lidz expects to begin intervention work based on evidence gathered on the MLERS (Lidz, 1989). As data from these and other future efforts become available, the practical usefulness and validity of this approach can be more objectively assessed.

NOTES

1. Although I can understand why Feuerstein and his associates would want to treat MLE as an entirely different concept from the general notion of child rearing or caretaking, I disagree with the connotation found commonly in the literature that MLE is a phenomenom that is either present or absent. For example, Chapter 3 of *Instrumental Enrichment: An Intervention Program for Cognitive Modifiability* (Feuerstein et al., 1980) is titled "Determinants of a Lack of Mediated Learning Experience." To the extent that every human child begins life in a social context, the earliest and fundamental being the infant-caregiver relationship, MLE is universally available to all humans. However, the quality of the

MLE to which individuals are exposed varies. It is appropriate, then, to talk of a continuum of the quality of MLE.

2. Scaffolding is used here to refer to the totality of support provided by an adult, in the context of ongoing social interaction, to extend the child's knowledge and skills to a higher level of competence.

REFERENCES

Bernheimer, L. P. and Keogh, B. K. (1986). Developmental disabilities in preschool children. In B. K. Keogh (Ed.), *Advances in special education* (Vol. 5) (pp. 61-93.) Greenwich, CT: JAI Press.

Bromwich, R. (1981). *Working with parents and infants: An interactional approach.* Baltimore: University Park Press.

Bronfenbrenner, U. (1979). *The ecology of human development.* Cambridge, MA: Harvard University Press.

______. (1989). Ecological systems theory. In R. Vasta (Ed.), *Six theories of child development: Revised formulations and current issues* (Vol. 6 of *Annals of Child Development)* (pp. 187-219). Greenwich, CT: JAI Press.

Consortium for Longitudinal Studies (1978). *Lasting effects after preschool.* Washington, DC: Department of Health, Education, and Welfare.

______. (1983). *As the twig is bent.* Hillsdale, NJ: Lawrence Erlbaum.

Dale, P. S. (1990, April). Cognitively and academically focused programs for young children: A re-examination of learner characteristics and program structure. Paper presented at the Annual Meeting of the American Educational Research Association, Boston.

Dale, P. S. and Cole, K. N. (1988). Academically-based and cognitively-based programs for young handicapped children. *Exceptional Children, 54,* 439-447.

Darlington, R. D., Royce, J. M., Snipper, A. S., Murray, H. W., and Lazar, I (1980). Pre-school programs and later school competence of children from low-income families. *Science, 208,* 202-204.

Drillien, C. M. (1957). The social and economic factors affecting the incidence of premature birth. *Journal of Obstetrical Gynaecology, British Empire, 64,* 161-184.

______. (1964). *The growth and development of the prematurely born infant.* Edinburgh: E. & S. Livingston.

Dunst, C. and Rheingrover, R. (1981). An analysis of the efficacy of early intervention programs with organically handicapped children. *Evaluation and Program Planning, 4,* 287-383.

Farran, D. C. (1990). Effects of early intervention with disadvantaged and disabled children: A decade review. In S. J. Meisels and J. P. Shonkoff (Eds.), *Handbook of early childhood intervention* (pp. 501-539). Cambridge: Cambridge University Press.

Feuerstein, R., Rand, Y., Hoffman, M. B., and Miller, R. (1980). *Instrumental enrichment: An intervention program for cognitive modifiability.* Baltimore: University Park Press.

Haywood, H. C., and Brooks, P. (in press). Theory development and curriculum development in cognitive education. In M. Schwebel, C. A. Maher, and N.

S. Fagley (Eds.), *Promoting cognitive growth over the life span.* Hillsdale, NJ: Lawrence Erlbaum.

Haywood, H. C., Brooks, P., and Burns, S. (1986). Stimulating cognitive development at developmental level: A tested, nonremedial preschool curriculum for preschoolers and older retarded children. In M. Schwebel and C. A. Maher (Eds.), *Facilitating cognitive development: Principles, practices, and programs* (pp. 127-147). New York: Haworth Press.

Haywood, H. C. and Switzky, H. N. (1986). The malleability of intelligence: Cognitive processes as a function of polygenic-experiential interaction. *School Psychology Review, 15,* 245-255.

Jensen, A. R. (1969). How much can we boost intelligence and academic achievement? *Harvard Educational Review, 39,* 1-123.

______. (1985). Compensatory education and the theory of intelligence. *Phi Delta Kappan, 66,* 554-558.

Kahn, R. (1990, May). The mediation of learning experiences: An early intervention approach for facilitating cognitive and socioemotional development. Round table presentation made at the 20th Anniversary Symposium of the Jean Piaget Society, Philadelphia.

Lazar, I. and Darlington, R. B. (Ed.) (1982). Lasting effects of early education: A report from the Consortium for Longitudinal Studies. *Monographs of the Society for Research in Child Development, 47* (2-3, Serial No. 195).

Lidz, C. (1989, August). Summary of research involving dynamic asessment with preschool children and parent-child interaction assessment with the Mediated Learning Experience Rating Scale. Paper presented at the Second International Conference on Mediated Learning Experience, Knoxville.

Lidz, C. S., Bond, L., and Dissinger, L. (in press). Consistency of mother-child interaction using the Mediated Learning Experience Rating Scale. *Special Services in the Schools.*

Mahoney, G. (1988). Enhancing the developmental competence of handicapped infants. In K. Marfo (Ed.), *Parent-child interaction and developmental disabilities: Theory, research, and intervention* (pp. 203-219). New York: Praeger.

Mahoney, G., and Powell, A. (1988). Modifying parent-child interaction: Enhancing the developmental competence of handicapped children. *Journal of Special Education, 22,* 82-96.

Marfo, K. (Ed. (1988a). *Parent-child interaction and developmental disabilities: Theory, research, and intervention.* New York: Praeger.

Marfo, K. (1988b). Enhancing interactions between mothers and their developmentally disabled children: A missing link in early intervention? In E. R. Boersma, H. J. Huisjes, and H.M.C. Poortman (Eds.), *A holistic approach to perinatal care and prevention of handicap* (pp. 231-239). Groningen, The Netherlands: Erven B. van der Kamp Publishers.

______. (1990). Maternal directiveness in interactions with mentally handicapped children: An analytical commentary. *Journal of Child Psychology and Psychiatry, 31*(4), 531-549.

Marfo, K., Browne, N., Gallant, D., Smyth, R., and Corbett, A. (1989). Child, program, and family ecological variables in early intervention. Unpublished manuscript, Department of Educational Psychology and Leadership Studies, Kent State University.

Marfo, K. and Cook, C. (in press). Overview of trends and issues in early intervention theory and research. In K. Marfo (Ed.), *Early intervention in transition: Current perspectives on programs for handicapped children.* New York: Praeger.

Marfo, K. and Kysela, G. M. (1985). Early intervention with mentally handicapped children: A critical appraisal of applied research. *Journal of Pediatric Psychology, 10,* 305-324.

McCollum, J. A. (in press). At the crossroad: Reviewing and rethinking interaction coaching. In K. Marfo (Ed.), *Early intervention in transition: Current perspectives on programs for handicapped children.* New York: Praeger.

Meisels, S. J. and Shonkoff, J. P. (Eds.) (1990). *Handbook of early childhood intervention.* Cambridge: Cambridge University Press.

Passamanick, B., and Knobloch, H. (1966). Retrospective studies on the epidemiology of reproductive casualty: Old and new. *Merrill-Palmer Quarterly, 12,* 7-26.

Rogoff, B., Malkin, C., and Gilbride, K. (1984). Interaction with babies as guidance in development. In B. Rogoff and J. V. Wertsch (Eds.), *Children's learning in the "zone of proximal development"* (pp. 31-44). San Francisco: Jossey-Bass.

Sameroff, A. J. (1975). Early influences on development: Fact or fancy? *Merrill-Palmer Quarterly, 21,* 267-294.

______. (1980). Issues in early reproductive and caretaking risk: Review and current status. In D. B. Sawin, R. C. Hawkins II, L. O. Walker, and J. H. Penticuff (Eds.), *Exceptional infant,* Vol. 4: *Psychosocial risk in infant-environment transactions* (pp. 343-359). New York: Brunner/Mazel.

Sameroff, A. J., and Chandler, M. J. (1975). Reproductive risk and the continuum of caretaking casualty. In F. D. Horowitz, M. Hetherington, S. Scarr-Salapatek, and G. Siegel (Eds.), *Review of child development research* (Vol. 4) (pp. 187-224). Chicago: University of Chicago Press.

Sameroff, A. J. and Fiese, B. H. (1990). Transactional regulation and early intervention. In S. J. Meisels and J. P. Shonkoff (Eds.), *Handbook of early childhood intervention* (pp. 119-149). New York: Cambridge University Press.

Schweinhart, L. J., and Weikart, D. P. (1980). Young children grown up: The effects of the Perry preschool program on youths through age 15. *Monographs of the High/Scope Educational Research Foundation,* No. 7. Ypsilanti, MI: The High/Scope Press.

______. (1985). Evidence that good early childhood programs work. *Phi Delta Kappan, 66,* 545-551.

Simeonsson, R. J., Cooper, D. H. and Scheiner, A. P. (1982). A review and analysis of the effectiveness of early intervention programs. *Pediatrics, 69,* 635-641.

Switzky, H. N. and Haywood, H. C. (1984). A biosocial ecological perspective on mental retardation. In N. E. Endler and J. McV. Hunt (Eds.), *Personality and the behavioral disorders* 2nd ed. (pp. 855-871). New York: Wiley.

Waddington, C. H. (1962). *New patterns in genetics and development.* New York: Columbia University Press.

Werner, E. E. (1984, November). Resilient children. *Young Children,* 68-72.

Wertsch, J. V. (1984). The zone of proximal development: Some conceptual issues. In B. Rogoff and J. V. Wertsch (Eds.), *Children's learning in the "zone of proximal development"* (pp. 7-18). San Francisco: Jossey-Bass.

______. (1989). A sociocultural approach to mind. In W. Damon (Ed.), *Child development today and tomorrow* (pp. 14-33). San Francisco: Jossey-Bass.

Wertsch, J. V. and Rogoff, B. (1984). Editors' notes. In B. Rogoff and J. V. Wertsch (Eds.), *Children's learning in the "zone of proximal development"* (pp. 1-6). San Francisco: Jossey-Bass.

Westinghouse Learning Corporation (1969). *The Impact of Head Start: An evaluation of the effects of Head Start on children's cognitive and affective development* (Report to the Office of Economic Opportunity). Washington, DC: Clearinghouse for Federal Scientific and Technical Information.

Woodhead, M. (1988). When psychology informs public policy: The case of early childhood intervention. *American Psychologist, 43,* 443-454.

Zigler, E., Balla, D., and Hodapp, R. (1984). On the definition and classification of mental retardation. *American Journal of Mental Deficiency, 89,* 215-230.

Zigler, E. and Berman, W. (1983). Discerning the future of early childhood intervention. *American Psychologist, 38,* 894-906.

Zigler, E. and Hodapp, R. M. (1986). *Understanding mental retardation.* Cambridge: Cambridge University Press.

Zigler, E. and Seitz, V. (1980). Early childhood intervention programs: A reanalysis. *School Psychology Review, 9,* 354-368.

Zigler, E. and Trickett, P. K. (1978). I. Q., social competence, and evaluation of early childhood intervention programs. *American Psychologist, 33,* 789-798.

Chapter 10

Help for the Runaway Child

Richard L. Jenkins

The term "running away," as it is used with children, usually means a departure from home, at least overnight, not authorized by the child's parents. This act is an offense in a child, but not in an adult. This, in turn, makes it a "status offense"—an offense only because it is committed by someone who has the status of being a child. As with other offenses, it also requires *intent* to run away. A child who is simply lost is not per se a runaway.

A runaway by a child is a signal that something may be seriously wrong in the life of the child, something that parents—and professionals, if they have any entree to the case—should be concerned about. The main cause or precipitant of the runaway is usually easy to ascertain and may range from something as minor as a verbal quarrel to something as serious as open rejection of the child by a parent or stepparent.

A majority of runaways run from an unsatisfactory home situation. If the home situation is not improved, running away may become repetitive. For example, Hartman, Burgess, and McCormack (1987) reported on 149 runaways who were in a shelter in Toronto in the summer of 1984. These children had run away an average of 8.9 times.

The U.S. Office of Juvenile Justice and Delinquency Prevention stated in a *Juvenile Justice Bulletin* (circa 1984, pp. 1-2) that

> well over one million children will run away from home this year. More than half will run from physical maltreatment inflicted by family members; a third will run from sexual abuse. Many will be "pushouts" or "throwaways," children whose parents encourage, even demand them to leave and never return. They may join thousands of other runaways who live on the streets or in abandoned

buildings and cheap hotels. The vast majority of those who remain at large for a few weeks will resort to theft or prostitution as a method of self-support. They will probably abuse alcohol and drugs and suffer from poor mental and physical health. Many runaways will survive this way for years. Some will not survive at all. . . .

No one has ever counted the runaways and homeless children in this country. The U.S. Department of Health and Human Services (HHS) has estimated that there are approximately 2 million, but it is a difficult number to ascertain. While some are successfully reunited with their families and others stumble upon an assistance program, an alarming number of runaways slip through the cracks of the system. A statistical survey conducted in California found that only one in six runaways is reported missing by parents or guardians. Moreover, HHS was consistently advised in interviews with police and juvenile authorities that only one in every four or five runaways and homeless children is ever arrested or detained. Thus, the remaining 75 to 80 percent of these youth are never officially acknowledged. A runaway's anonymity is further enhanced by the throng of the streets, the comfort of being but one face in a thousand, or by the screen of bogus identification. Some of them never surface. Some join the estimated 2,000 unidentified children's bodies buried annually by police.

The current attitude of the juvenile justice system towards runaways can be described as one of apathy—more specifically, apathy by statute. The fault lies behind the well-intentioned passage of the Juvenile Justice and Delinquency Prevention Act of 1974. In an effort to correct the ills of a juvenile justice system which incarcerated youth convicted of minor offenses, Congress effectively tied the hands of juvenile authorities, leaving runaways, quite literally, out in the cold.

The "apathy by statute" that "tied the hands of juvenile authorities" was the result of a movement articulated by the National Council on Crime and Delinquency (1974), which viewed the work of the juvenile court as primarily or exclusively punitive. It objected to the jurisdiction of the juvenile court over status offenders, "who had broken no law." The sentiment was reflected in the Juvenile Justice and Delinquency Prevention Act of 1974, which pressured states to "deinstitutionalize" status offenders as the price of maintaining federal assistance in juvenile justice. In its conclusion the *Juvenile Justice Bulletin* (1984, p. 9) states that "an overwhelming majority of the authorities interviewed agree that deinstitutionalization has had an adverse effect on the runaway problem."

The occurrence of running away is infrequent before the teen years. The average age is 15 (Angenent and Beke, 1984; Flowers, 1986). Both Angenent and Beke as well as Flowers report that running away is more frequent in girls than in boys, although *repetitive* running away is more frequent in boys (Hartman et al., 1987). As one gets into more severe and repetitive involvement, the proportion of boys increases. A majority of runaways return home within a short time. Girls return more often than boys, and among runaways who have been on runaway from home for more than a year, the boys outnumber the girls nearly three to one (Hartman et al., 1987).

Angenent and Beke report that running away appears to be somewhat more frequent in more closed, cold, and authoritarian households than in more open, warm, and democratic ones. Since the goal of growing up is to achieve an adequate and independent adulthood, some instances of running away may be viewed as simply premature efforts to assert independence before the teenager is fully equipped to be independent.

DIAGNOSTIC CONSIDERATIONS

Running away is a behavior ascribable to any one of many causes. Repetitive running away from home may become a grave concern. It seems desirable to consider running away in relation to the diagnosis of mental disorder.

In DSM-III-R, the current revision of the Third Edition of the *Diagnostic and Statistical Manual of Mental Disorders of the American Psychiatric Association* (1987), running away from home overnight at least twice (or once without returning) is one of 13 diagnostic criteria of which at least three must be present to justify the diagnosis of *conduct disorder*. "The essential feature of this disorder is a persistent pattern of conduct in which the basic rights of others and major age-appropriate societal norms or rules are violated. The behavior pattern typically is present in the home, at school, with peers, and in the community" (p. 53). DSM-III-R recognizes the following types of conduct disorder:

> 312.20 *Group Type.* The essential feature is the predominance of conduct problems occurring mainly as a group activity with peers. Aggressive physical behavior may or may not be present.
>
> 312.00 *Solitary Aggressive Type.* The essential feature is the predominance of aggressive physical behavior, usually toward both adults and peers, initiated by the person (not as a group activity).
>
> 312.90 *Undifferentiated Type.* This is a subtype for children or adolescents with Conduct Disorder with a mixture of clinical features that cannot be classified as either Solitary Aggressive Type or Group Type (p. 56).

Conduct disorder is a diagnosis determined by conduct alone. It may or may not overlap with psychotic or other psychiatric diagnoses. All warranted diagnoses should be made according to the DSM-III-R.

The diagnosis conduct disorder appears first in DSM-III (1980). It was formed to include three separate diagnoses from DSM-II (1968)—the group delinquent reaction of childhood (or adolescence), the unsocialized aggressive reaction of childhood (or adolescence), and the runaway reaction of childhood (or adolescence).

As early as 1944, two subtypes of conduct disorder were recognized: the socialized delinquent and the unsocialized aggressive (Jenkins and Hewitt, 1944; Hewitt and Jenkins, 1946). The family backgrounds of these types are quite different. The socialized (group) delinquent develops most frequently in an impoverished large family in a deteriorated crime-ridden neighborhood. An absent or alcoholic father is also a factor (Jenkins, 1966, 1967). The unsocialized aggressive child, by contrast, develops in all social levels but has typically been an unwanted child experiencing parental rejection, particularly maternal rejection. In contrast with the large family typical of the group type of conduct disorder, the unsocialized child is very frequently an only child of an unmarried or divorced mother (Hewitt and Jenkins, 1946).

An unsocialized runaway group was clearly differentiated in a statistical study of 300 boys admitted to the New York State Training School for Boys at Warwick (Jenkins and Boyer, 1970). This study made it very clear that the background of the unsocialized runaway child (runaway reaction, DSM-II, conduct disorder, unsocialized nonaggressive, DSM-III), is even more deprived of the socializing effects of early nurturing than is that of the unsocialized aggressive child. The unsocialized runaway group has a higher percentage of unwanted children, of children of unmarried mothers, and of only children. It has clearly higher rates of parental rejection, and of both past and present foster placement.

Individuals growing up in rejecting homes are often unsocialized and fearful. They may develop the pattern of the *runaway reaction* as described in DSM-II (1968, p. 50):

> 308.3 *Runaway Reaction of Childhood (or adolescence).* Individuals with this disorder characteristically escape from threatening situations by running away from home for a day or more without permission. Typically they are immature and timid, and feel rejected at home, inadequate, and friendless. They often steal furtively.

This diagnostic category became conduct disorder, undersocialized, nonaggressive in DSM-III (1980). Unfortunately, this needed category is omitted from DSM-III-R (1987).

The home background of children who run away has been studied and compared with clinic children who do not run away, as well as with children with and without the entry "group stealing." In a study involving 1,500 child guidance cases, 67 runaways were compared to the remainder of the subject population with respect to behavior and parental factors (Jenkins, 1986). Runaways were distinguished from other subjects by inadequacy of the mother-child relationship. Study results give a picture of a frequent relative lack of maternal interest in and emotional support for runaways, from an immature, unmarried mother, herself without emotional support. A question that arises is, "Could this inadequate mother become a more adequate mother if given support?" Additional questions might be, "What help can be given this child directly as well as indirectly through a parent or parents?" "How does it happen that some children succeed despite such adverse elements?"

The background typical of runaways reminds us of children's need of parental acceptance and security in a home environment. It should come as no surprise that runaways are likely to be slow to trust a home that is offered to them. This is where the authority to hold a runaway in a suitable secure setting until someone can develop a relationship with him may become essential. The recognition by the Office of Juvenile Justice and Delinquency Prevention (OJJDP) of the need for providing for the detention of some runaways is stated as follows in the *Juvenile Justice Bulletin* (1984, p. 9): "By no means do all runaway and homeless children need to be confined. But some do, if only for their own protection. Unfortunately, the Federal deinstitutionalization mandate prevents the juvenile justice system from providing that which many runaways need most."

Also, unfortunately, despite this recognition, there has been as yet no change in the federal policy against the involuntary detention of runaway or other status offenders. It is further unfortunate that this policy seems to be anchored to a moral conviction that children should not be "penalized" for actions that would not be criminal if they were performed by an adult. As a consequence, the *protective* function of the juvenile court is often denied the child.

When the misbehavior of the child exceeds the tolerance of the parents, the outlook is bleak. From my own clinical experience some years ago, I reported an example of a chronic runaway (runaway reaction, DSM-II) with a fairly typical background (Jenkins, 1974).

Lewis was one of four children born to parents, both of whom were in military service. His parents were divorced after 11 years. Lewis and his older brother remained with the father, who remarried, but showed little interest in his sons and apparently made little or no effort to supervise them. Lewis had a psychiatric examination and was placed in a "boy's ranch" as a dependent and neglected child. He was transferred to a coeducational treatment center where the children attended public school. Later, by court action, over the father's objection, Lewis was placed with his mother in Arizona. He ran away repeatedly and on the fourth runaway was picked up in Texas. He had two unsuccessful foster home placements and was repeatedly in the youth shelter. He was then hospitalized in the children's unit of a state mental hospital. He seemed proud of his success in stealing and of the fact that he had run from placements on a number of different occasions. He claimed that he had been physically abused by his father who, he said, had repeatedly stuffed a towel in his mouth and beaten him with a belt. He complained of beatings by his stepfather, his mother's second husband. There seemed no occasion for his further hospitalization, and he was sent to the state training school. He had been there intermittently 21 months at the time of writing.

TREATMENT CONSIDERATIONS

When a teenage runaway first occurs, it is desirable that the parent or parents report the matter to the police and to a social agency, and seek professional help. Unless the youngster has stolen or otherwise broken the law, in many states the police no longer have the power to hold the youth, but it is worthwhile to advise the police of the youth's runaway. According to the figures of the OJJDP, reporting the runaway is the exception rather than the rule. In approximately three out of four cases, the runaway voluntarily returns home, often making the first contact by telephone.

When a runaway is reported to a social or professional agency for help, it is desirable that all members of the family of a runaway be interviewed, as well as friends and associates, teachers, and other adults who are important in the life of the child. When the child surfaces, careful interview with the child is desirable, and will need to be done on more than one occasion. Some reasons for a runaway, such as physical or sexual abuse, are often easy to identify; but one should be aware that an insecure child may seek to protect an abusive parent. Sexual abuse in the home is a frequent problem, especially with girls. In cases in which a parent has been abusive, and especially in cases in which a parent has been or is rejecting, the possible alternatives to the return of the child to the home should be canvassed and considered. Of course, it is necessary to work with the parents, who are frequently angry, frustrated, fearful, and more defensive than cooperative, especially at first. Assigning blame is to be avoided and implying blame may result in a withdrawal of cooperation.

Failure to resolve a family conflict is likely to result in a repetition of runaway behavior. It may become clear that this runaway adolescent cannot make an adjustment in this home. Then the alternatives of the home of a relative (a grandparent?), a foster home, a group home, or an institution may have to be considered. If the runaways become repetitive, then sooner or later the runaway will have some collision with the law, which will give the juvenile court jurisdiction. When there is a basis for juvenile court intervention, the problem is somewhat simplified for the power of the court may be needed.

Naturally, the homes of runaways are more frequently in conflict than the homes of children who do not run away. The child is especially likely to have conflict with a new member of the household, such as a stepparent or stepsibling, or transient members of the household, such as boyfriends of the mother.

Runaway children are especially frequent in households lacking strong and dependable parent-child and child-parent bonding (Angenent and Beke, 1984). Runaway children tend also to be lacking in friendships and in peer bonding. They are seldom well-adjusted in school. Any ties to home or community that can be cultivated by and for the runaway improve his or her chances of *not* becoming a repetitive runaway.

In general, a runaway from home usually reflects some home condition that needs change. There are, however, some runaways that result not from morbid relations in the home, but simply from desire for adventure or to escape from boredom. Homer (1973) was able to sort cases of runaway girls into those who were running *from* and those who were running *to.* Of 20 runaway girls in the study, 7 were classified as running from an unhappy home situation, while 13 were classified as running to the company of friends (including boyfriends), parties, liquor, drugs, and sex.

Each girl was seen in treatment once a week for individual therapy, twice a week in a co-ed counseling group led by a therapist in conjunction with other staff, and every other week in family therapy. "There was also built into the role that of advocate with the schools and other community agencies on an as-needed basis" (Homer, 1973, p. 474).

The success of this program in resolving the problem of running away, for the 7 girls running from an unhappy home situation, was conspicuous and impressive. Of the 7 girls, 5 did not return to the juvenile court. One returned to court on another charge that was dismissed after she had kept out of trouble for six months. The seventh girl kept running from a family situation that she could not tolerate and that was not ameliorated. She was committed to an institution, because of a lack of community alternatives.

The lack of success of this treatment program for the 13 girls who were running to the runaway subculture was deplorable. Only one of these 13 girls never returned to court. Nine of the 13 ultimately required an institutional commitment. In these cases, the effort to awaken and stimulate internal controls in these girls in the open community was not successful, and the imposition of external controls became necessary as a part of treatment.

Linda Reppond, executive director of the Seattle Youth and Community Services, reported favorably on the success of a shelter with an "open door" policy in working with runaway children. "The Shelter" is the name of The Shelter Runaway Center in Seattle. Reppond (1985) wrote that "last year 10 percent of the runaway and street kids we served ran from the program. Many returned within several days. Similar locked facilities in our community reported a 30 percent run rate, with almost no youth returning voluntarily." It would appear that some repeated runaways can be worked with in an open setting that seeks to meet their needs.

Of course, if runaway youth engage repetitively in serious delinquent behavior, the juvenile court may find it necessary to commit such youth to institutions without an open door. Some runaway children succeed with an open door policy, but at some point the door may need to be closed and locked.

When runaways repeat, it is highly probable that there is pathology in the home relations of the runaway. The longer the time until these relations are resolved or at least improved, the greater the likelihood of further runaways—and the worse the adult prognosis. The earlier the intervention, the better the prognosis. I find the story of Robert Thornton (1988) a particularly fascinating one. As an illegitimate child, Robert was placed in an orphanage, where he remained about three and a half years. As an adult, he had no memory of any human contact during this period.

From the orphanage he was adopted into a family of two parents and an adolescent girl 11 years his senior. This girl was introduced in the role of a younger sister of the adoptive mother, but was in fact her illegitimate child. This adoptive mother, the dominant member of the family, was an emotionally unstable woman with violent outbursts of anger. From Robert's account, it is clear that he never developed an attachment bond to her. He was apparently starting to form an attachment bond with his adoptive father, but this was terminated by the sudden death of the adoptive father from a fatal heart attack.

Robert ran away from his home twice in his early adolescence. Both runaways were planned. The first was with one friend, and they took a bus from Seattle to San Francisco. They were returned after they ran out of money and eventually went to Traveler's Aid. The second runaway was with two friends and involved stealing a car. They were stopped by the State Police after they crossed the Oregon state line. After his release, Robert embarked on another car theft, and in detention he developed a solid identification as a delinquent. His socialization and loyalties developed within a delinquent group. When committed to the Green Hill School, a training school for delinquent boys, he rapidly rose to becoming a leader in rebellious behavior. With six others, he ran from the school on one occasion, and then, when assigned to a forestry camp, he ran four times with another boy. He was always caught.

Robert Thornton's turnaround from delinquency came when (1) he realized that he had tested the outer limits of the tolerance of the training school and was facing prison, and (2) he clearly realized that he had the acceptance, support, and help of strong adult men he had come to admire—a cottage father who visited with him in his own home after lights out; the assistant superintendent; a coach; and his parole counselor. These men he came to trust as well as to admire. Later, as a result of catching the spirit of these men, Robert successfully entered the helping professions.

There remains a basis for hope at any time that the child runaway decides that he or she wants to make a change. This is nowhere better illustrated than in the classic volume, *The Jack-Roller, A Delinquent Boy's Own Story,* which was published by Clifford Shaw in 1930. It is abstracted in this volume in Chapter 11, "Socializing the Unsocialized Delinquent." See also Snodgrass et al. (1982).

The professional worker who is called upon to give help after a child runs away from home should recognize that, with appropriate help, this can be a turning point in the life of a child. Sometimes a problem precipitating a runaway may be easily resolvable. Sometimes it may seem insolvable without the intervention of the juvenile court. Repetitive running away strongly suggests the need for such intervention.

REFERENCES

American Psychiatric Association (1968). *Diagnostic and statistical manual of mental disorders,* second edition (DSM-II). Washington, DC: American Psychiatric Association.

______. (1980). *Diagnostic and statistical manual of mental disorders,* third edition (DSM-III). Washington, DC: American Psychiatric Association.

______. (1987). *Diagnostic and statistical manual of mental disorders,* third edition, revised (DSM-III-R). Washington, DC: American Psychiatric Association.

Angenent, H. and Beke, B. (1984). *Runaways.* Nijwmegen, Holland: Institute of Orthopedagogics.

Flowers, R. B. (1986). *Children and criminality.* Westport, CT: Greenwood Press.

Hartman, C. R., Burgess, A. W., and McCormack, A. (1987). Pathways and cycles of runaways: A model for understanding repetitive runaway behavior. *Hospital and Community Psychiatry, 38,* 292-299.

Hewitt, L. E. and Jenkins, R. L. (1946). *Fundamental patterns of maladjustment: The dynamics of their origin.* State of Illinois.

Homer, L. E. (1973). Community-based resources for runaway girls. *Social Casework, 54,* 473-479.

Jenkins, R. L. (1966). Psychiatric syndromes in children and their relation to the family background. *American Journal of Orthopsychiatry, 36,* 551-560.

______. (1967). The varieties of adolescent behavior problems and family dynamics. In S. J. Shamsie (Ed.), *Adolescent psychiatry.* Montreal: Schering Corp.

______. (1974). Deprivation of parental care as a contributor to juvenile delinquency. In A. Roberts (Ed.), *Childhood deprivation.* Springfield, IL: Charles C. Thomas.

______. (1986). Antecedents of running away from home and of group stealing. *The Differential View, 15,* 107-125.

Jenkins, R. L. and Boyer, A. (1970). Effects of inadequate mothering and inadequate fathering on children. *International Journal of Social Psychiatry, 16* , 72-78.

Jenkins, R. L. and Hewitt, L. E. (1944). Types of personality structure encountered in child guidance clinics. *American Journal of Orthopsychiatry, 14,* 84-94.

National Council on Crime and Delinquency (1974). *Jurisdiction over status offender should be removed from the juvenile court: A policy statement.* Paramus, NJ: Author.

Office of Juvenile Justice and Delinquency Prevention, U.S. Department of Justice (not dated, circa 1984). Runaway children and the Juvenile Justice and Delinquency Prevention Act: What is the impact? *Juvenile Justice Bulletin.*

Reppond, L. (1985). Speaking out. *In Justice for Children, 1,* 19.

Shaw, C. R. (1930). *The Jack-Roller: A delinquent boy's own story.* Chicago: University of Chicago Press (reprinted 1960).

Snodgrass, J., Geis, G., Short, J. F. Jr., and Kobrin, S. (1982). *The Jack-Roller at Seventy: A fifty year follow-up.* Lexington, MA: Lexington Books.

Thornton, R. (1988). People do make a difference. In R. L. Jenkins and W. K. Brown (Eds.), *The abandonment of delinquent behavior: Promoting the turnaround.* New York: Praeger.

Chapter 11

Socializing the Unsocialized Delinquent

Richard L. Jenkins

Our juvenile justice system is geared to a pattern of gradualism, of repeated warnings and gradually increasing sanctions. This pattern was devised to interfere no more than necessary, and to use sanctions as sparingly as is compatible with some protection of the community. Most of us will find no fault with the foregoing as a general model for juvenile justice proceedings. However, there are instances in which it is wasteful, and sometimes it is dangerous. It is my thesis that, in a significant number of recognizable cases, this delay is at a human and financial cost to the public and contributes to a continuing problem.

SOCIALIZED VERSUS UNSOCIALIZED DELINQUENTS

In a broad sense, delinquents may be divided into two different categories—the socialized and the unsocialized. The socialized have ties of affection and loyalty to family and friends. They may be hostile, intolerant, and unfair toward those they regard as the enemy, but they are willing to make some sacrifices for the feelings and welfare of those they believe and feel to be of their own group.

By contrast, the unsocialized care only about themselves. They are ecocentric and narcissistic. In interviewing delinquent boys in a training school, one of my questions was: "Who is the person you care the most about?" The socialized delinquents usually responded, "my mother" or "my father" or perhaps "my baby sister." Those with strong religious training might respond with "Jesus" or "God"; but if asked whom they cared next most about, they responded with a family member, or occasionally with a boyfriend or a girlfriend. With the socialized delinquents, if the first choice was "myself," there was invariably a human second choice behind it.

The unsocialized delinquent gives a different set of responses. One unsocialized delinquent, after responding to the question, "Who is the person you care most about?" with "myself," when asked, "Who is the person you care next most about?" responded quite aggressively with the counter question, "Why should I care about anyone else?" A fairly frequent response was "nobody." Reform is difficult or impossible for the delinquent who cares about no one else.

The socialized and unsocialized (or undersocialized) groups of delinquents are dealt with at more length elsewhere (Jenkins, Heidemann, and Caputo, 1985). Notably, the socialized delinquents tend to be motivated toward understandable gains, as most of us are. The unsocialized delinquents are typically reacting to frustration with frustration behavior, behavior occasioned by emotion, but *behavior without a goal.*

These two types of delinquent behavior are different in their antecedents, and presumably in their causes, different in their prognosis, and different in their resistance to treatment. The socialized delinquent may be regarded as a youngster socialized within a delinquent group and behaving according to the norms of that group. Such a youngster offers a much more favorable prognosis than the unsocialized delinquent (Henn, Bardwell, and Jenkins, 1980).

The circumstances under which socialized delinquency most often arises include the large impoverished family living in the inner city or other delinquency area, and in which the parents lack the energy, the power, and perhaps the motivation to properly supervise their children. The father is very likely to be absent from the home, but harsh, brutal, and intoxicated when he is present. Conflict between the children (particularly the sons) and the father appears to be an important element.

The circumstances under which the unsocialized delinquent develops are quite different. Stated most simply, no one ever wanted him or loved him and he knows it. The poorly socialized, unmarried, underage, unwilling mother, not ready for responsibilities of motherhood and unwilling to accept them, is conspicuously frequent and is certainly a very prominent factor in the background of this child (Hewitt and Jenkins, 1946; Jenkins and Boyer, 1967). How important genetic factors may be and how they interact with environmental factors are unknown.

It seems clear that socialized delinquent behavior is associated with parental negligence and exposure to delinquent behavior, while unsocialized delinquent behavior is associated with parental rejection and particularly with maternal rejection. Granted that in one sense they are the two ends of the same spectrum, their backgrounds, and presumably their causes, are quite different.

Hewitt (Hewitt and Jenkins, 1946, p. 88) characterized the rejected, unsocialized child as follows:

The product of this background is a child of bottomless hostilities and endless bitterness, who feels cheated in life, views himself as the victim although he is constantly the aggressor, is grossly defective in his social inhibitions, or if you prefer, in his superego, and is grossly lacking in guilt sense over his misconduct. We may think of his hostility as springing from three sources. First, there is the hostility of the individual who has a need for and, by common judgment, a right to expect love from his parents and receives none. Even adults who have developed a good deal of social restraint often become hostile and sometimes even violent when they find themselves rejected in a love relationship, and certainly the reaction of resentment and bitterness is natural to a child who is rejected by his mother. Secondly, this child has lacked an effective affectional tie to any adult through which he could incorporate standards of behavior or from whom he could develop a superego. In the third place, the example of behavior this child sees before him is one which is highly selfish and inconsiderate and, by our conventional standards, objectionable if not delinquent. This background has developed a hostile, uninhibited personality, tending to act with direct violence at any provocation or desire. He has cause for insecurity and cause for anxiety, but the anxiety usually leads him to attack.

A subsequent study (Jenkins and Boyer, 1967) revealed that although our original group of unsocialized subjects was highly aggressive, among boys committed to a training school, another cluster of unsocialized boys was found, whose family backgrounds tended to be even more rejecting than those of the aggressive group. This new cluster was of boys who were timid and fearful. This finding led to the recognition of the *runaway reaction* of DSM-II, the revised *Diagnostic and Statistical Manual of Mental Disorders of the American Psychiatric Association* (1968).

The two groups of unsocialized disorders described in DSM-II, the aggressive and the runaway, differ conspicuously in the tendency to attack versus the tendency to run away. Otherwise, their character trends and behavior are quite similar. Both are unpopular, both project blame onto others, both lack guilt feeling, and both see the world as a hostile place. One attacks. The other runs away. Of course, we may expect good musculature (mesomorphism) to be associated with the aggressive disposition to attack, and poor musculature to be associated with the disposition to run away. Parental shielding of the boy from the natural consequences of his actions is also associated with the defiance and overaggressiveness of the aggressive group and is presumably a contributing factor (Jenkins and Boyer, 1967).

The adolescent who has loyalties to delinquent friends in the community may need to be separated geographically from those friends for some time in order for treatment to be successful. Such a child or adolescent is not truly unsocialized, but is perhaps socialized within the delinquent group. Such delinquents do not offer a bad long-term prognosis and are good candidates for contributing to their own success, especially if some of their loyalty can be won.

The unsocialized delinquent trusts no one and may attack without provocation if he dares, or run away if he does not dare. Treatment may be impossible outside of a controlled, secure situation. In a secure disciplinary unit in a training school, many unsocialized delinquents were reluctant to leave for the freer life in the regular cottages.

One unstable adolescent expressed his sense of security in this closely supervised unit, as well as his recognition of his own instability in the following pathetic verse, which, I hope makes up in human quality for all it lacks in poetic technique:

Want to Stay

I been in Quarantine about twelve weeks,
When I hear about leaving it gives me the creeps.
Sometimes I get bawled out and locked in my room,
But I don't mind it at all than to get swept out
with a broom.
I work all day long and have no time to play,
And at meal times bring around the tray.
Once in a while I go out for a smoke
Until one of these days I am going to choke.
I'd rather stay in jail than go out and fail,
Because I know that they will soon be following my
trail.
There is no use of me going out
When I'll be back in (Jenkins, 1954, p. 24).

Jenkins (1954) contains much material on the unsocialized delinquent, including a case in which army service marked the transition from severely unsocialized delinquency to acceptable army service.

STANLEY'S STORY

The most celebrated case of effective treatment of an unsocialized delinquent in the open community is that of Stanley, the Jack-Roller, treated by Clifford Shaw (1930) and his associates.

Stanley, the name Shaw gave to his subject, was a child of an immigrant, unskilled Polish laborer in Chicago. Stanley was first picked up by the police at age six years and six months, when he was found with an older boy sleeping under a doorstep, late at night, several blocks away from his home. He was returned home, but again picked up by the police for runaway six more times before he was seven years of age. Stanley's problem was his relationship with his stepmother, whom he completely rejected, and who he believed rejected him.

After being picked up for runaway three additional times, Stanley was arrested for shoplifting at a five-and-ten-cent store. This was the beginning of a long series of arrests, chiefly for stealing. Stanley was committed to the Chicago Parental School as a truant and was three times committed to Illinois Training School for Boys. At the age of 15, but claiming to be 18, he was committed to the Illinois State Reformatory for a year for "jack-rolling" (robbing drunken men) and for burglary. At 16 years of age he was back in court for jack-rolling and burglary and was sentenced to the House of Correction for a year. It was in the House of Correction that Clifford Shaw first visited Stanley and offered to help him on his release if Stanley would come and see him. Stanley, who had no other resources, did so.

Rehabilitation in the field of penology, restoration to a previous satisfactory state, is possible only when there is an acceptable life pattern to which the subject can return. Stanley never had such a life pattern, so the problem was not one of rehabilitation but one of habilitation. Habilitation is more difficult than rehabilitation. It has been stated that the rehabilitation of an offender requires the resolute and lasting effort of at least two people—the offender himself plus someone who can create opportunities for the offender. If the latter is working initially without the former having yet made a commitment to change, the task is immeasurably more difficult, for little progress is possible until the offender is committed to a determination to change.

Stanley seemed about as unlikely a candidate for habilitation as one could find in the criminal field. That he was in fact habilitated by Clifford Shaw and others is a monument to the inexhaustible goodwill, endless patience, and the pragmatic determination of those who succeeded in the job. The story is well recounted in *The Jack-Roller* by Shaw. Stanley's further story is told in *The Jack-Roller at Seventy* by Snodgrass et al. (1982).

Shaw was able to provide a foster home for Stanley in a community with little delinquency. Over the next two years, Shaw was instrumental in getting Stanley many of the 19 jobs Stanley lost or left. The median time before Stanley quit or was fired was three weeks.

While Stanley's later life was better than the conspicuous failure of his childhood years, Stanley was sentenced to another year in the House of Correction for attempted armed robbery, after the publication of his story in *The Jack-Roller*. Stanley's adult life involved no further criminal convictions, but did involve two periods in a mental hospital, at least in part as a result of conflict with his wife. He escaped twice from the mental hospital. The first time he just walked away. The second time, with a companion, he sawed out a bar from a security unit and made off in a stolen automobile.

In retrospect, it does not seem possible that Stanley could have given up his early pattern of delinquent and criminal behavior for more law-abiding behavior, without the experience of being confined in a security institution as a part of his treatment. In such cases control is an essential part of treatment. It is better when control and compassionate human acceptance can be simultaneous, rather than successive.

THOUGHTS ON TREATMENT

In the controlled environment of a training school it is possible to limit an adolescent to the extent that he poses no threat to anyone, and to use limited release from the severity of such restraints as a motivating force toward a change in behavior. In the absence of opportunity for behavior destructive or disturbing to others, the adolescent is less able to carry on an effective challenge to authority. At the same time, it is important to convey to the adolescent that the controlling individuals are really interested in his welfare. This may be a difficult message to get across under such circumstances, but it has certainly been accomplished many times, usually with quite positive results.

Success of treatment does demand that the treater maintain and extend a friendly acceptance in the face of a hostile attitude and hostile behavior. When under control, the subject is also vulnerable, for inevitably he wants some relief from restrictions. Always some things can be done, short of removing his restrictions, to make them less unpleasant and more bearable. This usually results in a kind of bargaining between treated and treater, in which the treater is in a position to withdraw any privileges that are abused. In the event of bad faith by the treated, the treater can always return him to square one.

A treater who wishes a change in the feelings or in the behavior of the treated can achieve at least some measure of success if he is consistent in his behavior and his values. If he really has the welfare of the delinquent at heart, he should ultimately be able to communicate this. This, in turn, should initiate the next stage, in which treater and treated collaborate to improve the chances and skills of the treated in dealing with life more successfully, while keeping out of trouble.

Since, by definition, the socialized adolescent considers the feelings and the welfare of those in his loyalty group, the group to which he feels he belongs, the problems of controlling his delinquent behavior may resolve into the problems of simply enlarging his loyalty group.

In general, in working with the unsocialized delinquent, real progress toward law-abiding behavior is possible only after the *treated* has made a decision to move in that direction. The treater can encourage that decision, but cannot make it. The problem is beautifully stated by Wiederanders (1988, pp. 209-210).

Project staff were first alerted to the importance of the decisional component by spontaneous remarks made by several youths who had done well on parole. When asked about various programs, events, or persons which we believed might have been important in the change process, these respondents would say something like, "No, that program didn't help me to change at all. *I* decided to change! But after I decided to change, then all of those programs helped. . . .

Perhaps for too long we have assumed that our offender-clients have been passively related to the change process, or that they have been mostly intransigent despite our extreme efforts to change them. A similar oversight has existed in the field of psychotherapy. In a review of the effectiveness of an exhaustive set of therapeutic variations on client improvement, one team of researchers (Smith, Glass, and Miller, 1980) concluded that the process of change, clearly, was set in motion by clients themselves: "What the client brings to psychotherapy—the will to solve a problem or be rid of it . . . the strength to face weakness, the confidence to trust another person—may contribute more to the success of the therapy than whether it lasts twenty hours or ten, whether or not there are other clients in the room" and other treatment variations.

To be successful, the socialization of the unsocialized delinquent *must* be a cooperative venture.

There is a measure of unpredictability about all human behavior. This is what we are talking about when we talk about "free will." It is impossible to predict how any given human being will react behaviorally or emotionally to any given experience. The most we can say about reaction to a specified experience is something like, "Most people would get angry and I would expect this person to get furious," or "Most people would be encouraged, but I do not think that this person would be encouraged."

A part of the skill of treatment is to be sensitive to and recognize when the treated is antagonistic, when he is indifferent, and when he is truly receptive. Limitations, such as confinement, may be necessary to bring about some receptivity, but they can achieve a constructive change in the treated only in combination with empathic human interaction.

Early indications that a delinquent may require treatment in a controlled environment are: gross lack of friends; gross conflict with parents, particularly the mother; and gross rejection or failure in all settings—home, school, jobs, and any social group or religious group or counselor. Any area of success in human relations improves the outlook for success in overcoming delinquent behavior.

REFERENCES

American Psychiatric Association (1968). *Diagnostic and statistical manual of mental disorders,* second edition (DSM-II). Washington, DC: American Psychiatric Association.

Henn, F. A., Bardwell, R., and Jenkins, R. L. (1980). Juvenile delinquents revisited adult criminal acting. *Archives of General Psychiatry, 37,* 1160-1163.

Hewitt, L. E. and Jenkins, R. L. (1946). *Fundamental patterns of maladjustment: The dynamics of their origin.* State of Illinois.

Jenkins, R. L. (1954). *Breaking patterns of defeat: The effective readjustment of the sick personality.* Philadelphia: J. B. Lippincott.

Jenkins, R. L., Heidemann, P. H., and Caputo, J. A. (1985). *No single cause: Juvenile delinquency and the search for effective treatment.* College Park, MD: American Correctional Association.

Jenkins, R. L. and Boyer, A. (1967). Types of delinquent behavior and background factors. *International Journal of Social Psychiatry, 14,* 65-76.

Shaw, C. R. (1930). *The Jack-Roller: A delinquent boy's own story.* Chicago: University of Chicago Press (Reprinted 1960).

Smith, R. L., Glass, G. V., and Miller, T. T. (1980). *The benefits of psychotherapy.* Baltimore: Johns Hopkins University Press.

Snodgrass, J., Geis, G., Short, J. F. Jr., and Kobrin, S. (1982). *The Jack-Roller at seventy: A fifty-year follow-up.* Lexington , MA: Lexington Books.

Wiederanders, M. R. (1988). Increasing the chances for reform among delinquents. In R. L. Jenkins and W. K. Brown (Eds.), *The abandonment of delinquency behavior: Promoting the turnaround.* New York: Praeger.

Chapter 12

Guidelines from Follow-Up Surveys of Adult Subjects Who Were Adjudicated Delinquent as Juveniles

Waln K. Brown, Timothy P. Miller, Richard L. Jenkins, and Warren A. Rhodes

This chapter is based on results obtained during a painstaking, long-term follow-up study of 500 randomly selected juveniles adjudicated delinquent in the juvenile court of Dauphin County, Pennsylvania. These adjudications occurred during the years 1960 to 1975. The study, described elsewhere (Brown and Miller, 1986), was successful in locating 376 out of the 500 cases, and was successful in securing filled-out survey forms from 204 of the original 500.

Extensive comparisons of these 204 participants with the original 500, on a large variety of data, failed to detect any systematic or selective differences, with one minor exception. There was a slight tendency for the subjects in prison to be overrepresented in the survey group. We believe this was because there was no problem in locating those in prison. They received their mail, and they did not lack time to fill out the survey questions, if they chose to do so. We do not believe that this slight tendency disturbed our findings in any significant way.

Among the 204 repondents were 64 who reported no record of arrest, conviction, or incarceration in adult life. This report was confirmed by a lack of any State Police record. We called this group A, our success group. Our failure group, which we called group F, contained 67 individuals. In these cases State Police records indicated arrest(s), conviction(s), including at least one felony conviction, and usually incarceration(s). The contrast of group A and group F provides a convenient and revealing test of the relation of various data to adult criminal prognosis.

The study described in this chapter was made possible through a grant from the Pennsylvania Commission on Crime and Delinquency.

In making our comparisons, we ignore the cases falling in outcome groups B, C, D and E, which are intermediate in their success between groups A and F. Our simple method, expressing group A as a percentage of group A + F, is used in the interest of clarity, and in the belief that it yields a sensitive result. Subgroups with a total of fewer than 20 A + F are omitted from our tables, but may be mentioned in the text.

It is well known that men are more prone to commit crimes than are women. Table 1 reveals the relation of gender to criminal outcome in adult life. Comparing only groups A and F, we find that only 36.6 percent of the males wind up in group A, those without even an arrest, while 90 percent of the females fall in group A. Of the males, 63.3 percent become adult criminals (group F), but only 10 percent of the women fall in group F. This trial, the "test run" of our method, reveals very strikingly the greater proclivity of males, as compared with females, for criminal behavior and consequent criminal conviction.

Table 1
Percent (Frequency) Distribution of Delinquents in A-Success and F-Failure Groups by Gender

	A	F	A+F
Male	36.6% (37)	63.4% (64)	100% (101)
Female	90.0% (27)	10.0% (3)	100% (30)
Total	48.9% (64)	51.1% (67)	100% (131)

THE DELINQUENCY

Having seen in our comparison of males and females that our method is a very sensitive indicator of criminal prognosis in adult life, we will now proceed to its application to other data, beginning with the delinquency itself. Some subjects have more than one referral to the juvenile probation department. It seemed that a useful and effective prognostic sign might be the level of the juvenile's most serious offense. The results are entered in Table 2. We see that, of those subjects adjudicated for only a status offense, 9.1 percent have an adult criminal career. Of those adjudicated for a felony, 68.5 percent have an adult criminal career.

Table 2
Percent (Frequency) Distribution of Delinquents in A-Success and F-Failure Groups by Delinquency

	A	F	A+F
Most severe referral			
Status offenses	90.9% (20)	9.1% (2)	100% (22)
Felony offenses	31.5% (28)	68.5% (61)	100% (89)
Number of referrals			
1	79.1% (34)	20.9% (9)	100% (43)
2	53.3% (16)	46.7% (14)	100% (30)
3	48.0% (12)	52.0% (13)	100% (25)
4 or more	6.1% (2)	93.9% (31)	100% (33)
Total	48.9% (64)	51.1% (67)	100% (131)

Clearly, serious delinquencies in juveniles predict a greater likelihood of criminality in adult life. The entry of misdemeanor-level delinquencies does not appear in the table, because there were only 8 instances in which the most severe delinquency was at the misdemeanor level. Of these 8 cases, only one fell in group F, which gives this misdemeanor group a %A of 87.5 percent. This falls between the status offenses and the felony level offenses. In the next four lines of Table 2, we see that as the number of referrals to juvenile justice increases, the %A diminishes. In our special population, more than two juvenile justice referrals indicates a more than 50 percent likelihood of serious criminal conviction in adult life. Of those with 4 or more referrals, only 6.1 percent avoid adult conviction.

AGE OF DELINQUENT REFERRAL

The younger the age at which a child is first referred to the juvenile justice system, the more serious the prognosis for criminal conviction in adult life. This is disclosed in Table 3. However, most delinquents are not detected, let alone referred, when they commit their first illegal act. Question 24 of our survey asks the respondent, "About how old were you when you *committed* your *first* illegal act?" The next two lines of Table 3 are based on the self-reports of respondents. Our divisions are age 12 or younger, compared with age 13 or older. The earlier the age at which delinquent acts begin, the worse the prognosis appears to be for serious criminal conviction in adult life. It is of interest that of 11 respondents who placed their first illegal act before 10 years of age, only 2 fell in group A, giving this group a %A of only 18.2 percent. We have shown

Table 3
Percent (Frequency) Distribution of Delinquents in A-Success and F-Failure Groups by Age at Initial Referral

	A	F	A+F
Age at initial referral			
12 and under	41.2% (14)	58.8% (20)	100% (34)
13 - 15	49.2% (32)	50.8% (33)	100% (65)
16 and over	56.3% (18)	43.8% (14)	100% (32)
Total	48.9% (64)	51.1% (67)	100% (131)
Age at first illegal act (self-report)			
12 or under	31.3% (15)	68.8% (33)	100% (48)
13 - 17	59.7% (40)	40.3% (27)	100% (67)

earlier that the greater the time lapse between detection of a delinquent act and juvenile court action, the greater the likelihood of criminal conviction in adult life (Brown et al., 1989).

THE DELINQUENT

We now turn to the delinquents themselves. Table 4 reveals that non-whites are overrepresented in adult criminal outcome. These findings are consistent with what one can observe throughout this country—that is, relative to the population, non-whites are generally overrepresented in jails, prisons, and the penal system. Non-whites (in this case almost entirely blacks) are overrepresented not only in those delinquents who go on to adult criminal behavior, but also in our original randomly selected group of delinquents. The one statement we can confidently make on this subject is that this overrepresentation in the population of delinquent juveniles is not due to any tendency of Dauphin County juvenile authorities to deal with non-white juveniles more severely than with white juveniles. In fact, the reverse appears to be true. Non-white juveniles are treated as younger children, and are less likely to be taken to juvenile court than are white juveniles of the same age. This is to the disadvantage of non-white juveniles, for those taken to court sooner do better in avoiding conviction in adult life than those for whom juvenile court action is delayed.

The next two lines of Table 4 reveal that those with an IQ of 91 or above do better in avoiding criminal conviction in adult life than those with an IQ of 90 or below. This is in accord with other studies. Table 4 also reveals that those juveniles whose parents were married did better in avoiding crime in adult life than those whose parents were not married. It is of interest that those who married but separated and/or divorced rank with the married, not with the never-married. The last two lines of Table 4 reveal that those in our group of adjudicated delinquents who grew up in a home shared with 1-3 other children did better in avoiding adult conviction than those who had to share their home with 4 or more other children. We ascribe this to a dilution of parental attention in larger families.

SCHOOL SUCCESS

Three elements relating to the subject's schooling now follow in Table 5: cases involving the entries suspended or expelled, failed one grade, and truant or chronically absent. All have less success in avoiding adult conviction than cases without such entries.

Table 4
Percent (Frequency) Distribution of Delinquents in A-Success and F-Failure Groups by Demographic Characteristics

	A	F	A+F
Race			
White	59.2% (42)	40.8% (29)	100% (71)
Non-white	36.7% (22)	63.3% (38)	100% (60)
Total	48.9% (64)	51.1% (67)	100% (131)
IQ (in record)			
90 or below	34.0% (17)	66.0% (33)	100% (50)
91 or above	47.1% (24)	52.9% (27)	100% (51)
Parents' marital status			
Married	51.6% (32)	48.4% (30)	100% (62)
Separated/Divorced	53.8% (21)	46.2% (18)	100% (39)
Never married	33.3% (7)	66.7% (14)	100% (21)
Number of other children living at home			
1 - 3	52.1% (38)	47.9% (35)	100% (73)
4 or more	42.9% (21)	57.1% (28)	100% (49)

REASON FOR CLOSING

Data in the first two lines in Table 6 did not become available on all subjects until they became adult. It is impressive that of the 50 juveniles whose cases were closed as not needing further supervision, 76 percent fell into success group A. Of the group for whom supervision was lifted because they reached adult age, only 34.3 percent avoided conviction.

THE ADULT

Table 7 presents data recorded on the status of our subjects at follow-up when they were adults. The first two lines in Table 7 reveal a strong

Table 5
Percent (Frequency) Distribution of Delinquents in A-Success and F-Failure Groups by School Success

	A	F	A+F
Suspended or expelled	32.6% (15)	67.4% (31)	100% (46)
Not suspended or expelled	57.6% (49)	42.4% (36)	100% (85)
Failed one grade	37.3% (19)	62.7% (32)	100% (51)
Never failed	56.3% (45)	43.8% (35)	100% (80)
Truant/ chronically absent	43.1% (28)	56.9% (37)	100% (65)
Not truant	54.5% (36)	45.5% (30)	100% (66)

Table 6
Percent (Frequency) Distribution of Delinquents in A-Success and F-Failure Groups by Reason for Final Termination of Supervision

	A	F	A+F
No further need	76.0% (38)	24.0% (12)	100% (50)
Became adult	34.3% (24)	65.7% (46)	100% (70)

relation between employment and success in avoiding adult conviction. The next lines also emphasize the value of stable employment. Table 7 next reveals the relation between successful marriage and avoidance of criminal conviction. In this comparison, unsuccessful marriage (separation/divorce) makes a showing slightly worse than the single state. Finally, the table reveals the strong relationship between home ownership and the avoidance of criminal conviction.

Table 7
Percent (Frequency) Distribution of Delinquents in A-Success and F-Failure Groups by Adult Functioning

	A	F	A+F
Employment			
Work for employer	61.0% (47)	39.0% (30)	100% (77)
Unemployed	27.8% (10)	72.2% (26)	100% (36)
Tenure with current employer			
Less than 4 years	43.6% (17)	56.4% (22)	100% (39)
5 years or more	78.9% (30)	21.1% (8)	100% (38)
Marital status			
Married	70.5% (31)	29.5% (13)	100% (44)
Separated/Divorced	34.8% (8)	65.2% (15)	100% (23)
Single	37.7% (23)	62.3% (38)	100% (61)
Home ownership			
Rent	49.3% (34)	50.7% (35)	100% (69)
Own	82.1% (23)	17.9% (5)	100% (28)

DISPOSITION

Evidence presented elsewhere showed that those juveniles who are brought to the juvenile court early do substantially better in avoiding criminal conviction in adult life than those for whom court action is delayed (Brown et al., 1989). Table 8 reveals that in those juvenile court cases that, on initial disposition, are simply closed with a warning, it is unlikely that the juvenile will avoid a criminal conviction in adult life. This is impressive, since we would expect that only the most favorable cases would be closed with only a warning. Apparently, such a warning is not likely to be taken seriously, even though it is usually given in the

Table 8
Percent (Frequency) Distribution of Delinquents in A-Success and F-Failure Groups by Initial Juvenile Court Disposition

	A	F	A+F
Type of disposition			
Warned and closed	20.0% (4)	80.0% (16)	100% (20)
Informal adjustment	44.4% (16)	55.6% (20)	100% (36)
Formal probation	79.1% (34)	20.9% (9)	100% (43)
Duration of disposition			
0 - 6 months	39.7% (23)	60.3% (35)	100% (58)
7 - 12 months	39.4% (13)	60.6% (20)	100% (33)
13 months or longer	70.0% (28)	30.0% (12)	100% (40)

presence of one or both parents. The best results on initial disposition are obtained by formal probation, with informal adjustment falling somewhere between these two. The final portion of Table 8 discloses that cases in which the initial disposition lasts 13 months or longer do better than those whose initial disposition lasts only 12 months or less. This is another indication that the first delinquent referral should be taken seriously by the juvenile court.

SUMMARY

The following items summarize the findings of our study of 500 randomly selected adjudicated juvenile delinquents in Dauphin County, Pennsylvania.

1. The delinquents whose most severe delinquent act was a status offense offer a more favorable prognosis for avoiding adult criminal conviction than those who commit felony-level delinquencies.

2. As the number of referrals to juvenile justice increases, the prognosis worsens.
3. The younger the age at which a juvenile begins illegal acts, the worse the prognosis for crime in adult life.
4. The prognosis is better for whites than for non-whites.
5. The prognosis is better for those with IQs in the average range or above than for those below the average range.
6. The prognosis is better for those whose parents married than for those whose parents did not marry.
7. The prognosis is somewhat better for those from households with 1-3 other children than for those from households of 4 or more other children.
8. Cases with the entries suspended or expelled from school, failed one grade, or truant or chronically absent do less well than cases without these entries. School success is important in avoiding adult criminal conviction.
9. The prognosis is better in those cases in which juvenile supervision is terminated because there is no more need for it, than in those cases in which it is terminated because the subject becomes an adult.
10. In the juvenile followed into adult life, employment, and in particular stable employment, are strong favorable prognostic signs.
11. Successful marriage (no divorce, no separation) is a strong positive sign.
12. Those for whom formal probation was the initial juvenile court disposition have a high degree of success (79.1 percent) compared to those cases closed with a warning. Apparently, the warning is not usually taken seriously (only 20 percent success).
13. Dispositions of 13 or more months' duration are much more effective in reducing adult criminal conviction than are dispositions of shorter duration.

We find nothing that would support a policy of "radical nonintervention" (Schur, 1973), but very clear indication that adjudication and formal probation on the first referral to the juvenile probation department result in a substantial reduction in criminal convictions in adult life.

REFERENCES

Brown, W. K. and Miller, T. P. (1986). Post-intervention outcomes of previously adjudicated delinquents: An overview. *A Report to the Pennsylvania Commission on Crime and Delinquency,* June 13.

Brown, W. K., Miller, T. P., Jenkins, R. L., and Rhodes, W. A. (1989). The effect of early juvenile court adjudication on adult outcome. *International Journal of Offender Therapy and Comparative Criminology, 13,* 177-183.

Schur, E. M. (1973). *Radical nonintervention: Rethinking the delinquency problem.* Englewood Cliffs, NJ: Prentice-Hall.

Chapter 13

Resisting the Powers of Religious Cults

Lita Linzer-Schwartz

Everyone experiences stress at some point in life, and, under certain conditions or in particular situations, is more vulnerable to outside influences than is normally true for them. Late adolescence and young adulthood are stages in which many changes are occurring as part of development and in which, therefore, vulnerability under stress may increase. Those most vulnerable to peer pressures, cult recruiters, and missionaries are not necessarily neurotic or from dysfunctional families. Rather, these young people find themselves in situations where they perceive themselves as being especially lonely, or are insecure or depressed and, therefore, may be vulnerable to the blandishments of another person or group.

For example, imagine yourself once again a bright, idealistic, 18 year old, newly arrived at a college campus. You're on your own for the first time in your life, a few hundred miles from home, ready and willing—though a trifle scared—to begin an exciting new phase in your life. Your roommate and the others on your floor seem nice enough, but you haven't really become friends yet. You have many questions, but the line to see the counselor is so long that you've given up waiting.

Walking back to the dorm, another student approaches you asking "Can I help you? You look a bit confused." This friendly overture leads to a conversation in which you share some of your hopes and ideals, as well as your questions, and ultimately to an invitation to join your new friend for dinner and a social evening. It seems that this new friend is part of a group working to help the homeless in the college town, certainly a worthy cause in which you're more than willing to become involved.

The scenario above may be "legitimate," or it may be the preliminary recruiting stage for one of the 2,000-3,000 cults functioning in the United States and abroad. And "you," the idealistic young college freshman, may be contributing to easing life for the less fortunate, or may be confronting a fork in the road that can lead either to a life-style that can become a nightmare for you and your family or to a reinforcement of the wisdom of listening to your own "inner ear." The route to deciding which fork in the road to follow begins in early childhood.

"Idealistic young adults" are focused on here because they have been the population most frequently attracted by the recruiters' messages of "good works" in which a particular cult movement participates. However, there is an equal need to avert vulnerability to satanic cults, which seem to be increasing in number and activity across the country. These groups exert strong "pulls," similar to those of religious-type cults, mostly in terms of peer pressure on young adolescents. Again, preventive measures taken by parents in the child's early years can increase invulnerability to these appeals.

The time to ward off vulnerability to cults—whether religious, satanic, political, or other—is in the early years. Just as parents make sure that their children are inoculated against measles and polio, or warn their preschoolers not to get into cars with strangers, so they must begin in toddlerhood to build those strengths that will enable even the most idealistic young adult to avoid entanglement in cult movements. But from what do these emotional "inoculations" save the young person?

Investigations of several researchers suggest that individuals who become cult members are confronted with a variety of problems both within the group and after leaving it. Within the group, they are typically pressed to conform totally to the ideology of the movement and the pronouncements of its leaders—i.e., to relinquish independent thought and judgment; to regard nonmembers, including their own families, as hostile figures; to subsist, in the case of communal living cults, on less-than-nutritious diets and little rest; to work devotedly for the group in fundraising and/or membership recruiting, often at below-minimum or no pay; and, varying with the group, to drop out of college or the work force in order to meet the expectations/demands of the group. At the extreme, cult members may engage in self-destructive behaviors at the direction of their leader, as was the case with the People's Temple (in Jonestown, Guyana).

Those who leave the cults on their own initiative, or after family members succeed in isolating them from the cult in order to have them "deprogrammed," often experience guilt, both for the grief they caused their families and for the friends they left in the group; thought diffusion, in which they are unable to focus their thinking on the task at hand; awkwardness in explaining the time period of cult membership when completing employment applications; physical ill-health from the poor diet and lack of sleep, although this is generally remediable; and some experience visual or auditory hallucinations that are both upsetting to them and that interfere with their daily functioning (Isser and Schwartz, 1988; Levine, 1984; Singer, 1979).

In keeping with the theme of this book, this chapter will discuss the nature of individual strengths and the techniques by which they can be developed. Information on the characteristics of these strengths will be drawn from professional literature on child development, locus of control, resiliency, and stress theories; from research on cult movements and their recruiting (as well as membership-maintaining) techniques; and from research with former cult members and those who were approached but resisted the call of the recruiter.

Most of the research on stress and vulnerability/invulnerability in humans looks to conditions of socioeconomic or cultural deprivation, to situations conducive to severe physical illness or psychological trauma, or to the unusual or abnormal family, and then seeks to discover why one child matures to healthy adulthood and another falls to the ground or turns to crime. When investigating invulnerability to cult recruiting, however, we are examining a largely middle-class population with intact families. The stresses with which these young people are confronted are usually not catastrophic, although they may be perceived as being traumatic at the time.

Anthony (1987, pp. 27-28) has proposed a "continuum of susceptibility" as well as a paradigm of vulnerability × stress interaction that can serve as background for this discussion. The model results in four categories:

> First, there are the hypervulnerables, who succumb to even "ordinary" and expectable life stresses. Second, there are the pseudoinvulnerables, who are vulnerable or extremely vulnerable individuals who have been "blessed" with an overprotective environment (particularly the material portion of it), and are relatively unchallenged and thriving until the environment fails, and they fail along with it. Third, there are the invulnerables with acquired resilience, who are exposed to cumulative traumas, but "bounce back" after each stress that they experience; with each successful rebound, they become increasingly resilient. Finally, there are the nonvulnerables, who seem robust from birth onward and continue to thrive and prosper within any "average expectable environment."

The goal of the discussion here is to identify means by which those in the first two categories might become members of the third category.

REVIEW OF THE LITERATURE

Cults and Cult-like Groups

The counterculture cults that flourished in the 1960s, and that have continued to recruit new members, seek young people, usually, who are reasonably intelligent, affluent, idealistic, and dependent upon or desirous of the approval of others (Isser and Schwartz, 1988). Intelligence is a requisite so that the new member can ultimately represent the group effectively and possibly become a member of its hierarchy. Affluence is necessary, for the group needs money, and one of the ways in which the new member proves "devotion" is to contribute all of his or her assets plus whatever the individual can persuade parents to contribute.

Idealism is often the "hood" by which the individual is attracted, for typically these are people who are "seekers." They are either looking for "something" in which to believe, for they may have been alienated from traditional religion, or for a "good cause" for which they can work. Finally, as Maslow (1968) taught, a sense of belonging and of being accepted is second only to survival needs in the hierarchy of motivation. Part of the cults' indoctrination technique is to overwhelm the recruit with acceptance and approval—"love-bombing" as it is known. This is continued throughout the membership period, as approval is contingent upon the individual's group-sanctioned behavior without deviation or question.

For the older adolescent or young adult, the precipitating factor in his or her vulnerability may be separation from the familiar, as in the opening example, or a broken romance, or an episode of academic failure. The recruiter is, in effect, saying that the individual is "worthy" of approval despite lack of knowledge or rejection by someone else. Thus the need for being accepted, for belonging, is met within the new group.

> In those few studies in which former cult members have been asked why they were attracted by recruiters' appeals, they reveal that idealism, the offer of a sense of purpose and commitment, and the opportunity to avoid feelings of loneliness were the dominant attractions. The religious ideology was not the primary factor, for indeed recruits were often unaware of the religious focus of the group in which they became enmeshed until a later time (Isser and Schwartz, 1988, p. 119).

It is well-known that a charismatic figure or a persuasive speaker can easily acquire followers and supporters. It is also accepted that not everyone who hears the "siren" call follows it. Even the "loners" may not be "willing to surrender their family ties and personal goals for a vague social cause, promised paradise, or a new religion" (Schwartz and Kaslow, 1982, p. 12). Why not? What characteristics does the "resister" have that the vulnerable "recruit" doesn't have?

For the younger adolescent who is drawn into satanic cults, peer acceptance is extremely important as part of his development. If not acceptable to "healthier" groups because he lacks some desirable form of competence, he may readily succumb to the appeal of an asocial group where different skills are approved.

Research Findings

There were several studies of cult members in the 1970s, all of which sought an answer to the question of differences between those vulnerable to cult recruiters and those who were apparently invulnerable. Looking back, one can see that many parents in those years were different about imposing their values on their children; that society was in flux with a strong strain of moral "relativism"; and that there were many diverse role models available, with little guidance for young people as to which might be most appropriate for a particular individual. Disputes over our involvement in Vietnam, political scandals in the Nixon administration, and multiple racial/ethnic/gender cries for recognition and rights abounded.

The result of many instances of conflict between the idealistic view of what society *should be* and the realities of what society *was,* and, closer to home, the hypocritical mouthings of parents that were at variance with their behaviors, caused resentment and disillusionment among young people. In some cases, for example, parents supported the civil rights movement in principle, but joined neighbors in opposing the sale of a nearby property to someone of a different race or religion.

The identity-seeking behavior of the adolescent, so well delineated by Erikson (1950, 1956), often led to identity diffusion instead. Without clear direction and models, the youth's difficulty in integrating his or her identity often was seen as the result of "a combination of experiences that demand his simultaneous commitment to physical intimacy (not by any means always overtly sexual), to decisive occupational choice, to energetic competition, and to psychosocial self-definition" (Erikson, 1956, p. 79). These factors combined to make many young people feel as if they were drowning in a sea of diffusion, and to welcome the certainties proposed by a cult recruiter as a lifeline thrown to save them. Levine and Slater (1976, pp. 413, 415), in a study of 106 cultists in nine cults, for example, found that 43 of their subjects had "joined" a cult because "life had no meaning, they were drifting," and the cults supplied "answers to identity-related and to existential questions plaguing the members."

In studies of alienated youth in the 1960s and 1970s, the Committee on Adolescence of the Group for the Advancement of Psychiatry (1978, p. 174) found that many parents, unsure of their own authority, often treated their teenagers as much younger children, giving them little opportunity to learn responsibility for decisionmaking. They concluded that "lacking experience with appropriate levels of shared responsibility, these youths are inadequately prepared to assume appropriate ranges of authority." Other parents resorted to dictatorial pronouncements to their adolescents, an equally inappropriate approach to preparing the youth for adulthood, or even for dealing with identity problems, peer relations, and decisionmaking.

In contrast to overprotective or dictatorial parents, but in keeping with the absence of clear value systems and role models, many of those who joined cults were found to have either weak or nonexistent relations with their fathers. This contributed to their ready acceptance of the strong father figure represented by the cult leader (Isser and Schwartz, 1988; Salzman, 1966; Schwartz and Kaslow, 1979; Spero, 1977). Note that these were not *physically* absent fathers; they were emotionally or morally absent. In Schwartz's (1983) study of 40 ex-cultists, for example, 75 percent of the respondents said that the most attractive aspect of their cult group for them was the feeling of closeness and belonging they gained, and 70 percent indicated that the cult gave them a sense of purpose that had been absent from their family life. Only one of the subjects came from a fatherless home, and that was because his father had died. The need among these subjects was for an *authoritative,* not authoritarian, father figure.

It is interesting to note a parallel in studies of parental discipline and children's anxiety in stressful situations (hospitalization for surgery, in this case). Zabin and Melamed (1980) found that modeling and reassurance helped to lower anxiety levels, but the correlation was stronger when fathers used these techniques than when mothers did. They commented that the stronger influence of the fathers might be related to the relative rarity of such paternal behavior.

By contrast, those who were invulnerable to the recruiters not only had a strong relationship with their fathers—either positive or negative—but also were self-directed. Their internal locus of control allowed them to say, in effect, "No one is going to tell me how to run my life except me." Even if they were "loners," disenchanted with their peers' antics, perhaps opposed to their parents' values, and maybe even a little low in self-esteem, they had developed enough coping strategies and resilience to have inner direction and the sense to listen to an "inner ear." They were not about to follow others blindly, like sheep (Schwartz, 1979).

FAMILY RELATIONSHIPS

"Developing effective early preventive models to short-circuit negative spirals in . . . youngsters before stressors of marked gravity permanently impair their lives can punctuate vividly the potential of a proactive health-building model for mental health" (Cowen and Work, 1988, p. 603), and for invulnerability to cults.

There are many kinds of families today—the traditional nuclear form, single-parent, step, foster, and so on—and, increasingly, they lack the support of the extended family in close proximity. The oldest generation may have moved to the Sun Belt, parents may have moved across the country from their hometowns because of careers, and aunts and uncles may well be scattered and involved with their own lives. This makes it more imperative than ever that the parents (biological, adoptive, foster, step) with whom children live provide consistent values, standards, and behaviors as guidelines for the children's own development.

Children, especially adolescents, may rebel against some of these guidelines, but the essential element is that there is something concrete to rebel against. Those cult recruits referred to earlier as being vulnerable because of absent or weak relationships with their fathers had no belief systems against which they fought; the value systems were frequently amorphous. The cults' systems and standards were therefore the more attractive because the young people knew what was expected of them. Thus, providing guidelines and behaviors consistent with them is an important factor in strengthening the youth's invulnerability to cult recruiting. As Hetherington (1989, p. 10) suggested in another context, "under stress, children gained security in a structured, safe, predictable environment." The key word would seem to be "structured," for neither family life nor the environment in which we live appears to be either "safe" or "predictable" in the early 1990s.

In a study of young adolescents aged 11-13 years, Krampen (1989) had the youths and their mothers complete a questionnaire involving child-rearing practices on two occasions, separated by a 10-month interval. He concluded that "emotional warmth and contingent reinforcement of positive behavior of the child was a developmental condition of children's internality in locus of control" (p. 187). On the other hand, "material reinforcement and noncontingent, demonstrative public praise of the child's achievement . . . [as well as] limited praise with reference to social comparisons of the child's behaviors and achievements" (pp. 187, 190) contributed to a more external locus of control. A more internal locus tends to be related positively to invulnerability as noted earlier.

Conversely, parents need to be alert to the effects of the too-frequent pattern of scolding children, or telling them that they're "stupid" or "clumsy," or "hopelessly wild"—the psychological abuse that lowers a child's self-esteem, increases feelings of anxiety, and contributes to vulnerability. Instead, as they teach children to cope, to "bounce back," to decide, they also need to teach them to "reach" a little higher each time they set a goal. As Vygotsky (1978) suggested, this use of additional clues helps them to solve problems that might otherwise overwhelm them.

Familial warmth, mutual honest communication, and respect for individual preferences within the family also strengthen the children's invulnerability. Satisfaction of the need for a sense of belonging, acceptance, and approval within the family will do much to avert the lure of peers or cult recruiters to satanic or other cultic groups.

COPING, RESILIENCE, AND LOCUS OF CONTROL

Coping Skills

Synonyms for "cope" include "handle," "deal with," "adapt to," "control," "manage," "weather," and "accomplish." These all imply some kind of difficult situation to which the individual must respond in an atypical way. That is, the usual responses do not apply, so different solutions must be sought. Can young children be taught how to cope?

What is being asked of the child in coping is the ability to perceive alternatives, to weigh them as to possible consequences, and then to choose one that has a high probability of resolving the problem. In Piagetian theory, it would seem unlikely that a preadolescent could do such abstract, and sometimes creative, thinking (Piaget, 1952). Yet, one can observe even toddlers at play pausing to consider which block should be placed next, which "tool" will help construct a sand castle, or which route to ride on a tricycle. Some children are more adept earlier than others at this kind of thinking, but most can be given opportunities to learn how to reason out answers to problems. The need is for them to develop a "sense of automony" in early childhood as preparation for initiative, industry, and identity integration as postulated by Erikson (1950), all of which contribute to reduced vulnerability in later years.

Creativity, like vulnerability/invulnerability, is on a continuum, and can be demonstrated by young children. Sometimes, in their naivete, they even suggest solutions that astonish their parents because of simplicity yet novelty. Creativity, combined with the ability to think about alternatives, increases the child's ability to cope with a large variety of problem situations.

Coping can be learned. Whether a "real" situation arises, or the parent/caretaker says "Let's pretend that . . . ," the youngster can work out a solution under supervision. *Example:* Perhaps the door has slammed, with the toddler on a porch and the adult inside. The toddler can stand there and cry, or figure out another way to capture the adult's attention. He might pull a chair over to a window, climb up on it, and bang on the window. *Example:* The child approaches a jungle gym in the playground that has several ways in which it can be climbed. She can be asked which approach she thinks might be easiest and why, or which route she'd take to reach the top most quickly. Given a variety of such experiences and opportunities, the child will be better prepared to think, rather than act impulsively, when confronted with a problem.

Resilience

Similarly, when things go awry and the child is confronted with disappointment, adults can help to build resiliency by encouraging the child to meet disappointment with a "shift in gears" rather than tears, anger, or sadness. Resilience is the ability to "bounce back," to recover from negative events with a degree of aplomb and possibly even a new and better plan. Garmezy (1980), a pioneer in studies of invulnerability, drew upon a quote attributed to Robert Louis Stevenson in discussing this trait: "Life is not a matter of holding good cards but of playing a poor hand well."

Whether we are dealing with a child who struck out in the Little League game or one whose day at the zoo has been washed out by heavy rain, there is a need to help the youngster recognize that this is not "the end of the world." The first child can be asked whether she learned anything about the pitcher's style that would help her at the next "at bat," and the second one might have an indoor visit with the animals at a museum of natural science or via videotape (complete with peanuts for the human rather than the animals).

The resilient personality, according to Flach (1988), has a strong yet supple sense of self-esteem, recognizes and develops his or her abilities, displays independence in thought and action, is open-minded, is willing to dream, and has a high tolerance for distress. This gives the resilient individual a sense of direction or focus, a commitment to life, and a framework within which personal experiences can be perceived and interpreted with meaning and hope, even when everything in one's life seems to be falling apart and hopeless.

It may be easier to teach resilience to the school-age child whose focus is on competence and effort (Erikson, 1950) rather than a young child, but a start can be made in recreational activities, as above, and then shifted to academic and social areas in the elementary school years. Even academically bright children have days when their test performance is not up to their usual standard, and, although they're entitled to be disappointed, they should be taught not to devalue their self-esteem as a result. Knowing that they really are capable, competent, loved, "good," and supported in their efforts, even when they fall short of the goal, gives people the positive sense of self-esteem that enables them to be resilient.

On the other hand, parental expectations of perfection may increase the youngster's fear of failure, leading to anxiety about his or her status in the event of imperfect performance, which, in turn, often leads to lower grades. If a parent responds negatively on such occasions, the child may seek acceptance elsewhere or withdraw into the world of fantasy, rather than develop motivation and resilience.

Locus of Control

Some people see themselves only in terms of others' perceptions of them; other people see themselves through looking inward. The first group tends to seek direction as well as approval from external sources; the second group tends to be more self-directed. Those in the first group are said to have an *external* locus of control; those in the second group have an *internal* locus of control. Krampen (1989) also has a third category called "chance control," which he says is a "fatalistic expectancy." This is, to my mind, closer to the external locus of control than the internal. It is likely that the second group will have better coping skills and resiliency than the first group. Indeed, coping skills and resiliency can help the individual to develop an internal locus of control.

One of the elements of an internal locus of control is decisionmaking. Parents can begin teaching their children quite early how to make *and live with* their own decisions by asking even toddlers to choose which of two T-shirts they prefer to wear each morning. If the child decides to wear an orange striped shirt with red plaid pants today, it's not an earth-shaking matter; tomorrow, the child may choose a solid white shirt to wear with the plaid pants. The important thing is to let the child express an opinion without being negatively criticized or berated. There will be thousands of choices to be made as the child grows up, and the more experience (within rational limits) that the child has with making decisions even on small matters, the more secure he or she will be when confronted with more critical decisions to make.

In an address summarizing locus of control research, Strickland stressed the relationship between locus of control and mental health, immunology, creativity, and even political activist behaviors (see Fisher, 1988). In future research, she anticipated, "psychology will doubtless continue to seek explanations for how cognitive strategies and self-schemas, or mental representations of one's mind, help people respond effectively to life events and disrupt dysfunctional behavior patterns" (Fisher, 1988, p. 14). It is the development of these strategies and self-schemas to which families and others must attend, from the child's early years, if invulnerability is to be strengthened.

Looking once again at the college freshman "at sea" on a campus, how much easier a negative response to a cult recruiter's invitation might be if this young adult had been prepared in earlier years. Reared in a family that provided warmth, acceptance, approval, and consistency in its value system, the freshman would have had basic psychosocial as well as survival needs met. A strong relationship with a father-figure, be it positive (preferably) or negative, would have obviated the need to seek such an authoritative person elsewhere. Learning opportunities, even in the preschool years, would have developed strategies for coping, decisionmaking, resiliency, and independent goal-setting.

CONCLUDING COMMENTS

As one looks at the life cycle, it is evident that coping skills and resiliency are needed at all ages. Even the elderly, often separated by hundreds of miles from their children and grandchildren, become lonely and have been prey for cult recruiters who flatter and attend to them for financial gain. While it may be difficult to avert such vulnerability in the aged, it is not as difficult with the young. The strengths discussed in these pages must be developed throughout the early stages of the life cycle to yield adolescents and young adults who are not only invulnerable to cult recruiters and others who would take advantage of them, but who are also capable of confronting life's stresses with the means to deal with them effectively.

REFERENCES

Anthony, E. J. (1987). Risk, vulnerability, and resilience: An overview. In E. J. Anthony and B. J. Cohler (Eds.), *The invulnerable child* (pp. 3-48). New York: Guilford Press.

Cowen, E. L. and Work, W. C. (1988). Resilient children, psychological wellness, and primary prevention. *American Journal of Community Psychology, 16,* 591-607.

Erikson, E. H. (1950). *Childhood and society.* New York: W. W. Norton.

______. (1956). The problem of ego identity. *American Psychoanalytic Journal, 4,* 56-121.

Fisher, K. (1988, October). Locus of control theory from formula to future. *APA Monitor,* pp. 14-15.

Flach, F. (1988). *Resilience: Discovering a new strength at times of stress.* New York: Fawcett Columbine.

Garmezy, N. (1980). Children under stress: Perspectives or antecedents and correlates of vulnerability and resistance to psychopathology. In A. Robin, J. Arnoff, A. Barclay, and R. Zucker (Eds.), *Further explorations in personality.* New York: Wiley.

Group for the Advancement of Psychiatry (Committee on Adolescence). (1978). *Power and authority in adolescence: The origins and resolution of intergenerational conflict* (GAP Report #101). New York: Author.

Hetherington, E. M. (1989). Coping with family transitions: Winners, losers, and survivors. *Child Development, 60,* 1-14.

Isser, N. and Schwartz, L. L. (1988). *The history of conversion and contemporary cults.* New York: Peter Lang.

Krampen, G. (1989). Perceived childrearing practices and the development of locus of control in early adolescence. *International Journal of Behavioral Development, 12* (2), 177-193.

Levine, S. V. (1984). *Radical departures: Desperate detours to growing up.* Chicago: University of Chicago Press.

Levine, S. V. and Slater, N. E. (1976). Youth and contemporary religious movements: Psychosocial findings. *Canadian Psychiatric Association Journal, 21,* 411-420.

Maslow, A. (1968). *Toward a psychology of being,* 2nd ed. New York: Van Nostrand.

Piaget, J. (1952). *The origins of intelligence in children.* New York: International Universities Press.

Salzman, L. (1966). Types of religious conversion. *Pastoral Psychology, 17,* 8-20, 66.

Schwartz, L. L. (1979), July). Cults: The vulnerability of sheep. *USA Today, 108,* 22-24.

______. (1983). Family therapy and families of cult members. *International Journal of Family Therapy, 5*(3), 168-178.

Schwartz, L. L. and Kaslow, F. W. (1979). Religious cults, the individual, and the family. *Journal of Marital and Family Therapy, 5,* 15-26.

______. (1982). The cult phenomenon: Historical, sociological, and familial factors contributing to their development and appeal. *Marriage and Family Review, 4* (3/4), 3-30.

Singer, M. T. (1979). Coming out of the cults. *Psychology Today, 12*(8), 72-82.

Spero, M. H. (1977). Cults: Some theoretical and practical perspectives. *Journal of Jewish Communal Service, 54,* 330-338.

Vygotsky, L. S. (1978). *Mind in society.* Cambridge, MA: Harvard University Press.

Zabin, M. A. and Melamed, B. G. (1980). Relationship between parental discipline and children's ability to cope with stress. *Journal of Behavioral Assessment, 2*(1), 17-38.

Chapter 14

Factors That Promote Invulnerability and Resiliency in At-Risk Children

***Waln K. Brown and
Warren A. Rhodes***

That some children succeed despite the odds is undeniable. The authors of the chapters included in this volume have supported this fact by outlining what the research literature has discovered in their particular areas of inquiry. They point to the interrelationship of three primary factors: family experiences, personal characteristics, and environmental circumstances. These factors heavily influence whether a youth will overcome—or be overcome by—the stressors that have put him or her at risk.

Family experiences play a major role in child development. This is true in regard both to causing stressful events and helping children cope successfully with them. The events that happen within the family can pose difficult problems for children; however, the character strengths learned from family members (most specifically, parents and other primary caregivers) can help determine how children adapt to, and consequently deal with, their difficulties. Furthermore, the support provided by family members—or lack thereof—can profoundly affect success or failure.

Personal characteristics include innate and acquired abilities and circumstances. Such factors as age, gender, intelligence, personality, special needs, individual strengths and weaknesses help determine the relative "vulnerability" of children to specific types of crisis situations. The interplay of these personal characteristics greatly influences how individual children adapt to different situations. In other words, the personal characteristics of some children make them better equipped to cope with and surmount certain events that for other children may prove devastating.

Environmental circumstances encompass events external to the child's nuclear family and his or her personal makeup. They include relationships with extended family members, friends, peers, teachers, coaches, clergy, and others. Also included are events that happen outside the home, such as school experiences, extracurricular activities, social pressures, and professional intervention. The potentially diverse influences of environmental circumstances can work in concert or individually to either promote or hinder resiliency.

Although the chapters contained in this volume cover different topics, each describes important findings about why some children succeed despite the odds. In many cases, regardless of the topic under discussion, there is collaboration about which factors help to "insulate" children from potentially dire consequences. A review of these findings may provide a clearer perspective of what factors promote resilience in at-risk youth.

Certainly, family experiences play a paramount role in how children handle life's adversities. Children with the good fortune to experience two-parent homes in which there are stable relationships, solid communications, appropriate role-models, consistent expectations, and support have an ideal foundation upon which to build their lives. These and other positive family experiences help protect children from succumbing to hardship.

But what happens to these children when the family experience is suddenly or dramatically altered? Or, for that matter, what happens to those children who have not had the advantage of the ideal family experience? Several chapters in this volume have addressed these issues.

Robson points out that children of divorce tend to cope well when they live with the parent of the same sex, when they maintain frequent and positive contact with both parents, or, if this is not possible, when they can develop a positive relationship with one parent.

Fine and Schwebel note the difference between white and black single-parent families. While white single-parent families are generally the result of marital conflict and divorce, black single-parent families usually occur because many black mothers never get married. Since single-parent families are the norm within the black community, extended family relationships and kinship support systems are often available to help children cope.

Coleman and Ganong cite the advantages of the stepfamily over the single-parent family. The added income, role-modeling, support, and supervision that are often provided by having two adult or parent figures in the home can make a positive contribution to a child's sense of stability. The authors are quick to note, however, that young children tend to make the most positive adaptation to the stepfamily situation.

For those children who do not have the advantage of living with at least one biological parent, and who are often moved from one setting to another, the potential to experience myriad difficulties is high. Fein and Maluccio discuss the many problems that can result from foster family care. These authors recognize the importance for children in foster family placement to be supported by policies and practices that enhance the child's sense of security, stability, and permanency within the foster family.

The support of family members is a crucial determinant of how children adapt in times of crisis. Rosen's look at children who lose a sibling shows how important it is that family members communicate among themselves to ease their grief and deal with their confused feelings. Sharing grief with family members can help children understand and cope with the loss.

The importance of support both inside and outside of the family is reviewed by Stevenson and Rhodes with regard to teenagers who avoid pregnancy. A strong relationship with a family member or friend plays a significant role in the female teenager's decision about sex and pregnancy. Other factors associated with a lowered risk of teenage pregnancy include church attendance, early sex education, and sex education that takes place both at home and at school.

Some children are born with or acquire emotional or behavioral problems early in life. Hechtman studied children who manifest a collection of dysfunctional symptoms termed Attention Deficit Hyperactive Disorder. Children with these symptoms are at risk to experience adjustment difficulties in many areas of functioning and throughout life. Hechtman found that children with this disorder are more likely to make a positive adjustment when they live in two-parent families with clearly defined rules and roles, where there is direct supervision and structure, and in which there are clear-cut, realistic expectations of the child and his responsibilities. Strong relationships with adult role models, such as teachers and coaches, were also cited as positive influences.

Along a similar vein, Marfo examined the topic of developmentally delayed children. These at-risk children, who experience difficulties mastering age-appropriate functions, have trouble with their cognitive functions. Timely, appropriate, consistent, continuing, and systematic mediation (provided by parents, teachers, or other significant adults) helps to cultivate the essential cognitive functions needed for these children to master their lives.

Some children, however, do not have the benefit of a safe, intact, nurturing home environment. Jenkins's chapter about runaway children reminds us of children's need for parental acceptance and security within the home. Chronic runaways are usually responding to family problems that remain unresolved. Early intervention and treatment are associated with a positive prognosis. The cultivation of meaningful relationships with family members or other adult role-models is essential to breaking the runaway reaction.

Jenkins also examined the unsocialized delinquent. These youths are egocentric and narcissistic. Their adaptation is associated with parental rejection, especially by the mother. Successful treatment of this disorder usually requires a controlled, secure setting. The formation of a meaningful relationship with anyone can help these delinquents become more socialized; however, it is also important for them to make a personal decision to change.

Expanding upon the theme of juvenile delinquency, Brown, Miller, Jenkins, and Rhodes surveyed adult subjects who were adjudicated delinquent as juveniles. The authors found that the first delinquent referral should be taken seriously by the juvenile court. Adjudication and formal probation on the first referral to the juvenile probation department resulted in a substantial reduction in criminal convictions in adult life.

Finally, there are also those whose vulnerabilities are not manifested until late adolescence or early adulthood. Linzer-Schwartz studied the powers of religious cults and found that those individuals most vulnerable to membership had weak or nonexistent relationships with their fathers. In turn, those who resisted the powers of religious cults had a strong sense of self-identity and had experienced strong family relationships during the early stages of life.

We have summarized some of the more generalizable findings presented in the preceding chapters concerning factors that promote resilience in at-risk youth. Although we have concentrated largely on the family as both the potential cause and cure for these childhood difficulties, personal characteristics and environmental circumstances also play important roles. The interested reader should review respective chapters for specificity.

Researchers in this area of inquiry are beginning to discover *what* the resiliency factors are. What is missing in this volume, and appears to be lacking throughout the resiliency literature, is an adequate understanding of *how* at-risk children integrate these factors to promote resiliency. Knowing that a stable family environment, meaningful relationships, early intervention, average or above intelligence, consistent discipline, and a host of other family, personal, and environmental factors is helpful; but these findings are, for the most part, predictable. What is less predictable is *how* and *why* some at-risk children succeed in overcoming the "odds."

We, the authors of this chapter, conjecture that the how and why of resiliency result from a mixture of the life experiences that children have to choose from. Some children are insulated by positive family experiences; others are not. Some children are protected by strong personal characteristics; others are not. Some children are bolstered by intervening environmental circumstances; others are not. Within this scenario the child makes decisions (both consciously and subconsciously) predicated upon an evaluation of past, ongoing, and current life experiences in the above-mentioned areas.

We are, however, aware that the proposed theoretical model has limitations. For example, it cannot account for serendipitous occurrences or other dramatic events that may either enhance or retard the potential for resiliency. Furthermore, neither can it weight the relative importance of individual factors for a particular child and his or her unique set of circumstances. However, the model may provide a valuable theoretical framework from which to begin studying and understanding *how* and *why* certain factors promote resiliency in at-risk youth.

In an attempt to clarify and more graphically represent the proposed theoretical model, Figure 1 and its explanation are offered.

Stressor(s): Childhood is filled with stressful situations. Usually chil-

Figure 1
The Process of Integrating and Adapting to Factors That Promote Resiliency

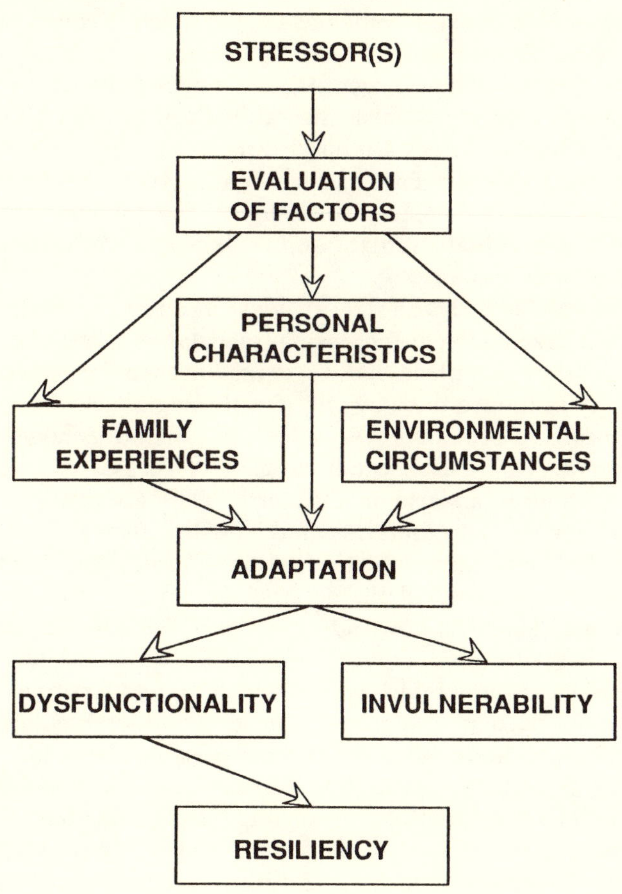

dren are able to quickly master or sufficiently deal with stressors such that they are not debilitating. But sometimes children face too many adversities at once or are overwhelmed by a single event. These are times of increased vulnerability; these are also times when children put their lives in perspective by consciously and subconsciously assessing what they have learned from their experiences.

Evaluation of Factors: Children faced with intense adversity assess the self-perceived gravity of the predicament and the options available to help them cope with it. Past, present, and ongoing family experiences, personal characteristics, and environmental circumstances are evaluated. An internal process (both conscious and subconscious) of weighting the relative impact of the above-mentioned factors occurs.

Family Experiences: For young children especially, life at home is not greatly distant from life in the womb. Home is the center of the universe, and what children experience within the family affects nearly everything they think and do. Children wrestling with difficulties draw upon their family experiences for guidance and perspective concerning how to handle a particular situation. They both rely upon and weight the relative importance of past, present, and ongoing family experiences. Positive family experiences act as insulators during difficult times, while negative family experiences are handicaps.

Personal Characteristics: Factors such as age, level of maturity, gender, health, physique, intelligence, self-esteem, mental state, personality, special needs, individual strengths and weaknesses work in combination to help determine options.

Environmental Circumstances: For older children especially, life outside the home takes on ever-increasing importance as they integrate into society and carve out a place in it. Circumstances in the general environment strongly influence the way children think and act. There are many people, places, and pressures with which to contend. Schools, jobs, relationships, responsibilities, expectations, goals, successes, and failures combine to give children a sense of self-worth. They are continually assessing what is happening around them and adjusting their lives accordingly.

Adaptation: The results of the evaluation of past, present, and ongoing family experiences, personal characteristics, and environmental circumstances are manifested in how individual children adapt to their unique situations.

Invulnerability: Some children seem to conquer adversity with ease. In evaluating their particular situations, these "invulnerable" children find reasons and implement ways to succeed despite the odds. This may include such factors as a positive home environment, a high IQ, a positive role model, a meaningful relationship, strong religious beliefs—or a combination thereof. Whatever the factors may be, they are the support mechanisms through which these children are able to implement ways to cope. In other words, the factors that promoted their invulnerability outweighed the relative impact of those factors that could have created dysfunctionality.

Dysfunctionality: Some stressors, or combinations of them, are more difficult than others to resolve. Furthermore, some children have fewer or less effective support mechanisms than others. These children are at high risk to experience problems coping with and surmounting their particular difficulties. In evaluating their particular situations, these "dysfunctional" children cannot find reasons or implement ways to make a successful adaptation to stressors such as family disharmony, having a low IQ, living in a dangerous neighborhood, experiencing low self-esteem, failing to form meaningtul relationships—or a combination thereof. In other words, the factors that created their dysfunctionality outweighed the relative impact of those factors that could have promoted resiliency.

Resiliency: Resilient children go through a period of dysfunctionality (either brief or protracted) before turning their lives around. At some point, however, factors change and their relative weight shifts (either suddenly or over time). This change may result from such factors as experiencing a more stable home environment, changing residence, maturing, forming an important relationship, the timely intervention of a therapist—or a combination thereof. In other words, the factors that created the dysfunctionality were redistributed in such a way that the balance of weight shifted to favor and promote resiliency.

According to our theoretical model, resiliency is not the avoidance of potential dysfunctionality (as is the case for invulnerability); rather, it is an adaptation away from a period of dysfunctionality—for that is when the "odds" are truly against them.

Perhaps the proposed theoretical model will in some way help provide a beginning framework from which to improve our understanding of *how* and *why* some children succeed despite the odds.

Author Index

Abend, S., 69
Abernathy, G., 82
Abernathy, V., 82
Acock, A. C., 26, 27
Adair, A. V., 30, 32, 33
Adams, G. R., 15
Adelberg, T., 31
Ahrons, C., 45
Akerman, P., 93
Aldgate, J., 63
Alexander, J. R., 17
Alexander, S. J., 80
Al-Khayyal, M., 70
Alpert, G. P., 88
Amato, P., 45
Ambert, A., 11
Amsel, R., 97, 99, 101
Anderson, P. G., 56
Angel R., 30
Angenent, H., 132-133, 136
Anthony, E. J., 2, 75, 99-101, 161
Aschenbrenner, J., 31
Awad, G., 7

Baldwin, W., 79
Ball, R. E., 33-34
Balla, D., 108
Bardwell, R., 142
Baydar, N., 45
Bebbington, P., 68
Beke, B., 132-133, 136
Bell, R. W., 49
Belmont, L., 79
Berman, W., 109
Bernheimer, L. P., 107
Bertrand, J. T., 83, 86
Bertsche, A. V., 63
Bianchi, S., 46
Billingsley, A., 31
Bleck, R. T., 19
Blish, D., 11
Bohannon, P., 48
Booth, K., 29, 31, 32
Bonagura, N., 96
Bond, L., 125
Borland, B., 96
Boswell, J., 55
Bowlby, J., 13
Boyer, A., 142-143
Bray, J., 45
Breiling, J., 57
Brenneman, F. S., 63
Bringle, R. G., 29
Brody, G., 50

Broman, C. L., 32
Bromwich, R., 124
Bronfenbrenner, U., 111-114
Brooks, P., 116, 119, 121, 123
Broudo, M., 43
Brown, D., 45
Brown, G., M., 8
Brown, P., 35
Brown, S. V., 81, 86, 88
Brown, W. K., 2, 3, 149, 153, 156
Browne, N., 110-111
Brunswick, A. F., 82
Bryce, M., 58, 63
Bumpass, L., 50
Burgess, A. W., 131-132
Burgess, R., 44
Burns, S., 116, 121, 123

Cain, H., 62
Cain, V., 79
Cantwell, D., 94
Caputo, L. M., 2
Carey, K., 63
Chandler, M. J., 111, 113-114
Cherlin, A., 48
Cherry, F., 83, 86
Chess, S., 15
Chilman, C. S., 79
Clark, F. W., 63
Cleminshaw, H. K., 26
Cline, D., 17
Clingempeel, G., 45
Cohen, J., 15
Cohen, P., 79
Cohen, S., 23
Cohler, B. J., 2, 100
Cole, K. N., 123-124
Coleman, M., 41-47, 51
Coles, R., 81, 88
Consortium for Longitudinal Studies, 109
Cook, C., 111
Cooper, D. H., 110-111
Corbett, A., 110-111
Cowen, E. L., 2, 164
Cox, M., 8, 11, 18, 26, 27, 45
Cox, R., 8, 11, 18, 26, 27, 45
Crossman, S. M., 15

Dale, P. S., 123-124
Dallas, J. R., 79
Dancy, B. L., 31, 32, 33, 54
Danzigor, P., 49
Darity, W. A., 33
Darlington, R. D., 109
Deford, C., 33
Delissovoy, V., 79
Demo, D. H., 26, 27
Denhoff, E., 96
Diagnostic and Statistical Manual of Mental Disorders (DSM-II), 133-135; DSM-III, 133-134; DSM-III-R, 133-134
Dissinger, L., 125
Dixon, V., 36
Dlugokinski, E. L., 2
Doherty, W., 45
Dorian, B. J., 8
Douglass, V., 93, 97
Drillien, C. M., 112
Dryfoos, J., 79
Duberman, L., 45
Dugan, T., 70, 75
Dukes, J. L., 31
Dunham, R. G., 88
Dunne, M. J., 62
Dunst, C., 110-111
Dykman, R., 93

Ehlert, C., 58
Elizur, E., 68
Ellison, E. S., 15
Emery, R. E., 27
Erikson, E. H., 163, 167

Fanshel, D., 57, 58, 60-62
Farran, D. C., 111
Federal Register, 57
Fein, E., 57, 60-63
Feldman, S., 96
Ferri, E., 43, 45
Festinger, T., 59
Feuerstein, R., 111, 117-121
Fiese, B. H., 111, 113
Finch, S. J., 60
Fine, M. A., 25, 26, 29, 51
Fisher, K., 168

Flach, F., 167
Flick, L. M., 81, 88
Flinn, M., 44
Flowers, C., 82
Flowers, R. B., 132
Ford, K., 81
Forehand, R., 50
Forste, R. T., 80, 85, 88
Frank, G., 58
Frate, D. A., 31
Freeman, R., 19
Freud, S., 70
Friedman, P., 30, 32
Fulton, R., 68
Furstenberg, F. F., 33, 46, 50, 81

Gable, R. L., 3
Galaway, B., 57
Gallant, D., 110
Gambrill, E., 57
Ganong, L. H., 41-47, 51
Gardiner, R., 16
Garfinkel, B. D., 8
Garmezy, N., 1, 2, 23, 24, 28, 30, 31, 69, 74, 85, 89, 99, 101, 167
Garnett, L., 62, 63
Geiss, G., 139, 145
Gerrard, M., 44
Gershenson, C., 57
Gilbride, K., 112, 121
Ginsburg, A., 29
Gittleman, R., 94, 96
Gittelman-Klein, R., 96
Glick, P. C., 7, 25, 41
Goldfarb, J. L., 82
Gottschalk, L. A., 82
Grad, J., 7
Green, C. P., 79
Greif, J. B., 17
Griffin, R. B., 2
Gruber, A. R., 57
Guidubaldi, J., 26, 27
Grundy, J. F., 60
Guttman, J., 43

Handel, P. J., 31, 32, 33
Harburg, E., 35
Hardy, J. B., 79
Hart, B., 83
Hartman, C. R., 131-132
Hartnagel, T. F., 28
Hartsaugh, C., 94
Hauenstein, L., 35
Hauser, S., 69, 75
Hawkins, R. P., 57
Haywood, H. C., 111, 116-117, 119, 121, 123
Heaton, T. B., 80, 85, 88
Hechtman, L., 95-97, 99, 101
Heckman, H., 96
Heidemann, P. H., 142
Henn, F. A., 142
Hess, P. M., 63
Hetherington, E. M., 8, 11-12, 18, 26, 27, 45, 165
Hewitt, L. E., 133-134, 142
Hilton, I., 83
Hobart, C., 45
Hoberman, H., 23
Hodapp, R., 108
Hoffman, M. B., 111, 117, 119-120
Homatides, G., 11
Homer, L. E., 137
Hoover, M., 23
Hopkins, J., 95-96
Hoppe, C., 94
Horejsi, C. R., 63
Hudson, J., 57
Hundleby, M., 62, 63
Hunt, J. G., 28, 29
Hunt, L. L., 28, 29
Huntington, D. S., 13-14
Hurley, R. B., 29
Hurry, J., 68

Ilfeld, F. W., Jr., 17
Ilfeld, H. Z., 17
Isaacs, M., 45
Isser, N., 161-162, 164

Jackson, A. D., 62
Jackson, E., 71
Jacobson, A., 69, 75
Jenkins, R. L., 3, 133-135, 142-144, 153, 156
Jensen, A. R., 109, 115

Johnson, L., 11
Johnson, S. T., 30
Jones, J., 70
Jones, J. B., 79, 82, 89
Jones, M. B., 56
Jorgensen, S. R., 80
Juvenile Justice Bulletin, 131-132, 135

Kahn, R., 125
Kalter, N., 8, 19
Kantner, J. G., 79-81
Kaplan, H. B., 82
Kasela, G. M., 111
Kaslow, F. W., 162, 164
Katz, M. H., 30
Kaufman, M., 68
Keane, A., 62
Kelly, J. B., 10, 13, 16, 18, 27
Keogh, B. K., 107
Kern, S., 15
Keshet, H. F., 15
Keystone, E., 8
King, J. R., 33
Kinnaird, K., 44
Kluger, M., 57, 60-63
Knobloch, H., 113
Kobasa, S., 23
Kobrin, S., 140, 145
Konig, P. H., 96
Kramer, J., 97
Kramer, P. A., 17
Krampen, G., 165, 168
Krieger, R., 63
Kurdek, L. A., 11, 26, 27
Kurland, J., 44

Ladner, J. A., 79, 87
Lambert, N., 94
Landry, E., 83, 86
Langer, T. S., 7
Lasley, J. H., 31
Lazar, I., 109
Leavey, J. M., 56, 58
Leon, G., 45
Lesowitz, M., 19
Levine, S. V., 161, 163
Lewis, R. J., 3
Lidz, C., 125
Lightcap, J., 44
Lightel, J., 26
Lindblad-Goldberg, M., 31
Lloyd, J. D., 63
Lochman, J., 82
Loney, J., 97
Lutsk, B., 57, 59

Maddi, S., 23
Mahoney, G., 124
Malkin, C., 112, 121
Malson, M., 31
Maluccio, A. N., 57, 60, 61, 63
Mannuzza, S., 94, 96
Mapes, D., 41
Marfo, K., 110-111, 124-125
Markusen, E., 68
Martin, D., 84, 89
Maslow, A., 162
Masten, A., 2
McAdoo, H., 31
McCollum, J. A., 124-125
McCormack, A., 131-132
McCoy, J. K., 81
McDermott, J. F., 7
McKenry, P., 29
McKenry, P. C., 80, 84-85
McLanahan, S., 29, 31, 32
McLaughlin, J. E., 29
Mech, E. V., 57
Meisels, S. J., 111
Melamed, B. G., 164
Menkes, J., 96
Menkes, M., 96
Metrakos, K., 96
Metz, R. J., 2
Michael, S. T., 7
Milardo, R. M., 31-33
Milich, R., 97
Miller, B. C., 81
Miller, R., 111, 117, 119-120
Miller, T. P., 3, 149, 153, 156
Mills, R. C., 88
Milman, D. H., 96
Milne, A. M., 29
Milroy, T., 96
Minde, K., 93, 97
Mittleman, M., 15

Moore, K. A., 81
Moreland, J. R., 26
Morris, R. B., 32
Moynihan, D. P., 25, 63
Mumford, D. M., 82
Murry, H. W., 109
Myers, D. E., 29
Myers, L. J., 25, 26
Myers, S. J., 33

Nagera, H., 68
Nagy, N., 68
Nastasi, B. K., 26
National Center for Health Statistics, 8
National Council on Crime and Delinquency, 132
Needle, R., 45
Nemeth, E., 93, 97
Neuchterlien, K., 2
Newbaum, E., 50
Nobers, D. R., 30
Nobles, W., 33, 34
Nord, C. W., 33, 46
Nordstrom, L., 2
Norton, A. J., 25

O'Grady, D., 2
Olmstead, K., 63
Olson, J. K., 81
Oplu, M. K., 7
Oppel, W. C., 79
Orlando, F., 11

Parish, E., 57, 59
Parish, T. S., 11
Passamanick, B., 113
Perlman, T., 95-97, 99, 101
Perry, J. D., 26, 27
Perry, L., 35
Pestrak, V. A., 84, 89
Peters, J., 93
Peters, M., 33
Peterson, J. L., 33, 45
Philliber, S. G., 79, 82, 89
Piaget, J., 166
Pickar, J., 19
Piker, H. N., 82
Pine, B. A., 63
Piotrkowski, C. S., 30
Pokorny, A. D., 82
Polit, D., 58
Pollock, G., 68, 75
Potteiger, K., 79
Powell, A., 124
Presser, H., 80
Proch, K. P., 63
Prom-Jackson, S., 30
Puig-Antich, J., 16

Radin, N., 30
Rae-Grant, Q., 7
Ralph, N., 82
Rand, Y., 111, 117, 119-120
Reeves, C., 63
Rennie, T.A.C., 7
Reppond, L., 137
Rheingrover, R., 110-111
Rhodes, W. A., 3, 79, 88, 153, 156
Rice, J., 83, 86
Robson, B., 8, 11-18, 20
Rogoff, B., 112, 120-121
Rosen, H., 71, 74, 75
Rosenthal, A. S., 29
Rosenthal, K. M., 15
Rowe, J., 62, 63
Royce, J. M., 109
Royston, A. B., 79
Rubin, R. H., 28
Rutter, M., 2, 7, 8, 11, 15, 16, 23, 24, 32, 69, 85-86, 88-89, 99-102
Ryan, P., 57

Salzman, L., 164
Sameroff, A. J., 111, 113-115
Sandoval, J., 94
Santrok, W. J., 11
Sassone, D., 94
Satterfield, B., 94
Satterfield, J., 94
Saucier, J., 11
Savage, J. E., 30, 32, 33
Scheiner, A. P., 110-111
Scheinfeld, D. R., 30
Schell, A., 94
Schur, E. M., 158
Schwartz, L. L., 161-162, 164

Schwebel, A. I., 25, 26
Schweinhart, L. J., 109
Scott, J. W., 80-81, 84
Segal, S., 45
Seitz, V., 109
Seltzer, J., 46
Shah, F. K., 79
Shaw, C. R., 139, 144-145
Shenker, R., 94, 96
Shimkin, D. B., 31
Shimkin, E. M., 31
Shinn, E. B., 57, 58, 61, 62
Shinn, M., 29
Shonkoff, J. P., 111
Short, J. F., 139, 145
Shum, C., 82
Siesky, A., 11, 27
Simeonsson, R. J., 110-111
Sinanoglu, P. A., 63
Singer, M. T., 161
Slater, N. E., 163
Slaughter, D., 30
Smith, B. A., 23
Smith, P. B., 82
Smith, R. S., 2, 69, 70, 99-102
Smyth, R., 110-111
Snipper, A. S., 109
Snodgrass, J., 139, 145
Spanier, G., 50
Spero, M. H., 164
Srole, L., 7
Stack, C. B., 31
Stainsbury, P., 7
Stanley, J., 79
Staples, R., 33
Statistics Canada, 7
Stein, M., 63
Stein, Z., 79
Steinberg, L., 47
Steinman, S., 17
Stevenson, H. C., 88
Stewart, S. S., 82
Stokes, G., 81, 88
Stone, H. D., 63
St. Pierre, M., 30
Su, S., 45
Sudarkasa, N., 34-35
Svanum, S., 29
Svobodny, L. A., 79
Swift, W. J., 17
Switzky, H. N., 111, 116-117
Szekely, L., 68

Takai, R. T., 31
Taylor, J. C., 11
Taylor, R. J., 31
Tennant, C., 68
Terrorese, M., 2
Thomas, A., 15
Thomas, T., 82
Thorley, G., 95
Tienda, M., 30
Titchener, J. L., 82
Trickett, P. K., 109
Triseloitis, J., 59
Tuck, D., 95-96

U.S. Census, 18, 25

Vieyra, M. A., 69, 75
Visher, E. B., 46, 48
Visher, H. S., 46, 48
Vygotsky, L. S., 112, 120, 165

Waddington, C. H., 116
Wallace, C. M., 81
Wallace, M. B., 30
Wallerstein, J. S., 9-10, 13, 16, 17, 18
Wallisch, L., 45
Walsh, J. A., 61
Walsh, R. A., 61
Walters, J., 80, 84-85
Walters, L. H., 80, 84-85, 137
Warshak, R. A., 11
Wedemeyer, N., 31
Weigel, R. M., 29
Weikart, D. P., 109
Weiss, G., 93, 95-97, 99, 101-102
Weiss, R., 27
Welcher, D. W., 79
Werner, E. E., 2, 23, 69, 70, 99-102, 108-109
Werry, J., 93, 97
Wertlieb, D., 69, 75

Wertsch, J. V., 112, 120-121
Westinghouse Learning Corporation, 109
Westman, J. C., 17
Whittaker, J. K., 63
Widom, C. S., 58
Wiederanders, M. R., 146
Wilkinson, G. S., 18-19
Williams, J. S., 32
Willie, C. V., 33
Wilson, M., 31
Wiltse, K. T., 57
Woodhead, M., 109
Work, W. C., 2, 164
Wynne, L., 70

Yahraes, H., 48

Zabin, M. A., 164
Zayac, S., 79
Zelnik, M., 79-81
Zigler, E., 108-109
Zill, N., 33, 43, 45
Zollar, A. C., 32

Subject Index

abandonment, 55, 67
abnormality, 10
academic difficulties, 79
academic performance, 19, 43, 94
academic problems, 18, 93; with hyperactives, 99
achievement, 29, 47, 82, 94; educational, 11; personal, 33; scholastic outcomes, 124; school, 30
acting-out, 70, 74
active modification approach, 118-120
additional adult hypothesis, 44, 47
Adoption Assistance and Child Welfare Act, 63
African cultural heritage, 25, 34-36
almshouses, 55, 56
anoxia, 113
auditory hallucinations, 160

behavior disorders, 10, 26
bereavement, 15
biological discrimination hypothesis, 44
black scholars, 35
boarding homes, 56
British foster care studies, 59

California, joint custody in, 16; runaways survey, 132
California Civil Code, Section, 16-17
California Personality Inventory (CPI) 103
Canada, DD children in, 123; remarriage in, 7
Casey Family Program, 60-61; in Idaho and Montana, 60-61
census, 25, 42
Chicago, black families study, 31
Chicago Parental School, 145
child-centeredness, 61
Child Psychiatry Department, 102
chronic illness, 69
classroom management techniques, 32
clinical intervention, 62
clinical observation, 67
clinical reports, 20, 26, 27
clinical services, 62
clinical writers, 46
cocaine addiction, in utero, 2
Cognitive Curriculum for Young Children (CCYC), 123
cognitive dissonance, 81
cognitive modifiability, 115-117, 125

cohabiting couples, 42, 50
cohesive family climate, 30
common-law union, 7
Committee on Adolescence of the Group for the Advancement of Psychiatry, 163
Commonwealth of Massachusetts, early foster home care, 56
conduct disorder, diagnosis, 133-134
Congress, 132
Connecticut, foster care, 57, 61
Consortium for Longitudinal Studies, 109
coping, 2, 3; attempts, 23; behaviors, 74; efforts, 23, 32; repertoires, 19; strategies, 9, 18, 70
counseling, 13, 16, 71-72
counselors, 14, 17, 18, 41, 73, 89, 138
court transcripts, 16
crack cocaine, 63
crisis intervention, 19
crisis theory, 15
custodial parent, 11, 18, 19
custody, 9-10, 16-17

Dauphin County, Pennsylvania, juvenile delinquent study, 149
deficit-comparison approach, regarding stepchildren, 42
developmental disruption, 26
developmental imbalances, 69
developmental interferences, 68
developmental stage, 9, 10, 15
developmental tasks, 19
diabetes, 8
disappearing fathers, 15
discipline, 10, 14, 20, 46

early childhood indicators, 1
early traumatic life experiences, 1
efficacy, 27. *See also* self-efficacy
electroencephalography (EEG), in ADHD adults, 96
emergent model, 25, 34
emotional adjustment, 58
emotional availability, 15
emotional coherence, 61
emotional deprivation, 27
emotional development, 83
emotional difficulty, 18, 94
emotional distress, 27
emotional enmeshment, 17
emotional expressiveness, 101
emotional intensity, 48
emotional involvement, 61
emotional liability, 97
emotional stability with hyperactives, 97
emotional well-being, 54-55
encopresis, 102-103
enuresis, 102-103
Experimental Educational Unit, University of Washington, 123

family: adopted, 7, 9; breakdown, 8; disruption, 24, 50; histories, 82; mediation, 16; milieu, 23, 28, 30, 31; modal, 31; nuclear, 30, 47-48, 171; stability, 85; structure, 29, 82; therapist, 17
Family Development Resource Center at St. Joseph College, 125
Florida, low-income black families in, 34
foundling home, 55
Friedman Developmental Level Scoring System, 83

General Cognitive Index, 123
Green Hill School, 138
grief and sibling loss, 67-76
growth enhancing process, 8

Head Start programs, 109
Holocaust, effect on DD children, 108
House of Correction (Illinois), 145
hypervulnerables, 161

identity, 16, 31, 58, 163
Illinois State Reformatory, 145
Illinois Training School for Boys, 145
incomplete institution hypothesis, 51
infant curriculum model, 124
interaction-focused early intervention, 125; model, 124
interparent hostility, 15, 19

intervention programs, 9, 109
intrapsychic factors, 71

Jack Roller, The, 139, 144-146
Jack Roller at Seventy, The, 145
Juvenile Justice and Delinquency Prevention Act, 132; Office of (OJJDP), 135-136

lawyers, 50
learned helplessness, 109
learning disabilities, 104
learning disabled, 94
litigation, 10, 16
locus of control, 15, 23, 27, 82; characteristics, 167-168; development of, 165; hyperactives, 100; invulnerables, 164
longitudinal data, 109
longitudinal investigations, 19, 26
longitudinal studies, 8, 9, 12, 27, 31, 35, 58, 61
Los Angeles, joint custody cases in, 17
low-level intimacy, 14
loyalty conflicts, 10, 16

main-effect model, 113-114
Massachusetts Visiting Agent, 58
maternal attitudes, 30
maternal deprivation, 109
maternal employment, 47
maternal rejection, 240
McCarthy Scales, 123-124
mediated learning experience (MLE), 117-119
Mediated Learning Experience Rating Scale, 125
mediators, 17
mental health professionals, 1
mental illness, 1, 3
mental retardation, 107, 116, 118
mentor, 11, 19
Mississippi, black familes study, 31
Moses, first foster child, 55
Mourning and Melancholia, 70
multimodal treatment, 94

narcissistic character disorder, 14
National Council on Crime and Delinquency, 132
National Survey of Black Americans, 32
National Survey of Families and Households, 29
neoplasms, 8
network, 13, 30-32, 82, 89
neurochemical and physiological aspects of stress, 2
New York City, foster care study, 59
New York sample of foster care children, 57
New York State Training School for Boys, 134
nodal developmental points, 19
no-fault divorce, 16
noncustodial fathers, 46
nonrecidivists, 3
nonvulnerables, 161
normative-adaptive perspective, 42-44, 52
North America, remarriage in, 7
nurturant caregiver, 13

oppositional behaviors, 60
orphanages, 55-56, 138
out-of-home placement, 57
out-of-wedlock, 25, 33

parent-absent families, 30
parent-incarcerated, 30
parental-alienation syndrome, 10
parental alcoholism, 69
parental careers, 44
parental death, 42
parental discord, 15, 27
parental education, 80
parental hostility, 15
parental occupation, 94
parental rejection, 134, 142, 173-174
parental remarriage, 42, 45, 47, 50
parental reports, 29
parental separation, 7, 8
parental supervision, 82
parental variables, 9
parenting styles, 31

participant-observation methods, 36
passive-acceptant approach, 120
passive aggressive, 61
pathology, 25-26, 69
peer, 18; group, 29, 74; interaction, 11; network, 86; pressure, 86, 158; relationships, 32, with hyperactives, 98, 100; self-help groups, 20; support, 11, 18
peer-bonding, 137
penology, 145
People's Temple cult members, 160
perinatal complications, 113
Piaget, Jean, 119
Piagetian theory, 166
poorhouses, 55
positive outcomes, 2, 3, 42; associated with child's age, 61; children at risk, 102; for developmentally delayed, 110-111; mastery of a death, 68; pregnancy risk, 79, 88; variables, 44
postnatal development, 113
prenatal development, 112-113
preventive programs, 9, 19, 89
primary prevention of mental illness, 1, 2
primary prevention specialists, 2
proactive health-building model, 164
problem-oriented perspective, 42-45
protective factors, 24, 34-36; work by Garmezy, 85
protective mechanisms, 24, 85-89
protective processes, 24
proximity seeking, 13
psychiatric disorders, 7
psychiatric inpatient, 82
psychiatric populations, 10
psychological abuse, 165
psychological conflicts, 70
psychological development, 13
psychological dysfunction, 1, 3
psychological intervention, 94
psychological parameters in hyperactive disorders, 95
psychosomatic symptoms of stepchildren, 42
psychopathology, 76
psychotherapy, 71-74, 147

radical nonintervention, 158
ratings: abnormal, 58; aggressivity, 97; behavioral, 43; scales, 96; teacher, 43
regression, 13
retrospective studies, 60
Rorschach test, 83

satanic cults, 160, 162, 165
schizophrenia, 67
Seattle Youth and Community Services, 137
self-concept, 11, 28
self-confidence, 10, 12, 49
self-control, 23
self-efficacy, 24, 85-86
self-esteem, 16, 23, 24, 28-29, 42, 45, 49; associated with resiliency, 167; developing, 89; enhancement of, 85; factors that lower, 165; hyperactive adolescents, 93, 95, 100; low, 82, 87, 93, 164; needs of, 86; protective mechanism, 86
self-image, 12, 19, 28, 62, 82
self-observation, 75
self-regulation, 83
self-worth, 12, 20
Sentence Completion Test, 83
Shelter Runaway Center, The, 137
sibling loss, 67-76
social facilitation programs, 15
social interaction-based mediational approach, 124
socialization hypothesis, 43-45
Social Security Act, 56
social skills, 74-75, 89, 96, 100
socioemotional adjustment, 28
status offenders, 132-135, 158
stepchildren, famous, 41
structural-functional model, 25
suicide, 8, 72-74, 96
superego, 143

Temple University, 125
Thematic Apperception Test, 83
Thornton, Robert (runaway child), 138
toileting problems, 9
Toronto, Canada, runaways in, 131

Toronto Family Study, 11, 18
traditional family, 7
transactional models, 111-118, 122

United States, 25, 107, 123, 160
universal unity, 36
Urist Mutuality of Autonomy Scale, 83
U.S. Department of Health and Human Services (HHS), 132
U.S. Office of Juvenile Justice and Delinquency Prevention, 131

Vanderbilt University, 123
visitation, 16

Westinghouse evaluation of Head Start, 109

zone of proximal development (ZPD), 112, 120-121

About the Contributors

WALN K. BROWN is founder and chairman of the William Gladden Foundation, Huntington, New York, a nonprofit organization dedicated to research of social and family issues, with special emphasis on juvenile delinquency and juvenile justice.

MARILYN COLEMAN is professor and chair of the Department of Human Development and Family Studies, University of Missouri-Columbia.

EDITH FEIN is research director at Casey Family Services, a long-term foster care and permanency planning agency in Hartford, Connecticut.

ROBERT D. FELNER is director, Center for Prevention Research and Development, Institute of Government and Public Affairs, University of Illinois, Urbana-Champaign.

MARK A. FINE is a licensed psychologist and associate professor of psychology at the University of Dayton, Ohio.

LAWRENCE H. GANONG is an associate professor, Department of Human Development and Family Studies, University of Missouri-Columbia.

LILY HECHTMAN is a psychiatrist on staff at the Montreal Children's Hospital.

RICHARD L. JENKINS is professor emeritus of child psychiatry, University of Iowa College of Medicine, Iowa City.

LITA LINZER-SCHWARTZ is a professor of educational psychology, Pennsylvania State University, Ogontz Campus, Abington, Pennsylvania.

ANTHONY N. MALUCCIO is professor of social work and director of the Center for the Study of Child Welfare, University of Connecticut, West Hartford.

KOFI MARFO is an associate professor of educational psychology, Department of Educational Psychology and Leadership Studies, Kent State University, Ohio.

TIMOTHY P. MILLER is director of research, William Gladden Foundation, York, Pennsylvania.

WARREN A. RHODES is professor of psychology, Department of Psychology, Delaware State College, Dover.

BONNIE E. ROBSON is an assistant professor, Department of Psychiatry, Faculty of Medicine, University of Toronto.

HELEN ROSEN is a clinical associate in psychoanalysis, Philadelphia Association for Psychoanalysis, and assistant professor at Bryn Mawr College, The Graduate School of Social Work and Social Research.

ANDREW I. SCHWEBEL is a professor of psychology, Ohio State University, Columbus.

HOWARD STEVENSON is a visiting professor in the Department of Education, University of Pennsylvania, Philadelphia.